Principles of Physical Education and Sports Studies, and Research in All Nations

Noriaki Osada

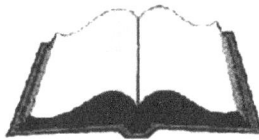

CCB Publishing
British Columbia, Canada

Principles of Physical Education and Sports Studies, and Research in All Nations

Copyright ©2010 by Noriaki Osada
ISBN-13 978-1-926585-68-0
Second Edition

Library and Archives Canada Cataloguing in Publication

Osada, Noriaki, 1949-
Principles of physical education and sports studies, and research in all nations /
written by Noriaki Osada – 2nd ed.
Includes bibliographical references.
ISBN 978-1-926585-68-0
1. Physical education and training--Social aspects.
2. Sports--Social aspects. 3. Physical education and training--Research.
4. Sports--Research. 5. International relations. I. Title.
GV706.5.O825 2010 306.4'83 C2010-900155-9

Cover design: Images utilized are in the public domain and are used without malice.

Publisher: CCB Publishing
             British Columbia, Canada
             www.ccbpublishing.com

To Baron DeCubertin of France,
who began the modern Olympic games,

and also my parents,
who passed away before this book was published.

Contents

Preface ix

Part I. My Memories 1

**Part II. Theory of Martial Arts Studies for the
    Achievement of Peace**
1. A Word from the Author 13
2. Establishing the Hypothesis for Creating Martial Arts Studies 14
3. The Movement-Cultural Ontology of the Martial Arts Human ...21
4. The Education Ontology of the Martial Arts Human 28
5. The Social Ontology of the Martial Arts Human 36
6. Generalizations from the Ontology of the Martial Arts Human ...46
7. The Teleology of the Martial Arts Human 49
8. The Methodology of the Martial Arts Human 60

**Part III. Theory of International Skating Studies for
    the Achievement of Peace**
1. A Word from the Author 69
2. Establishing the Hypothesis for Creating Skating Studies 70
3. The Movement-Cultural Ontology of the Skating
    Human (or Ice Human) 77
4. The Educational Existence of the Skating Human
    (or Ice Human) 84
5. The Social Ontology of the Skating Human (or Ice Human) 92
6. Generalizations from the Ontology of the Skating Human
    (or Ice Human) 102
7. The Teleology of the Skating Human (or Ice Human) 105
8. The Methodology of the Skating Human (or Ice Human) 116

**Part IV. Theory of International Gymnastics Studies for the
    Achievement of Peace**
1. A Word from the Author 125
2. Establishing the Hypothesis for Creating Gymnastics Studies 126

3. The Movement-Cultural Ontology of the Gymnastics Human 133
4. The Education Ontology of the Gymnastics Human 140
5. The Social Ontology of the Gymnastics Human 148
6. Generalizations from the Ontology of the Gymnastics Human ... 158
7. The Teleology of the Gymnastics Human 161
8. The Methodology of the Gymnastics Human 172

**Part V. Theory of International Skiing Studies for the
     Achievement of Peace**
1. A Word from the Author 181
2. Establishing the Hypothesis for Creating Skiing Studies 182
3. The Movement-Cultural Ontology of the Skiing Human
     (or Snow Human) 189
4. The Education Ontology of the Skiing Human
     (or Snow Human) 196
5. The Social Ontology of the Skiing Human (or Snow Human) 204
6. Generalizations from the Ontology of the Skiing Human
     (or Snow Human) 214
7. The Teleology of the Skiing Human (or Snow Human) 217
8. The Methodology of the Skiing Human (or Snow Human) 228

**Part VI. Theory of International Dance Studies for the
     Achievement of Peace**
1. A Word from the Author 237
2. Establishing the Hypothesis for Creating Dance Studies 238
3. The Movement-Cultural Ontology of the Dance Human 245
4. The Education Ontology of the Dance Human 251
5. The Social Ontology of the Dance Human 259
6. Generalizations from the Ontology of the Dance Human 268
7. The Teleology of the Dance Human 271
8. The Methodology of the Dance Human 281

**Part VII. About Physical Education and Sports Studies
     in Each Nation in the World** 289

Part VIII. What Is the True Principle of Physical Education and Sports Studies?

1. About the Function and Shape of the Principle in Reality 311
2. Establishment of World Academy of Physical Education and Sports Studies 314

Part IX. Our Social, National, and World Responsibilities 321

Afterword 337

Bibliography 341

Preface

This book is my second book to be published. It is also a continuation of my first book, *Theory of International Physical Education and Sports Studies for the Achievement of Peace*. I could say this book concerns the principle of physical education and sports studies in each nation in the world. This principle is connected with all questions of physical education and sports in all nations. (See figure 1.) This principle functions definitely to the reality of physical education and sports practices, theory, and research programs. This principle shows all researchers of physical education and sports how to create a national theory in their nations, including the correct method of all research, the compass of the responsibility of the research, and the purpose' of all research papers in relevance to the physical education and sports studies. This book has a universal character that goes beyond different countries, different national languages, and different eras in the world because the word *principle* refers to a basic, universal, and unchangeable theory of physical education and sports studies in each era and in each country. This is also a book that I have to offer for beginners, students, and researchers of physical education and sports studies in all nations.

The theory and the opinions or review (level of hypothesis) are quite different. The opinions cover the facts of physical education and sports practices. They do not in fact sanction support of physical education and sports practices. That means they act to avoid the responsibilities of physical education and sports practices. The opinions go to just display abilities without the responsibilities of the fact. They demand limitlessly of the researchers a lot of speaking and writing of papers as if the researchers had done a lot of work. On the other hand, the theory is a thing that goes to the fact of physical education and sports and explains the fact of physical education and sports. So the theory is a thing to take for the responsibilities of the fact of physical education and sports practices. Therefore, the former is a way that demands irresponsibility in the realities. I always take the standpoint of the latter, and my opinions are always connected to the principles or the theory because I am always a scholar of physical education and sports who can teach people in all nations of the world.

I have been deliberating on physical education and sports studies being of peace in order to continue these studies forever and secure many minds of sports events and applied practices for sports in the practice of physical education in reality. However, all general studies have certainly been tainted so much because all studies have not been created from the universal blueprint before the establishment of the study's name in public. Therefore, they bring about an abuse of the national language as a result of the real education in all nations. They also bring the educational phenomenon of students randomly having to memorize a lot of knowledge given by a professor. This phenomenon would evoke mental torture, but not education. Professors and students would be tired because there is no universal blueprint of study before they talk to each other about study in college and graduate school. For example, there are many books titled *Principle of the Study of Education* (pedagogy) in all nations, with these books expressing and explaining the author's thoughts in each national language, yet we have still not discovered the true principle of the study of education. Why is it so? The contents of all the books have come from the personal plans of authors but not from proof of real necessity. This word *principle* means there is absolutely only one theory in the world and in each era, because it means the true knowledge that all people can trust and learn from.

Our physical education and sports study can be only one true study in the world, because we have constructively created it toward our goal, "the study of peace." We can expect that our study promises a brilliant future to all scholars of physical education and sports, as I mentioned in my first book. Furthermore, we have to create internal principles of physical education and sports studies, which mean the partial principle (theory) of philosophy, the partial principle (theory) of sociology, the partial principle (theory) of physiology, the partial principle (theory) of psychology, and so forth, in order to establish a more solid study in all nations. I will expect all scholars in all nations to establish the national theory of peace in their own national languages.

My study has not come from books but through the fact of physical education and sports in the United States and in Japan, where I have been living. I can perceive the phenomenon of physical education and sports through my eyes. I believe that seeking the truth or the facts becomes a true study for students. A "true study" means a study that goes to all students in all nations, beyond different countries and different languages. I also believe that college and graduate school must be connected to real society, the nation, and the world, because we cannot think of education without the real society, real nation and real world. Prof. Earle F. Zeigler suggested about how education should be in reality. He mentioned, "experiences basic to peace in the sports and physical education program" (*ISCPES Journal*, 1992, p. 12). He will seek a true study of physical education and sports through breaking out an isolation of the education in the real society, nation, and world. The late professor Hideo Kawamura, a person who had contributed to the principles of physical education as a leading runner in Japan, said: "Physical education principle is always our theme and connected actual and essential issue of the practices." Therefore, we primarily have to see the facts of physical education and sports through our eyes.

All governments have evoked colonial war in the national languages in real education throughout world history because there has not appeared a universal study of the educational programs that the government has really offered in public. The national language is a language that gives profits to the nation. For example, American English is a language that brings profits to America, Japanese is a language that brings profits to Japan, and other national languages are also languages that bring their nations profits. Therefore, the education by the government is not able to make peace in the world, even though the government is not able to make a national theory to support the government and the people in the nation. These situations in the nation have brought a lot of waste of money that people pay as taxes to the government in each nation and the waste of efforts of the researchers and professors who have just felt a sense of fatigue coming from ineffective research education. We think of all national languages being equally unique expressions of human existence in each nation. It means that humans use the words in a national language as an expression of human existence, but must not be used by the words that humans in each nation have technically created, a lot of words in each national language. Human existence should be more advantageous than words in reality because of ensuring the prosperity of mankind, including all nations on the earth.

As mentioned above, this book was published for all scholars of physical education and sports in all nations because we need excellent scholars, professors, and national doctors, who can serve as qualified lecturers in all nations. In the future we will hold "Olympic-type competitions" every four years sponsored by the World Academy of Physical Education and Sports. We will play the national anthem and hoist the national flag. These symbols mean the national anthem of human nation and the flag of the human nation. The differences between national flags and national anthems in all nations in the world mean "goodness and uniqueness," as former president of the USA Richard Nixon said in public statements (*Time* May 2, 1994, p. 39). The excellent scholar means a person who supports the human nation and human world, who supports all people in each nation, who brings a peace to his nation and the world, who brings true acknowledgment of students, and who eventually supports the practices of physical education and sports through theory. These works of scholars can truly provide support to governments in all nations and to people in all nations on the earth.

I have presented five principles of physical education and sports studies in all nations in the world in this book. They are the principles of gymnastics studies, the principles of dance studies, the principles of martial arts studies, the principles of skiing studies, and the principles of skating studies. Beside them, I covered three principles in my first book, Theory of International *Physical Education and Sports Studies for the Achievement of Peace* (New York: Vantage Press, 1992). They are the principles of ball game studies, the principles of track-and-field studies, and the principles of swimming studies. These principles became complicated and have a contradictory structure. Why is it so? Because the facts of the physical education and sports practices are very complicated and have contradictions. "The principle must follow truth like the fact." If my attitude toward the principle tends to reject that, my principle will not become the principle by which I am able to lead all people in all nations in the world. That means the opinions in public that have personal values for just me. Therefore, I think that I have to explain in more detail so that readers can understand the principles in order to begin research and studies, in order to begin the lectures and the practices, and in order to begin to devise a program of physical education and sports courses in college and graduate school in all nations in the world.

I appreciate that I am standing on the stage on which Prof. Earle F. Zeigler in the United States and Prof. Hideo Kawamura in Japan contributed to the principles of physical education in our past history. I think that we are running on their contributions for the principle. "Our contributions of peace," which Professor Zeigler mentioned, and "our contribution of actual, essential issue of physical education," which Professor Kawamura mentioned, are making an international line so that we are able to show common point. We want to raise up the hands of both high in public because of breaking out of all the differences (for example, history, language, traditions, races, etc.) between the United States and Japan.

Furthermore, I must mention that our principle of physical education and sports must be independent from the government in each era and protected by law forever on behalf of all scholars of physical education and sports in all nations in the world. And I hope our principle will be used for peace within nations and peace in the world. And all papers and books that scholars of physical education and sports have published must be returned to all people and our nations, like "the reduction to the phenomenology" that a great philosopher, Edmund Husserl, mentioned in his book. Why do we have to do so? Because we finally must support human existence (all people) in all nations on the earth by all national languages in the world.

I know that education in all nations must return to true education, including love of the truth (the principle) and skills in the national language, as I have learned from the struggle between proponents of different ideas, sophistry and the thought of Socrates, in ancient Greece. I know that harmony of both elements brings development of national education. We need a dynamic harmony between skills in the national language and love of truth (principle) on behalf of the new generations (particularly of the twenty-first century). The skills of

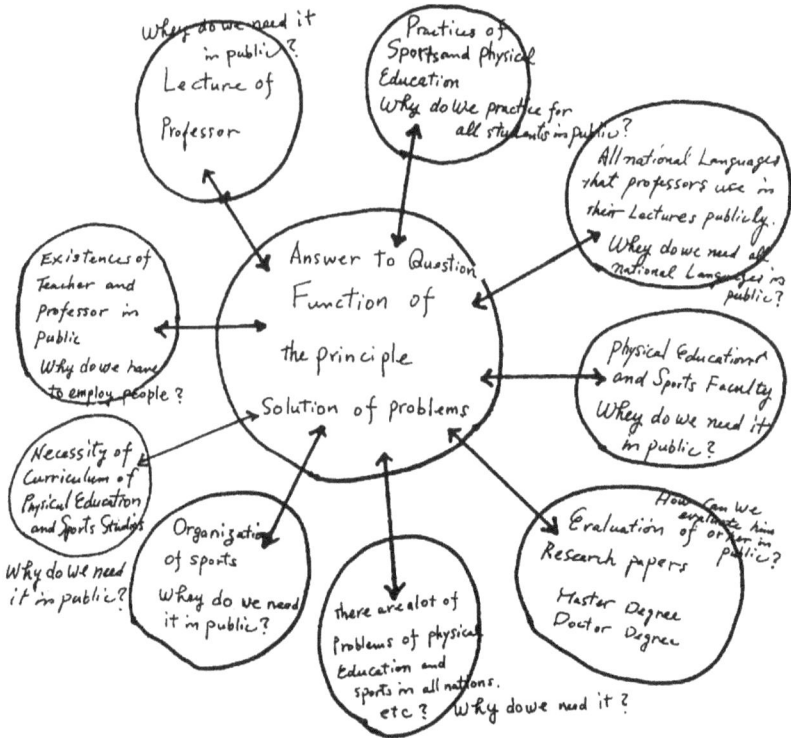

Figure 1. Relations between the principle of physical education and sports studies and all questions connecting physical education and sports in fact in all nations in the world

national language do abundantly prove the existence of the human as a cultural, social, and educational existence, but they are proof of human existence in the nation, too. We must adjust and harmonize powerful relationships of all national languages by all governments, because all national languages are just methods in order to build the national theories in all nations for realization of peace in the world.

Therefore, the papers and the books written in American English must return to human existence in the United States (American people) because American English is a proof of American people who are living and were living on the North American continent. Therefore, the research papers and books written in another national language must return to sports and physical education practices (phenomena) in all nations on the earth in each era. It would make international order or stipulation for all researchers and promise the developments of physical education and sports studies and research in all nations in the world.

The United States has been leading all nations to freedom and democracy. If I had to add another word to describe its role, I would choose this word: *responsibility,* for the human nation, in connection with rights of human existence in all nations on the earth. I think that we must share happiness and responsibility with our wisdom, the principles. I have been doing my best for the establishment of physical education and sports studies and research with sacrifice of my private life. Therefore, I really pray that peace in the world will come true in all nations in the world. I love the United States, but I cannot love just the United States. I love Japan, but I cannot love just Japan. I want to love all nations in the world equally as long as they are doing the practices of physical education and sports. I strongly believe that the healthy love of all nations brings peace in the world. The peace goes to the existence of specific humans (all people) in the practice of physical education and sports in all nations in the world. All people have a right to get peace. I know that learning all national languages is important (because learning the national language is a method for doing something on behalf of development of the human nation and human world) particularly for the realization of national peace and world peace. We humans must emphasize peace in the world to the people of the world. Our friends are not people who just talk to us in our common national language but people who have contributed to our profession, because physical education and sports studies work on behalf of realization of peace in the world.

Part I

My Memories

In this book, I have done my best to back up my theories with factual evidence. I clearly mention the places (actual nations) and objective (specific human existence) of research and studies for which we must be responsible for all nations.

Now that I feel I have really settled down to live in New York City, I am reminded of a terrible episode in my life when I look back on my past in Japan. After I finished my studies at a graduate school of education in Osaka, I felt that it was necessary to continue my research in order to develop my theory. Even though my theory went to development and I have had opportunities to make presentation of my theories at the Japanese Society of Physical Education several times, my research situation went badly and I was coldly ostracized by many Japanese professors, despite the fact that I, as a scholar, was doing the most important tasks. I sometimes criticized researchers' work at the Japanese Society of Physical Education from the public responsibility as a scholar of physical education because they did not know what research is, they did not know what their national language (Japanese) is, they did not have a blueprint before they did the research, and they acted irresponsibly with the national language, with the laboratory, with social examinations, with computers, and so forth. Their efforts toward physical education study seemed useless for scholars of physical education and sports. Professors, doctors, those words of authority must mean people who contribute to people in all nations in the world when we call them "Professor" or "Doctor" in public. In fact, those words mean a person who contributes to his family and his personal benefit but not a person who contributes to the human nation and human world. The cause comes from lack of principles of study (medicine, education, philosophy, etc.). This tendency will certainly lead to destruction of mankind.

I was so isolated that I felt I could not continue the research in Japan anymore. My research was clearly considered a social crime, to be destroyed by some groups of Japanese professors. In Japan, there was still not the democratic situation of young scholars researching freely in graduate school. The young Japanese scholars were like slaves of the professors. They were not able to criticize other research papers in those days. Professors had a right to adopt them directly and indirectly in college through personal connections among professors in Japan after they graduated from their college and graduate school. The Japanese Society of Physical Education has not had a strong power in order to foster future professors of physical education. Therefore, professors have personally utilized the Japanese Society of Physical Education through presentation of their research. A group like the Japanese Society of Physical Education encourages professors to gather just in order to make sticky friendships. The Japanese Society of Physical Education still does not fulfill social functions in order to foster scholars. The appearance in society is like a rubber balloon. The organization loses social responsibility as our profession's represent-tative. In fact, it kills the social function of members of the Japanese Society of Physical Education. The cause that we must consider important is a lack of principles of physical education in the Japanese Society of Physical Education. Therefore, the Japanese Society of Physical Education cannot evaluate all the research papers regarding our profession in public.

Japanese professors currently have so much power in colleges that students must obey them. The professors' attitudes come from abuse of their social position. There are so many professors who don't produce professional knowledge. Moreover, they are strangely employed as professors in the Japanese educational system. They have a right to give jobs in college to students they are involved in personal relationships with, without public standards of evaluation. So there is a situation that ensures excellent young scholars in the future will never be educated well in college and graduate school. The relationship between student and professor is very sticky, like a relationship between a renter and landlord. In my case, my papers and my speech were denied to the public by Japanese professors in those days in order to defend a boss of the physical education world in Japan. The thought of democracy was crushed in our profession. I remembered that when I was about thirty-two years old I felt as if I had been thrown into hell by professors. And I knew that the Japanese Society of Physical Education was in deep corruption, in fact. They did not have responsibilities as professors of physical education in college and in graduate school for students and for the Japanese people at all. All school curricula of physical education were irresponsible. I must show the Japanese shame to people in the world in order to love my homeland Japan, even though I still have such passion that I bring up Japanese professors of physical education nationally and internationally for future generations.

Japan is a country that abhors negation even if the negation has a valid reason. However, I, as a scholar of physical education, must have been denied, on the condition of the physical education studies in those days, a sense of social responsibility in Japan. At the same time, I felt that I must build up our national theories in the actual nation as a scholar of physical education and develop them in public more despite the Japanese government and the college I graduated from never helping me. I expected our theories to bring the real scholars of physical education out in order to protect all people in all nations. Our theories should be the most powerful thing in the world, because they bring peace and justice in reality.

When I think of Japan after the Second World War, my head aches with so many considerations. I was born in Japan after the Second World War. When I was an elementary school student, our class had provisions for school lunch (*kuwshoku* in Japanese) every school day after we finished the studies of the morning schedule. I remember the lunch almost always came with milk. The milk of the school lunch I had was brought from the United States because Japan was under reconstruction after the Second World War. I grew up with the American milk of my childhood.

Also, I think that the recent prosperity of the Japanese economy has depended very much on aid from Americans. I feel that the United States has a friendly attitude toward Japan despite its own problems in domestic issues. I personally appreciate American people for helping the Japanese people, in ruin after the Second World War.

I have to mention another aspect of Japanese society. In fact, Japan has been very dependent on the United States after the Second World War. Therefore, Japanese people's minds have leaned toward the United States. Japanese people have not been able to judge or decide on many aspects internationally, independently by ourselves on behalf of the imbalance of power of relationships between both countries. I think that Japanese people after the Second World War were influenced spiritually, more or less. The relationship between the United States and Japan has brought a power relationship in one way only. There was no thought of coexistence and fair competition. And the matters the United States emphasized were just competition among nations. It brought development of technology to the United States. The thought of coexistence has gone toward death, in fact. Therefore, the American English and Japanese that people express themselves in has gone to technical ostentation through individualism.

This also means that Japan was not a nation to support true democracy as a modern nation should. I think that really modern nations abhor hypocrisy, because *modern nations* means mature nations that can try to understand other nations in a rational manner and decide independently. Therefore, the relationship between the United States and Japan has been taking on a distorted nature, unfortunately. This has brought a lack of wisdom going to harmonized prosperity of the entire world on the earth. The international educational issues in the United States and Japan at present have come from this point made by the political world. Therefore, both national languages in education have become irresponsible for real human life.

In Japan, words of authority, for example doctor, professor, etc., have never been defined in order to indicate responsibility for the human nation and for mankind. They have been running the Japanese educational system without theory that can guarantee the authorized words. Therefore, it has caused a sense of distrust of them that people in Japan have in reality I see that aspect of Japan in that the Ministry of Education does not recognize each special field of physical education scholars, without the minister of education holding the principle (theory) in fact. At least, I think that our field must become part of a democratic situation so that all people have an equal hope in the educational system. The Japanese bureaucracy in education has obstinately been taking a hard line in public to take formalism, but it has certainly prompted distrust about Japanese education inter-nationally until now after the Second World War.

In Japan, a professor can take his position in college as a professor without demonstrating his own theory, despite his salary coming from payments from the people who pay taxes and students or students' parents who pay the tuition in college and in graduate school. Japanese professors have an absolute right in that college students and graduate school students must obey his teaching. I must say in public that professors in Japan have been made by strong secret relationships (like *dango* by Gakubatsu in Japanese) without their own theory. In fact, our faculties in Japan, as the United States takes the same way, recognize doctoral degrees coming from other faculties such as Tukuba University and Tokyo University, etc. That means abuse of the doctorate. All terms connecting physical education and sports phenomena in all nations belong to us as scholars. I must say in public that the Japanese professors must serve all the Japanese people as a professional obligation without personal demonstration of the Japanese language in front of students in college and in graduate school. Professors must produce a national theory of physical education and sports studies to support all Japanese people and the government. We must check all Japanese professors' achievements in physical education faculties of all colleges and all graduate schools under our true principle of physical education. They must submit to all Japanese people and all students a "universal blueprint" in order to explain the physical education studies and sports practices of public education in college. In fact, educational doctors, medical doctors, etc., have reigned as leaders of physical education, despite nobody creating a responsible doctoral program in Japan. Therefore, we really need national physical education and sports doctors in Japan. It would be a national issue and international issue that people cannot trust the recent situation of physical education at all.

I think we must establish the Japanese Academy of Physical Education and Sports by public necessity, notwithstanding the existence of the Japanese Society of Physical Education in Tokyo, because it does not function for Japanese society as a preparer of people for the physical education instruction. It is just a place where many professors in Japan assemble and make a secret group relationship (*dango* in Japanese). The organization itself I1 could not have taken responsibility for Japanese society because there was no principle of physical education study.

I flew from New York to Tokyo and met a professor and president

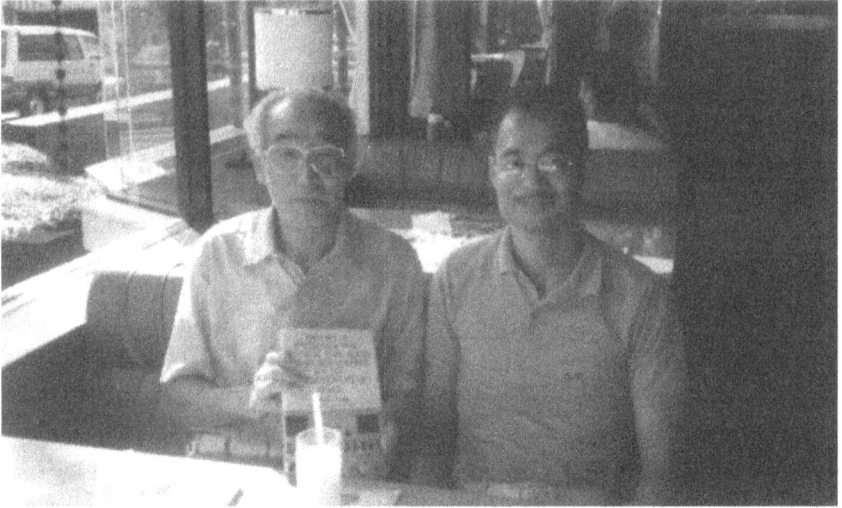

I met my professor Kenzo Kashiwabara in Osaka, Japan, August 12, 1993.

I met Prof. Earle F. Zeigler on September 30, 1989,
at Western Ontario University in Canada.

of the Japanese Society of Physical Education, Shinobu Abe, at the Japan College of Physical Education on August 6, 1993.I have had constructive talks with him there. These were meaningful talks. We made sure of the responsibility of our profession there.

When I moved to Osaka, I met my former professor Kenzo Kashiwabara at Ikeda in Osaka on August 12, 1993.I had an opportunity to talk frankly with him for a few hours about social, national, and world issues concerning physical education and sports studies in the future. I was enjoying our memories also. I emphasized that our theories do not belong to all governments in all nations in the world but belong to all scholars of physical education and sports studies in all nations in the world, in order to take the responsibility for practices of physical education and sports without and within schools.

In June 1993 I joined the National Association for Sport and Physical Education (NASPE) of American Alliance for Health, Physical Education, Recreation, and Dance (AAHPERD). I am looking forward to seeing other members. I also exchange letters every year with former professor Earle F. Zeigler. I have a picture that he sent to me before. It is a precious memory, taken when I participated in his retirement party at Western Ontario University in Canada. I think that I have been doing my best as a scholar of physical education and sports studies. And I promise that I will continue to put my efforts toward it until I die. From now on I intend to make more wide friendships internationally.

Part II

Theory of Martial Arts Studies for the Achievement of Peace

1

A Word from the Author

The term *martial arts human* is a symbolic term that works toward a national peace and a world peace. We, the world's physical education and sports scholars, must treat this term as dearly as our own lives. This is because, without the existence of the martial arts human, none of the language concerning martial arts and research concerning martial arts could be formed. The existence of the martial arts human builds and determines it all. The existence of martial arts humans creates many national languages. However, the national languages are not able to create the human existence in all nations. The human existence in all nations produce American English, Japanese, German, French, Italian, Korean, British English, Spanish, Chinese, etc. The martial arts humans in China speak Chinese. The martial arts humans in Russia speak Russian. The martial arts humans in the United States speak American English. The martial arts humans also make other words like sound (noisy or nice), imitation sound, onomatopoeic words, in the phenomenon of martial arts. All national languages involved in the phenomenon of martial arts are a proof of existence of martial arts humans in each nation. The term *martial arts human* is part of the universal language of the world's physical education and sports scholars as long as the phenomenon of martial arts continues actually in all the nations. It is a specialized term, even a holy term.

I present this book for the benefit of all the physical education and sports scholars of each of the world's nations alike.

2

Establishing the Hypothesis for Creating Martial Arts Studies

The following questions are the fundamental motives for attempting to create the theory of international martial arts studies for the achievement of peace (principle of physical education and sports studies and research for all nations in the world):

1. Why, in the scholastic physical education programs of the education ministries of each country in the world, are teachers or professors using any types of martial arts as the educational resources to lead students?
2. Why are the physical education and sports researchers of each country in the world conducting research concerning any types of martial arts?
3. Why are physical education teachers and physical education and sports researchers and professors of every country in the world conducting classes in schools, colleges, universities, and graduate schools concerning the theory of any types of martial arts?
4. Why does the IOC (International Olympic Committee) adopt any types of martial arts and include martial arts in the Olympics?
5. Why does the research concerning martial arts belong to the physical education and sports studies?
6. Why is the research concerning the martial arts worthy of doctorates or master's degrees in the physical education and sports studies?
7. Why do we need physical education faculties in colleges, universities, and graduate schools in the nation and the world?
8. Why do we physical education scholars need professors who take lectures for their studies to the public and to employ them?

We physical education scholars ask the above-mentioned questions in order to restore public social, national, and world trust for our profession. It means that we physical education scholars have social, national, and world problems. It also brings what education is in reality.

Currently there is no theory in the world's physical education and sports research that can answer these fundamental questions of martial arts research and practices. It is the most important problem that I have to take a responsibility as a physical education scholar in public. Therefore, I try to think that I undertook the problem and tried to solve the problem and build the theories so that I could answer all of the questions. The motive that I have to try the theory for studies of martial arts is mentioned above.

Here, in order to ask myself and answer the question: "What are all types of martial arts and, more generally, what are the martial arts?" I have formed the following hypothesis. "When a human does the martial arts that human becomes a martial arts human. (When a human does martial arts is not when a human becomes a human.)" As a reason for the formation of the hypothesis, I believe that to do martial arts is to do martial arts, and to do martial arts is not to not do martial arts. To do is to become.

This new term (which will become a specialized term used among physical education and sports scholars) has been created in order to convert terms such as *martial arts* and the terms included in it (*judo, boxing, karate, sumo, kendo, fencing, wrestling, naginata,* etc.) into moving, living words. Also, the world's physical education teachers must take responsibility for the social reality of martial arts being taught by sports leaders to sports students and followers.

Also in this book I have used the term movement human. When we perceive the phenomenon of the martial arts, we see people moving. In order to express the existence of the moving human being (apart from the technique one may have in one's arms and legs) in one noun phrase, we say "movement human." This term refers to the entire existence of the human (individual) and some other (another person or something else) dynamically working together in both a passive and active relationship.

The term *martial arts human* is used to collectively represent all of the various types of martial arts, such as boxing human, judo human, karate human, archery human, fencing human, etc. Each of these terms refers directly to the existence of the acting relationship between a movement human (oneself) and movement human (opponent) in each type of martial art. It is this relationship, too, which gives life to and maintains the socially significant term *martial arts*.

Next I would like to explain in detail what the term *martial arts human* refers to. The object to which the words *martial arts human* refers is the entirety of the acting relationship between a movement or non-movement human (oneself) and a movement human (opponent) in the phenomenon of the martial arts or in the applied phenomenon in which martial arts is dealt with. In the world of the martial arts, the movement human (oneself) and movement human (opponent) together make up the martial arts human. In this situation, the movement human is a movement human (oneself) related to a movement human (opponent) and the movement human (opponent) is a movement human (opponent) related to movement human (oneself). Therefore, the two share a common point that connects them together. Specifically, this common point is the existential form in which the martial arts human acts together in mutual independence and in certain aspects moves in a uniform motion. However, if we look objectively at them, we can divide the martial arts human into a martial arts human as a movement human (oneself) and a martial arts human as a movement human (opponent).

Therefore, in presenting the theory, in order to refer directly to both the martial arts human as a movement human (oneself) and the martial arts human as a movement human (opponent), we will use the term *martial arts human* for simplification. Only when we wish to make an explicit distinction between the two sides will we use the expression *martial arts human as a movement human (oneself and martial arts human as a movement human (opponent).* Therefore, the expression *martial arts human* refers to both the movement human (oneself) and movement human (opponent) sides of the martial arts.

There were many reasons for the creation of the special term *martial arts human*, but the most important of these was the need to distinguish the general human existence from the existence experienced in the special world in which martial arts is dealt with in physical education and sports studies and to make this special independence clear. In addition, it serves to help construct national theories (martial arts studies) to explain the unique practice of martial arts.

The next matter with which we must concern ourselves is the development of all types of martial arts phenomena and phenomena that involve the applied exercises of martial arts in every country in the world. Specifically, in what form does this living phenomenon appear to our eyes? In other words, which actions in the living phenomenon of the martial arts are essential and which are nonessential? Understanding this distinction and synthesis will lead to a clear insight into this living phenomenon of martial arts. ,

In order to answer these questions, I will examine the living phenomenon of the martial arts themselves, relying on intuitive analysis and the integrated judgment method. As was stated in the hypothesis, the essence of the existence of the living phenomenon of the martial arts and the phenomenon in which the applied exercises of martial arts are dealt with and the nonessence of that existence (auxiliary actions to the existential essence) are manifested in the various aspects of the martial arts human, such as the track-and-field human, ball human, flying human, dance human, etc. Please see figure 2 for an explanation of this idea. There are, in other words, all the essential structural elements that form the living phenomenon of the martial arts.

If we analyze the primary factors that form the movement relying on our perceptions of the martial arts phenomenon and then integrate these back together, we can come to understand the movement itself. For example, if we look at the action of the martial arts human, we see that he acts on the ground, the air, the image, the ball, etc., in reality, to form the living phenomenon of the martial arts, The instant the martial arts human acts in relation to the ground he begins to exist as a track-and-field human. In that instant the martial arts human acts momentarily in relation to another image, he begins to exist as a dance human.

Furthermore, in the instant the martial arts human acts momentarily in the air, he begins to exist as a flying human. There are the auxiliary actions in the living phenomenon of the martial arts that

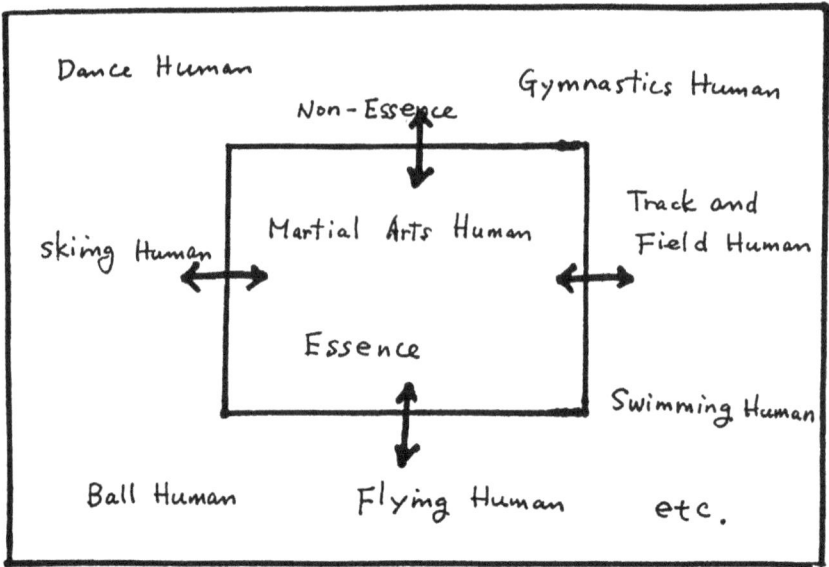

**Figure2. Formation elements of the living phenomenon of
martial arts in each nation in the world**

Furthermore, in the instant the martial arts human acts
momentarily in the air, he begins to exist as a flying human. There are
the auxiliary actions in the living phenomenon of the martial arts that
create motion and that act indirectly on the movement of the martial
arts human.

In order to determine if figure 2 is true or false, let us try to return
to the living phenomenon (fact) of each type of martial arts. For
instance, to explain the living phenomenon of the boxing human in the
martial arts using this figure, we can say that in the actions of the
boxing human the boxing human appears as the existential essence. At
the same time, the phenomenon appears as a composition of transient
aspects of the nonessential, such as the dance human (he may be
momentarily doing boxing with some of his image), the track-and-
field human (he may perform boxing with acting on the ground or the
artificial ground, like a rink), the flying human (he may perform
boxing with acting in the air,), etc. The phenomenon of the martial arts
human is, most importantly, the actions of the martial arts human as
movement human (opponent), in which there are made movements as

18

a martial arts human. I can explain concrete matters of actual martial arts with figure 2. It means figure 2 is true. So we need many kinds of special terms in order to construct national martial arts studies. If the boxing is performed outdoors, the boxing human may act momentarily in rain and water (like swimming human) or snow (like skiing human). The determining factors in the valuation of the martial arts, above all, are the actions of the martial arts human between oneself and opponent. Therefore, the martial arts human in the phenomenon of the martial arts is essential existence. Why? I explain it in evidence of existence of martial arts human, because existence of the martial arts human creates all of these things: national language, special terms of martial arts, actual sounds of the phenomenon of martial arts, etc. The actions of the martial arts human mean movement human (opponent) for the sake of doing martial arts and movement human (oneself) for the sake of doing martial arts.

Therefore, it is possible to say that all the living phenomena of the various types of martial arts can be found in every country in the world, being formed by a mixture of the characteristics of the living phenomenon of the martial arts human, the track-and- field human, the flying human, the dance human, etc. Most important, all are formed from the existential essence of the martial arts human, namely, the living actions of the martial arts human that determine the process and result of the martial arts. As evidence for this we can say that the points scored in martial arts, which depend upon the actions of the martial arts human between oneself and opponent in martial arts, provide dynamic variation to the aspects of the phenomenon and the result of martial arts is determined by them. They also produce a lot of words (specific terms) in relation to the martial arts in national languages and nonwords like sounds and imitation sounds in the phenomenon of martial arts. Therefore, the action of the martial arts human determines everything in the phenomenon of the martial arts.

I would like to put forth the idea that the phenomenon of martial arts is formed by the mutual actions of specific humans, that is, martial arts human (oneself) as a movement human and material arts human as a movement human (opponent), namely, the martial arts human in the form of a hypothesis. However, in order to do this I must provide some clear evidence that is able to confirm that this is the existential essence in the phenomenon of martial arts. This would be the factual grounds for the formation of these words. In order to speak scientifically about the phenomenon of the martial arts and phenomenon in which movement human as martial arts human (opponent) is dealt with, we must make this existential essence that will be the object of the analysis very clear. In other words, it is necessary to confirm whether or not the term *martial arts human* is a term that possesses realistic qualities in the phenomenon of the martial arts.

Thus I began to think that I could incorporate this method into an ontology of the martial arts human. In other words, using the term *martial arts human*, I will explain in detail the reality of the martial arts. Thus, should it be possible to prove this hypothesis, the martial arts human would be the existential essence in the phenomenon of the martial arts and *martial arts human* would become specialized terminology whose use would be required any time martial arts research is being conducted. Furthermore, we would begin down the road toward the construction of a theory of martial arts studies dealing with the entirety of martial arts practice and theory. It would be possible to advance the national theory by means of a teleology and a methodology and, finally, form martial arts theory (in a world united and different).A distinction would be made in the aspects of martial arts studies that affect the daily lives of actual humans and special areas of the martial arts studies and the practices. When names are given to these boundaries, martial arts studies will be formed.

I have ascertained that the existence of the martial arts human can be grasped as three aspects, and in this way I hope to make this existence clear. Specifically, these are the movement-cultural existence of the martial arts human, the educational existence of the martial arts human, and the social existence of the martial arts human. These all point to the fact that in every country in the world the martial arts human exists in many ways and forms a special world. I will begin my undertaking from my understanding of the existence of this martial arts human–the martial arts human that exists in every country in the world.

3

The Movement-Cultural Ontology of the Martial Arts Human

The martial arts human lives in the movement culture and the martial arts human exists possessing movement-cultural aspects in all nations in the world. This comes from a connotative structure and a denotative structure. Together they maintain independent functions while living and existing as a whole.

The Connotative Structure

The martial arts human as a movement human is organically composed with a head, a torso, hands, and feet. Internally, he is partially muscles, bones, organs, a brain, etc., which all rely on blood for their actions. However, the martial arts human as movement human is actually made of many materials, such as a certain amount of air and various other objects, all of which will be acted upon by the existing life energy. This is based on factors of nature, which include gravity, temperature, climate, sunshine, rain, snow, etc., and artificial factors, which include gymnasiums, ground, lighting, etc., and act on individual or group behavior and skill. However, these factors act together with factors dependent on the martial arts human as a movement human himself, such as perception, thought, emotion, etc. Therefore, the martial arts human as a movement human exists as a complex synthesis of the various factors that make up each specific human.

There are other aspects of the martial arts human as an object movement including karate human, judo human, fencing human, wrestling human, boxing human, kendo human, *naginata* human, sumo human, etc. Therefore, this term, *martial arts human*, means specific human existence in the phenomenon of martial art.

As individual actions, the two sides, the martial arts human as a movement human (oneself) and the martial arts human as a movement human (other), approach each other, come into contact, and separate from one another. These actions consist of various types, such as pushing, touching, grasping, kicking, punching, jumping, striking, holding, thrusting, etc.

As group actions, the two sides, the martial arts human as a movement human (oneself) and the martial arts human as a movement human (opponent), approach each other, come into contact, and separate from one another. These group actions consist of various types, such as yelling, using signals, watching, etc.

The actions of individual and group technical skills are based on the actions of the eyes, ears, tongue, skin, etc., of the martial arts human as a movement human and the actions of bones, bowels, and organs such as the heart, lungs, etc. Finally, the actions of thought, emotion, etc., also contribute. In other words, while the sensation/thought/emotion systems' parts have independent functions, they are organically and dynamically related and participate in the skilled actions of the martial arts human as a movement human. In making value judgments about skilled actions, such as good/bad, achieved/not achieved, the martial arts human as a movement human relies greatly on the actions of the sensation/thought/emotion system. The decisions and conflicts are that "my head hurts, but I have to keep performing hard," "I'm tired, so I may quit soon," "if I challenge to him as a judo human, I shall do my best," "my hands hurt, but I have to try harder," "my teacher sees the performance of my fencing, so I try to do my best," etc. Those phrases point to the dynamic actions of martial arts humans of sensation/thought/emotion, sensation/emotion, sensation/thought, thought/sensation, emotions/sensation, emotion/thought/sensation, and so on (figure 3).

The Denotative Structure

The martial arts human as a movement human exists in various movement-cultural aspects in all nations in the world. If we were to classify these movement-cultural aspects, we could classify them in the following four types, because basic forms of all movement humans are composed by approaching actions to someone and some substances

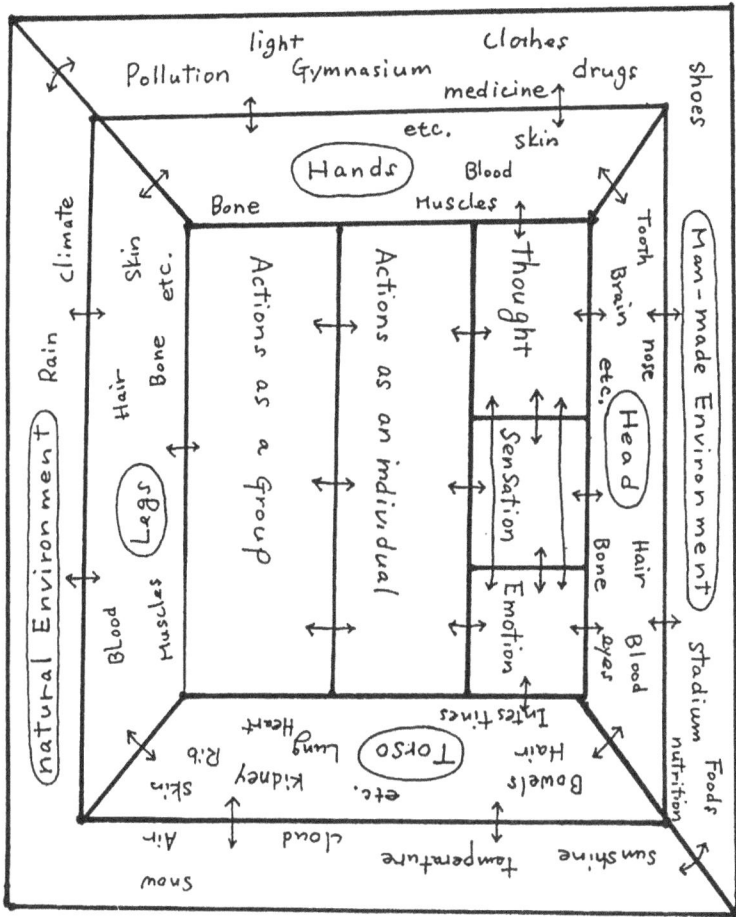

Figure 3. The many kinds of actions of the connotative structure of the martial arts human in each nation in the world

(including water, image, air, ball, human, etc.), touching actions to someone and some substances, and separating actions to someone and some substances in fact. When we watch all actions of movement human we can confirm three kinds of characterized actions through existence of movement human in physical education and sports practices.

The first type includes a kind of martial arts event in which either the movement human as martial arts human (oneself) just approaches the movement human as martial arts human (opponent) or the movement human as martial arts human (opponent) just approaches to the movement human as martial arts human (oneself). There is archery human as movement human like this type nowadays. However, this kind of martial arts event might be r o more increased by some martial arts specialists in the future.

The second type includes martial arts events in which the action of the movement human (as the martial arts human oneself) and the movement human (as the martial arts human opponent) are mutually disjunctive and conjunctive, such as judo human as movement human, wrestling human as movement human, sumo human as movement human, karate human as It movement human, fencing human as movement human, boxing human as movement human, etc.

While both types 1 and 2 deal with individualistic movement-cultural properties, both types 3 and 4 deal with movement-cultural properties that are oriented by the group of more than two people from the movement human (as martial arts human).

The third type includes martial arts events in which the actions of the group martial arts human as a movement human attempt to approach the other group of martial arts humans or separate from the other group of martial arts humans. Today martial arts of this type do not exist in reality but remain a possibility, like boxing human as movement human, archery human as movement human, in a competition among groups.

The fourth type of martial arts human in the phenomenon of martial arts is the martial arts human in which the martial arts human as a movement human in the group and martial arts human as movement human in the group repeat actions of mutual approach, separation, and contact. The martial arts human as a group has events.

For example, there are possible judo humans as movement humans in the group, wrestling humans as movement humans in the group, in a competition among more than two groups belonging to this fourth type.

In this manner, it is possible to classify the movement-cultural existence of every martial arts phenomenon based on the substance and type of actions of the martial arts human. (Refer to figure 4.) However, each martial arts human as a movement human exists in a manner that presents unique aspects. (The boxing human as movement human exists with unique aspects not found in the judo human as movement human. The boxing human as movement human is absolutely boxing human as movement human.) The karate human as movement human exists with unique aspects not found in wrestling human as movement human. (The karate human is absolutely karate human as movement human, in fact.) Therefore, each type of martial arts human appears in his own unique movement-cultural aspects.

Boxing-ness (the Boxing Human as Movement Human)

The boxing human as a movement human exists in aspects of boxing. For example, there is either a direct or indirect relation to the apparatus of boxing, the rules of boxing, the facilities of boxing, the terminology of boxing, etc. The appearance of the boxing human as a movement human forms the unique world of boxing.

Kendo-ness (the Kendo Human as Movement Human)

The martial arts human as a movement human exists in aspects of kendo movement. For example, there is either a direct or indirect contact with the apparatus of kendo, the rule of kendo, the facilities of kendo, the terminology of kendo, etc. The appearance of the kendo forms the unique world of kendo.

Fencing-ness (the Fencing Human as Movement Human)

The martial arts human as a movement human exists in aspects of fencing. For example, there is either a direct or indirect relation to the

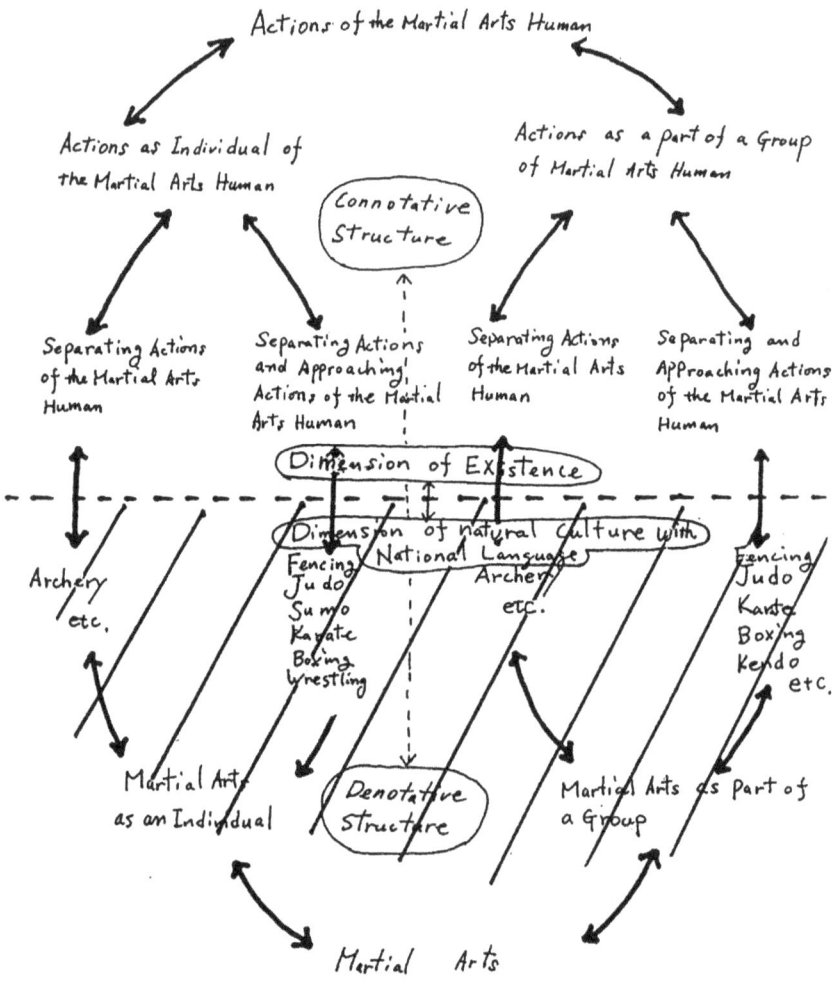

Figure 4. The movement-cultural existence of the
martial arts human in each nation in the world

apparatus of fencing, the rule of fencing, the terminology of fencing, the facilities of fencing, etc. The appearance of the fencing human as a movement human forms the unique world of fencing.

Sumo-ness (the Sumo Human as Movement Human)

The sumo human as a movement human exists in aspects of sumo. For example, there is either a director indirect contact with the apparatus of sumo, the rule of sumo, the facilities of sumo, the terminology of sumo, etc. The appearance of the sumo human forms the unique world of sumo.

As there are several martial arts events that have been introduced in the above-mentioned, the number of martial arts events may increase in the future to include new martial arts events that we have never seen before in this way, the martial arts humans as movement humans exist in all various movement-cultural aspects in every country in the world. In the United States as Americans, in Russia as Russians, in France as the French, in England as the English, and in China as the Chinese. The martial arts human exists in these various movement-cultural aspects.

4

The Educational Ontology of the
Martial Arts Human

In the special society of physical education in every country in the world, the martial arts human as a movement human exists possessing an aspect of the physical education. Every type of martial art is evaluated educationally. Certainly, opinions are formed about whether a martial arts human builds a certain strength, develops character, fosters mental growth, fosters creativity, etc. The educational existence of the martial arts human as a movement human comes from a connotative structure and a denotative structure. Each works based on an independent structure, and as a whole they exist educationally.

The Connotative Structure

In order to make clear the actions of the martial arts human, we will analyze them and use integrated judgment, by both looking from the social actions of the martial arts human toward the living energy and from the living energy toward the social actions of the martial arts human. In this manner, we can fully grasp the entire substance of the actions of the martial arts human. We have some factors that are expressed, such as body strength, flexibility, etc., while in contrast, some factors are expressive, such as the mind, soul, character, personality, condition of character, morale, flexibility, etc. These factors work in a living separate manner, and at the same time the actions of martial arts human are in the integration of all of these living elements. By using these words to inquire about the nature of the actions of the martial arts human, we can elucidate the concept of the martial arts human. Therefore, these words refer to the various partial factors that make up the martial arts human, and they are living words. The source of these words is based upon the supply and demand of living energy produced by the unification (actions of digestion, actions of oxidation) that takes place inside the individual of the mutually conflicting elements of air and fwd, and the martial arts human. In other words, the source is the transformation of the various elements, such as body strength, flexibility of body, physique, physical condition, mind, soul, morale, flexibility of mind, personality, condition of character, etc., into a living entity. Therefore, the words *body, body strength, flexibility of body, physique, physical condition, mind, soul, morale, flexibility of mind, personality, and condition of character* are all living words and are words that have come to refer to reality.

On the other hand, we have said that the action of the martial, arts human is formed from a synthesis of the various types of actions of the martial arts human expressed in terms of mind, body, soul, physique, physical condition, body strength, flexibility of body, condition of character, morale, and flexibility of mind. It should be noted that in our analysis of the actions of the martial arts human we said that there is both a movement human as a martial arts human and another movement human as a martial arts human, with mutually different objects. Since this is the case, it may not be appropriate to use the same type of language to explain both. However, based on the common point of view that both share as the martial arts human, we will use the same language to explain them.

The analysis and synthesis of these two sides, the martial arts human as a movement human and the martial arts human as a movement apparatus, are shown in figure 5 and figure 6.

Also making up the actions of the martial arts human are skilled actions, which express technique. However, if we analyze these skilled actions, we can see that they are made up of actions of the conduct of the martial arts human and the substance of the kind of technique being expressed. In other words, the actions of the conduct of the martial arts human, together with the substance of the technique, make up the reality of the skilled action of the martial arts human and exist united in reality. These exist in a relationship that is mutually life-giving and enlivened, creating the phenomenon of the skilled existence of the martial arts human.

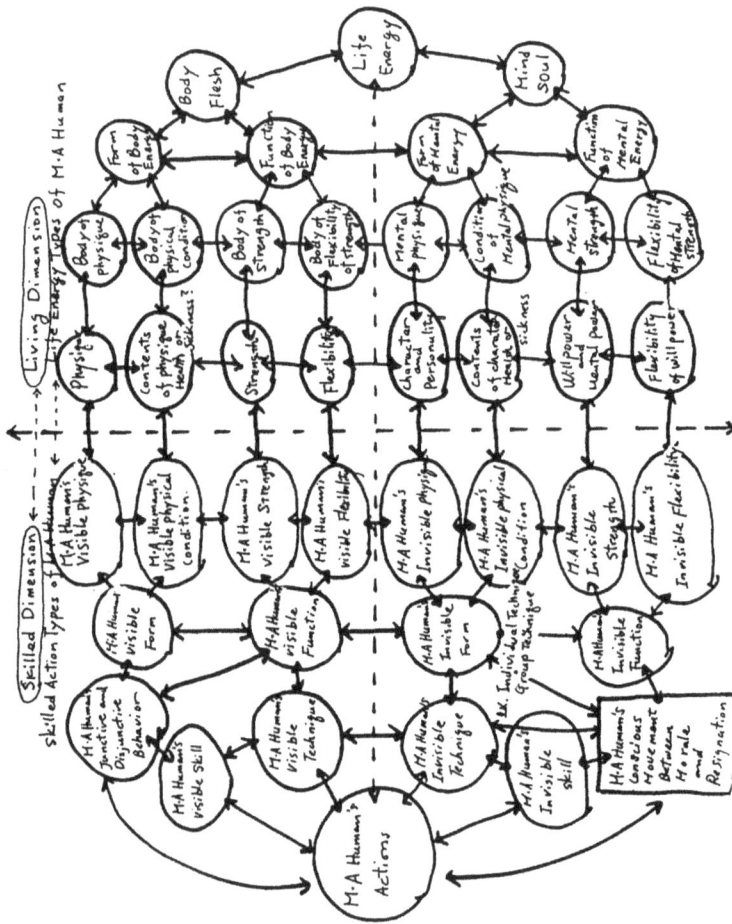

Figure 5. Types of actions of the martial arts human in each nation in the world

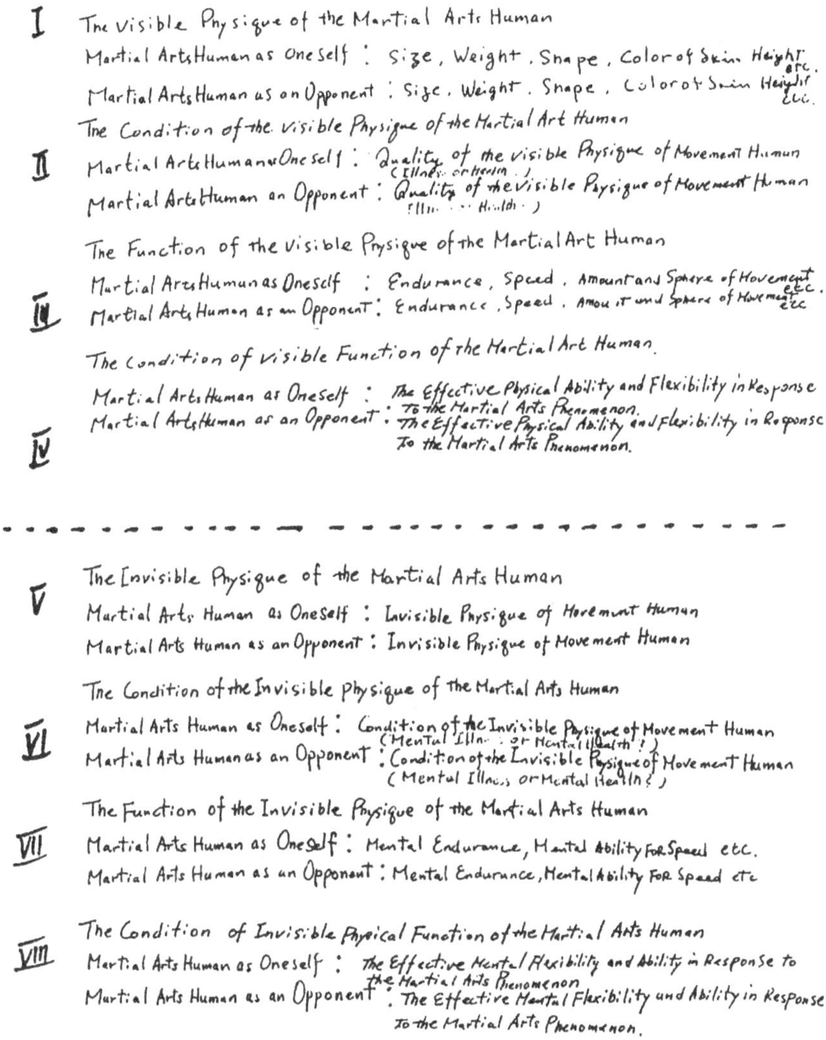

I The Visible Physique of the Martial Arts Human
Martial Arts Human as Oneself : Size, Weight, Shape, Color of Skin, Height etc.
Martial Arts Human as an Opponent : Size, Weight, Shape, Color of Skin, Height etc.

The Condition of the Visible Physique of the Martial Art Human

II Martial Arts Human as Oneself : Quality of the Visible Physique of Movement Human (Illness or Health)
Martial Arts Human an Opponent : Quality of the Visible Physique of Movement Human (Illness Health)

The Function of the Visible Physique of the Martial Art Human

III Martial Arts Human as Oneself : Endurance, Speed, Amount and Sphere of Movement etc.
Martial Arts Human as an Opponent : Endurance, Speed, Amount and Sphere of Movement etc.

The Condition of Visible Function of the Martial Art Human.

IV Martial Arts Human as Oneself : The Effective Physical Ability and Flexibility in Response To the Martial Arts Phenomenon.
Martial Arts Human as an Opponent : The Effective Physical Ability and Flexibility in Response To the Martial Arts Phenomenon.

- -

V The Invisible Physique of the Martial Arts Human
Martial Arts Human as Oneself : Invisible Physique of Movement Human
Martial Arts Human as an Opponent : Invisible Physique of Movement Human

The Condition of the Invisible physique of the Martial Arts Human

VI Martial Arts Human as Oneself : Condition of the Invisible Physique of Movement Human (Mental Illness or Mental Health)
Martial Arts Human as an Opponent : Condition of the Invisible Physique of Movement Human (Mental Illness or Mental Health)

The Function of the Invisible Physique of the Martial Arts Human

VII Martial Arts Human as Oneself : Mental Endurance, Mental Ability For Speed etc.
Martial Arts Human as an Opponent : Mental Endurance, Mental Ability For Speed etc

The Condition of Invisible Physical Function of the Martial Arts Human

VIII Martial Arts Human as Oneself : The Effective Mental Flexibility and Ability in Response to the Martial Arts Phenomenon
Martial Arts Human as an Opponent : The Effective Mental Flexibility and Ability in Response To the Martial Arts Phenomenon.

Figure 6. The types and contents of the actions of the martial arts human in each nation in the world

The Denotative Structure

In regard to the denotative structure of the educational e of the martial arts human, I have attempted some a1 speculation that will explain it, as shown in figure 7.

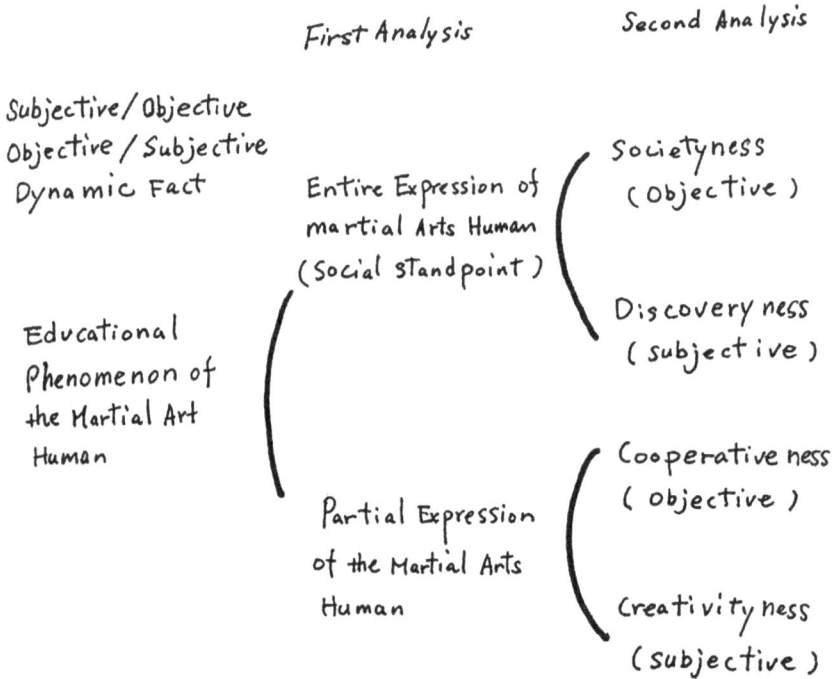

First Analysis   Second Analysis

Subjective / Objective
Objective / Subjective
Dynamic Fact

Entire Expression of martial Arts Human (Social Standpoint)

Societyness (Objective)

Discovery ness (subjective)

Educational Phenomenon of the Martial Art Human

Partial Expression of the Martial Arts Human

Cooperative ness (objective)

Creativity ness (subjective)

Figure 7. The educational existence of the martial arts human in each nation

Here I will explain each of the educational elements of the martial arts human dealt with in the second analysis of the educational phenomenon of the martial arts human.

Society-ness

The martial arts human functions in the special society of the martial arts. However, in order to create this special society, all of the factors must be accepted and approved. Specifically, the martial arts human as a movement human that takes on the special social role as player acts both socially and morally. The martial arts human as a movement human acts in participation with the humans that take on the social roles of judges, teachers, leaders, students, etc., and even with things that are set up for the purpose of becoming a martial arts human as a movement human, such as unique facilities, equipment, rules, etc. In this manner, the phenomenon of the martial arts is when the martial arts human as a movement human is enlarged from some person to some thing and from some thing to some person, he acts both socially and morally. However, while the society of the martial arts human as a movement human provides the nature of a special society, in order that martial arts occur in general society, they exist in the twofold relationship with general society and the special society of the martial arts.

Discovery-ness

The martial arts human as a movement human acts creatively. At the same time, another martial arts human (opponent) as a movement human also acts creatively. In the action of the martial arts human, there are situations in which new technical content or form, of which no similar example existed in the past, is added. These new techniques are conceptualized and given special names. This itself points to the discovery-ness of the martial arts human. For example, names in the events of martial arts itself point to the discovery-ness of the martial arts human.

For example, we are able to find so many things from the martial arts of the Olympics. The original words for martial arts that the Olympics created are proof of the discovery-ness of martial arts human. There is a certain way that Olympics brought about the birth of the new martial arts. In this way, there are situations in which a new martial arts human given movement-cultural existence in history is formed. The discovery-ness of the martial arts human consists of both the creative and historical expansion aspects of these actions.

Cooperativeness

In the phenomenon of the martial arts there are many cases in which the martial arts human acts in a group. In these cases, cooperative intentions are demanded of the martial arts human. This cooperativeness depends on the mutual relationship between acting martial arts humans that have taken on the social role of the competitors, and therefore this is a social action. There is cooperativeness from a unified standpoint and cooperativeness from a different standpoint. For example, the general factors of the school associated with the individual human: the religion, age, sex, etc., may be identical or different. Also, the various factors of the special standpoint of the martial arts such as skill level of the martial arts human, the competitor, companions, etc., may be identical or different.

In this way, the actions of the cooperativeness of the martial arts human exist as the nature of the identities and differences of the special things limited only to the martial arts. So if we try to limit it to only the cooperativeness in the special society of the martial arts, the cooperativeness of identity recognition of the martial arts human is based on the recognition of technical standpoint and the cooperativeness of difference recognition is based on the recognition of the existential standpoint.

Creativity-ness

The martial arts human, in the living, always-changing space of the martial arts, acts while at every moment being faced with the problem: "in what way should I best handle another martial arts human (rival or opponent) I encounter?" The martial arts human as movement human who has been acted on by martial arts human as a movement human (opponent) is a concrete expression of the skill of the martial arts human as a movement human himself. It is something that indicates the level of skill. Therefore, the martial arts human as movement human demands skill from the martial arts human as a movement human, and conversely, the martial arts human as a movement human exists while demanding skill from the martial arts human (opponent) as a movement human. Through the skill demands of these two sides the martial arts human creates. For example, the martial arts human (opponent) as a movement human is thrown by the martial arts human (oneself) as a movement human, which requires the social role of martial arts as an athlete and a skill. Then the martial arts human as a movement human tries to face this movement human (opponent) and through the martial arts human of movement human (opponent) as an extension of the individual body tries to respond to the skilled action of the martial arts human as opponent. As a result, the excellent performance as a martial arts human, tools, special terms of martial arts, and so forth, will be created.

The creativity of martial arts human can be seen in the creativity of the partial cause/effect action of playing and the action of going inside and the action of doing well and the action of failure. Through this partial cause/effect process, the action of winning, the action of losing, and the action of a draw was created. Creativity can be seen in the partial cause/effect actions in the entire process of the martial arts, from start to finish. Furthermore, the creativity generates the subjective emotions of happiness, vexation, anger, and sorrow at every instant in the martial arts human as a movement human (oneself) and the martial arts human as a movement human (opponent). In the special living space of the martial arts the unknown space of the martial arts, and regulated space of the martial arts is acting creatively in an original way. These actions bring about a reformation of the self-consciousness of the possibilities of ability in the martial arts human that have taken the special role of performer. In this special society, it gives meaning to life.

In this way, the martial arts human exists educationally. At the same time, he exists as the educational being in scholastic physical education in every country in the world and is an expression of every country in the world (each national language) in his existence.

5

The Social Ontology of the
Martial Arts Human

The martial arts human exists within general society. There he exists in each nation while possessing an aspect of social existence in which he lives trying to plan original plans. For example, from the factual phenomena of the martial arts all kinds of words have been derived, such as *physical education, recreation,* etc. On the other hand, in social actions of martial arts human there are various kinds of sociological terms that have been created, such as *fair, unfair, cooperative,* etc. This can be said to be implicit proof that the martial arts human exists socially. Concerning the social existence of the martial arts human, in order to grasp his factual living state as a living state, I will divide this into a connotative structure and a denotative structure and explain each. Therefore, the social existence of the martial arts human is the entirety of the independent actions of connotative structure and denotative structure.

The Connotative Structure

Let us consider the basic aspects of the actions of the martial arts human. In the case of the individual, it is the actions of mutual separation-contact within the martial arts human. In the case of the group, it is the actions of mutual separation-contact among many martial arts humans. In other words, the basic principle is the entirety of the motion that occurs when the martial arts human as a movement human (opponent) and the martial arts human as a movement human (oneself) mutually separate, approach, and contact.

If we apply this fact to each kind of the entire phenomenon of the martial arts it will be understood easily. This is shown in figure 8.

In other words, in order to grasp this dynamic separation-contact

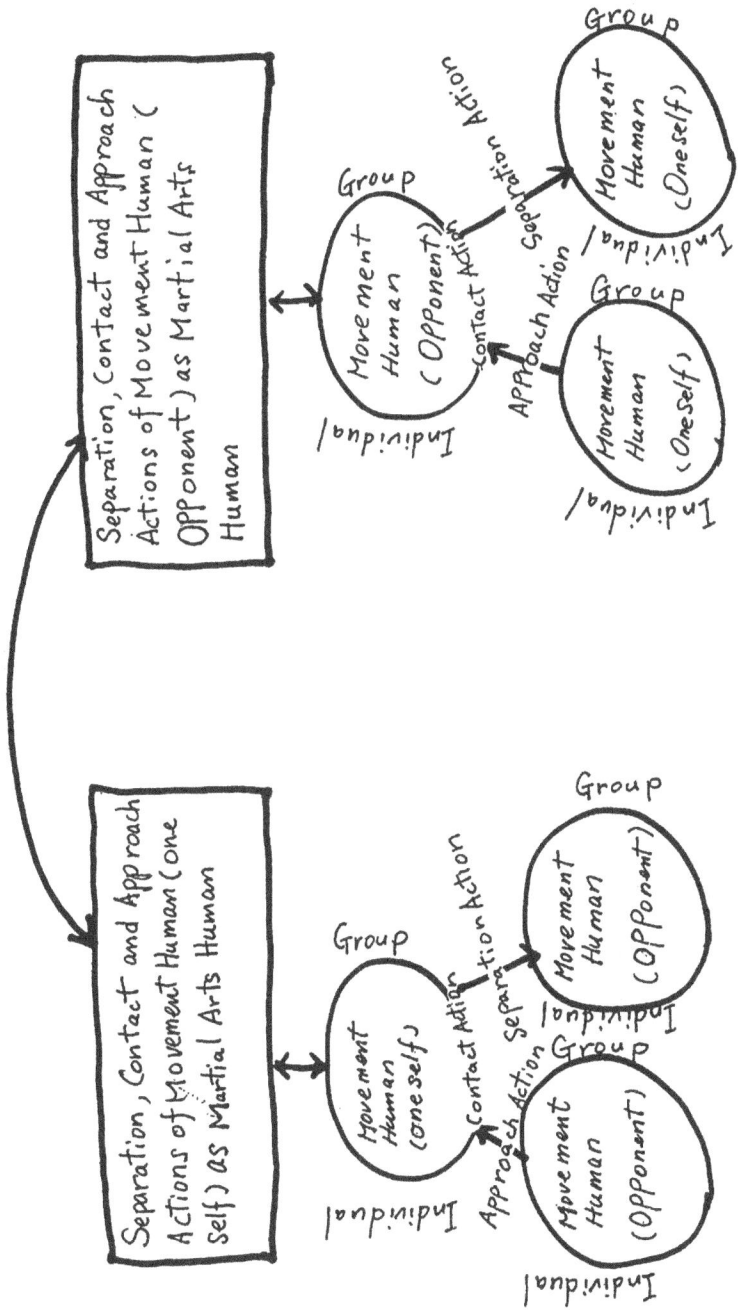

Figure 8. The separation/contact/approach actions of the martial arts human in each nation in the world

relationship within the martial arts human, one must begin by looking objectively from the actions of the body of the martial arts human. Meanwhile, there are also the actions of the mind of the martial arts human, namely the separation-contact movement of the consciousness. Those actions come from the fact that when dealing with the apparatus, the martial arts human as a movement human recognizes another martial arts human (opponent) by the action of unconscious-conscious. The strength, or perhaps weakness, of the actions of the consciousness of the martial arts human as a movement human is located in the polarized structure of the morale and resignation of the consciousness. The strength or weakness depends throughout on the manner in which the consciousness moves between those polarizations (figure 9).

As the martial arts human as a movement human lives, breathes, and goes to another martial arts human as movement human (opponent) and as another martial arts human as a movement (opponent) lives, breathes, and goes to the martial arts human as a movement human, the morale strengthens the consciousness. In other words, the morale strengthens the unified perception of both sides of the martial arts human, the martial arts human as a movement human and the other martial arts human (opponent) as a movement human. It also promotes the manifestation of living as a martial arts human. For example, in a hotly contested martial arts competition, the performer himself and each act that the performer does come to be perceived as a unified dimension.

Because the morale is a living thing, it promotes flattering aspects, but since it is caused through the consciousness's condition of resignation, it moves to the resignation, which is a different kind of element. Primarily, the morale of the martial arts human is in the dimension of time, which hap a passive nature and has some bad points, but in the dimension of space the morale has an active nature. The morale possesses these kinds of properties.

However, the resignation of the martial arts human is the condition of the consciousness of the preparatory steps for displaying the consciousness of morale. Therefore, the resignation of the martial arts human, in relation to the morale, is an element of denial, but on the other hand, it provides a kind of quality that serves to support morale

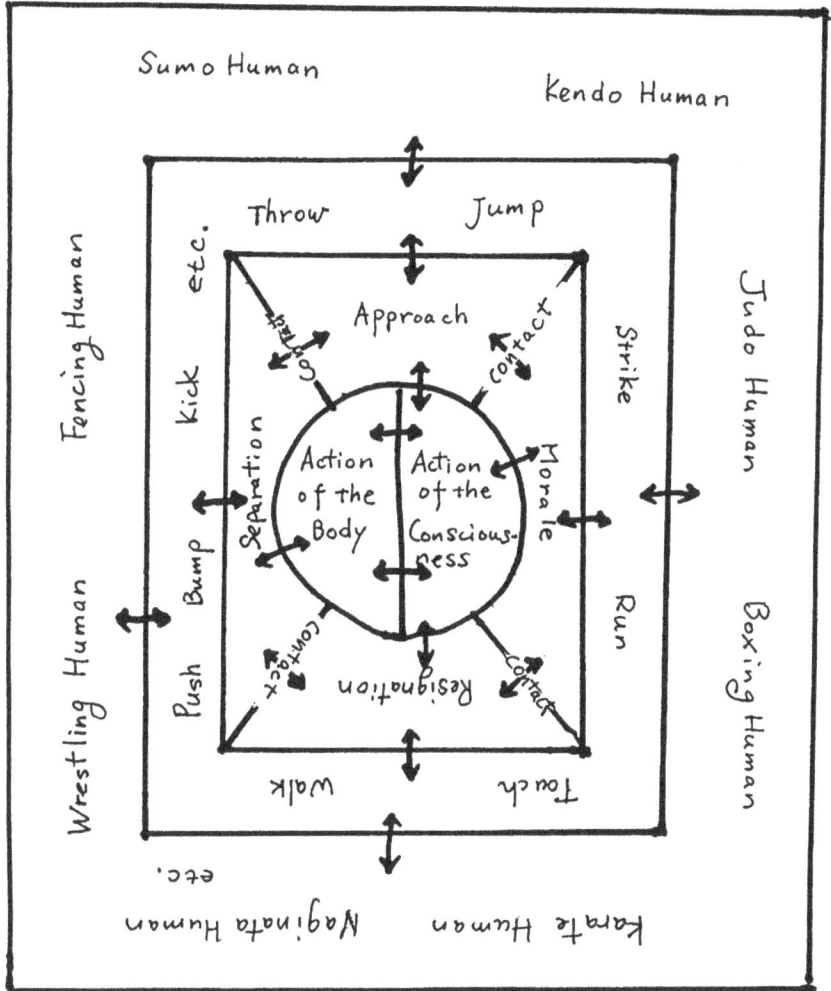

Figure 9. Relation between existence of the martial arts human and the words or language connecting phenomena of the martial arts in each nation in the world

39

as well. In the realm of space the resignation of the martial arts human is weak and passive, but in the realm of time it is strong and active.

The connotative structure of the social existence of the martial arts human presents the mutual actions of separation-contact between the martial arts humans. Objectively, the body acts by the separation-contact actions, and at the same time, subjectively, the mind acts by the separation-contact actions. Together they act as a whole. Within these actions, the changes in consciousness are acting, namely by presenting the aspects of morale and resignation.

Concerning the actions of the martial arts human, we use many different expressions to indicate them. These different expressions all rely on the aspects of the actions of the martial arts human. (Refer to figure 10.)

For example, in order to create sentences for classifications within the types of martial arts human, such as the action of the martial arts, one would proceed in the following way.

The judo human as a movement human grasps the clothes of the competitor at the same time another martial arts human as a movement human (opponent) is grasped by the competitor (the action of the judo human). The boxing human as movement (human) jumps the competitor at the same time another boxing human as a movement human (opponent) is jumped by the competitor.

In the preceding manner, the actions of the connotative structure of the martial arts human themselves act in an original way. At the same time, they also act with aspects of the denotative structure.

The Denotative Structure

In the following way, I have analyzed and gained insight into the denotative elements of the social existence of the martial arts human and I have attempted to extract the denotative elements themselves. (See figure 11.)

Using figure 11 I will show each of the social factors of the martial arts human listed in the second analysis.

Names of Actions of the Other Martial | Names of Actions of the Martial
Arts Human as a Movement Human | Arts Human as a Movement
(Opponent) | (Oneself)

$$
\begin{pmatrix}
\text{being moved} \\
\text{being bounced} \\
\text{being creeped} \\
\text{being rolled} \\
\text{being jumped} \\
\text{being grasped} \\
\text{being touched} \\
\text{etc.}
\end{pmatrix}
\quad \text{and} \quad
\begin{pmatrix}
\text{moving} \\
\text{bouncing} \\
\text{creeping} \\
\text{rolling} \\
\text{jumping} \\
\text{grasping} \\
\text{touching} \\
\text{etc.}
\end{pmatrix}
$$

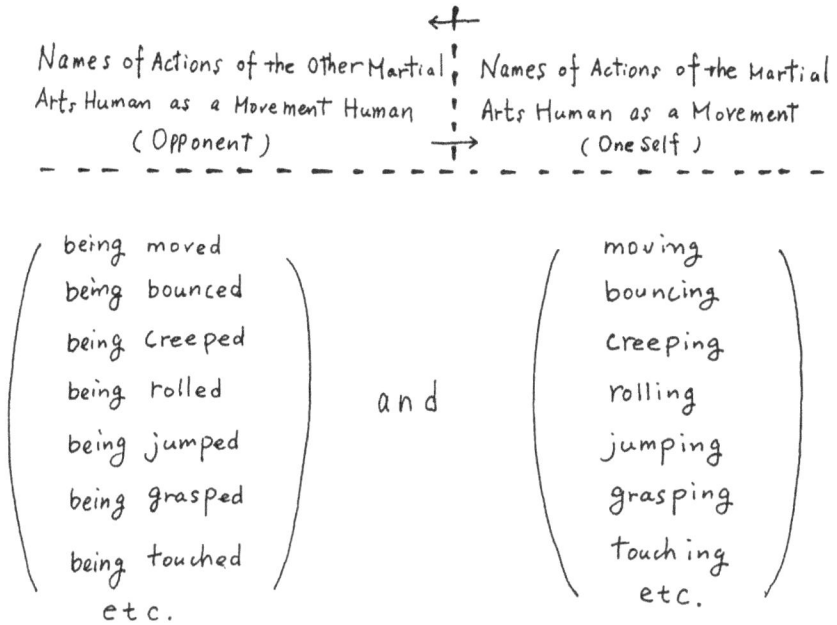

Figure 10. Natural expressions related to the actions of the
martial arts human in each nation in the world

Recreation-ness/Competitiveness

First there is recreation-ness, in which the martial arts human amuses himself with entertaining martial arts, such as when a group of coworkers or a family enjoys martial arts. There is also competitive-ness, which includes tension of seriousness such as when competitive leagues are sponsored by all kinds of competitive groups. The recreation-ness of martial art humans fosters a place for the meeting of the hearts of the martial arts human as a movement human comrade and the martial arts human as a movement human and the martial arts human as a movement human comrade. It is a softening aspect that encourages mutual understanding. Then there is competitiveness, which is the aspect of the martial arts human where, within the rules of competition, a martial arts human as a movement human comrade or perhaps a martial arts human as a movement human and a martial arts human as a movement human comrade, facing on another, act with

First Analysis   Second Analysis

Recreation ness –
Competitive ness

Entire Expression
of the Martial Arts
Human

Sports ness – physical
Education ness

The Aspects of
the Social
Existence of
the Martial Arts
Human

Partial Expression
of the Martial Arts
Human

Combative ness –
Cooperative ness

Primitive ness –
Modernity

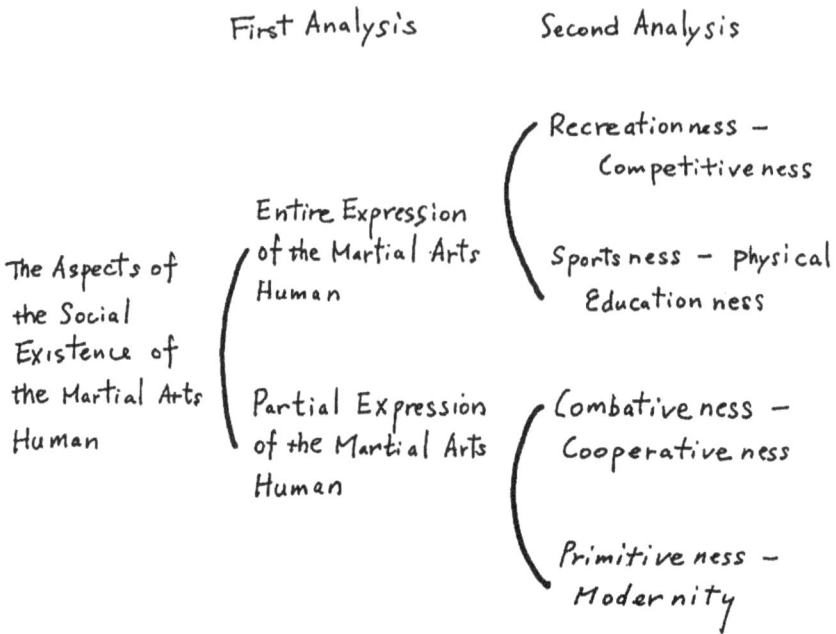

Figure 11. The social existence of the martial arts human
in each nation in the world

bravery and valorous determination. The greater the scale of the competitive league, the more the spirit intensifies, and the competetiveness of the martial arts human appears more conspicuous. For instance, this is the case in all the types of martial arts in international leagues, etc.

Sports-ness/Physical Education-ness

In the phenomenon of martial arts based on the fundamental structure of the teacher and pupil, the educational environment and content are given in the school's gym or a corresponding place. This is the physical education-ness of the martial arts human performing in each martial art event. The physical education-ness of the martial arts human is an educational phenomenon that depends on the sum total of the teacher and pupil. This is an aspect of the special society called school and an aspect of the actions of the martial arts humans as teacher (or professor) and students (as they are driven by sociological terms) that comes from a regionally narrow scope. The student who is recognized by the school side, perhaps specially selected, from nursery school through elementary, junior high, and high school, will be acting the role of the physical education-ness of the martial arts human. On the other hand, the phenomenon of martial arts in general society is an expression of the sports-ness of the martial arts human. We can see the sports-ness of the martial arts human because the sphere of martial arts belongs to sports. It is of course possible for martial arts to belong in the realm of sports. If that is the case, the sports-ness of martial arts humans would be the aspect of the martial arts human in which, in the social phenomenon that relies on the sum total of leaders and followers, a wide range of many kinds of martial arts would be developed with no relevance to sex, age, or occupation. Furthermore, there are the phenomena of judo, kendo, fencing, karate, etc., expressions of the sports-ness of martial arts human.

Combativeness/Cooperativeness

In the actions of the martial arts human, there are the elements of the contrasting actions of combativeness and cooperativeness. The action of behavior (or performance) of an individual martial arts human as a movement human on a team of martial art humans is an expression of cooperativeness. This action of the behavior between companion martial art humans creates a oneness of the team/individual and builds many conscious states. It conspicuously expresses the cooperativeness of martial arts humans. This aspect can also be seen in the phenomenon where a group performs a martial art, whereas actions of the martial arts human, the skilled actions of the martial arts human, as an individual, are sublimated to the skilled actions of the martial arts humans as a group. Namely, when there is a lack in the skilled actions of one martial arts human as a movement human, it is compensated for by the skilled actions of some other individual martial arts human as a movement human. In addition, there is also the aspect in which in order for one martial arts human as a movement human as an individual to do skilled actions, some different martial arts human as a movement human as an individual tries to give assistance. In these forms, this aspect appears.

In contrast to this, there are also times when, with a severe attitude toward other martial arts humans (competitors), the martial arts human as an individual feels that the other martial arts humans are rivals or opponents. This is an expression of the combativeness of the martial arts human. It is most conspicuous in the setting of vehement competition between martial arts humans. Combativeness can be seen in every phenomenon of martial arts and every phenomenon in which the other martial arts human (opponent) is dealt with. It is the moment when the skilled actions of the martial arts humans as an individual are strong opposed to the skilled actions of some other martial arts human as an individual and they feel each other to be rivals. It also can be the movement of rivals that appears between the skilled actions of martial arts humans of a group.

Primitiveness/Modernity

In martial arts, there is the primitiveness of the martial arts human, in which the martial arts human directly engages the other martial art human (as opponent) in contact momentarily In martial arts such as karate, judo, sumo, wrestling, etc. (barefoot, uncovered palms of the hands, etc.) there is momentary direct contact with the other martial arts human in the actions toward the martial arts human as a movement human that has taken on the role of competitor, such as the situations of hand grabbing, touching, kicking, etc. Therefore, the primitiveness of the martial arts human involves giving a direct impact to the body of martial arts human, but the opportunities to handle the other martial arts human (opponent) are relatively frequent.

On the other hand, there is an aspect of modernity of the martial art human which in the relation between martial arts human (oneself side) and the martial arts human (opponent side) equipment, gloves, uniforms, shoes, music, etc., are used. Judo, fencing, kendo, etc. by using specific uniforms, wooden swords (called *shinai* in Japanese), metal swords, etc., are martial arts events that conspicuously express the modernity of the martial arts human. In the modernity of the martial arts human, the impact of the opponent received by the body of the martial arts human as a movement human is small. The handling of the competitor is relatively rare, and the freedom of the martial arts movement is limited.

Moreover, to say that here in the denotative structure we have come up with a comprehensive list of all of the words that refer to the social existence of martial arts human would be added. I have aimed only for a coordinated understanding of the social existence of the martial arts human and understanding of it as a living existence. Furthermore, if we look at all the various elements of the social existence of the martial arts human, such as the amateur-ness or professional-ness of martial arts human, the fair play-ness of the martial arts human and the playfulness of the martial arts human, we can see that these elements are vital elements that act to stir up the social aspects of the martial arts human. In this manner, in every country in the world, the martial arts human expresses the originality of each country and carries on a social existence. In the stream of time of past-present-future, this existence lives in the present as realistic beings and this existence is variable and alive.

6

Generalizations from the Ontology
of the Martial Arts Human

Up to this point, the three existences of the martial arts human, namely, the movement-cultural, educational, social existence, have been explained clearly The *martial arts human*, when taken as in the hypothesis, is language that refers to the existential essence of the phenomenon of the martial arts and the phenomena in which a competitor is dealt with. In other words, we have confirmed the fact that the words *martial arts human* are alive and exist, forming the special expanding world of martial arts and dealing with competitors in martial arts in every country in the world. We have also confirmed the fact that these words refer directly to a special kind of human. The martial arts human exists as the expression of each country (national language) in the world, in the United States as an American, in the Soviet Union as a Soviet, in China as Chinese, in Japan as Japanese, in Sweden as Swedish, etc. The martial arts humans speak American English, Chinese, Korean, German, British English, Italian, French, Spanish, etc., in the phenomena of martial arts. In the presence of the ever-flowing stream of past-present-future, with living and variable aspects, it exists and lives.

Now, as a result of the clear evidence of the existential essence of the martial arts and the clear evidence of the existence of the martial arts human in phenomena of the martial arts, the following kinds of questions can now be answered:

Question1: What is the phenomenon of the martial arts?
Answer: The phenomenon of the martial arts is the phenomenon in which a human and another human become martial arts humans through doing the martial arts. It is a special world in which the martial arts human performs (or acts).

Question 2: What does it mean to perform martial arts?
Answer: This is when some humans become martial arts humans that can be divided into, on the one hand, a martial arts human as self and, on the other hand, a martial arts human as opponent, for performing a martial art.

For example (more concreteness):

Question 1: What is the judo?
Answer: Judo is a practice by which a human and another human become judo humans.

Question 2: What does it mean to perform judo?
Answer: This means becoming a judo human that can be divided into a movement human as a judo human and an another judo human as an opponent.

Question 3: What does it mean to perform martial arts in physical education?
Answer: This is the conduct in which the human and another human as an opponent become martial arts humans (as movement human and another movement human as an opponent) and both of these are physical education-ized and try to become physical education-ized.

Question 4: What does it mean to perform martial art in sports?
Answer: This is the conduct in which the human and another human a san opponent become martial arts humans on both sides, and both of these are sports-ized and try to become sports-ized.

For any other questions concerning the phenomenon of the martial art itself, they can be answered from the movement/cultural, educational, and social ontologies previously presented.

Furthermore, this martial arts human encompasses every type of martial arts human. Namely, it is the existence of fencing human, the existence of *naginata* human, the existence of karate human, the existence of boxing human, etc. Also depending on the differences in sex, age, race, school, occupation, etc., the specific humans in phenomena of martial arts exist as different expressions.

In the above manner, through the movement of speculation, the establishment of the ontology of the martial arts human, from both an abstract standpoint and a concrete standpoint, from the existence to being and from being to existence, become possible. Here we can generalize this system as the ontology of the martial arts human.

Finally, while I have referred to the existence of the martial arts human as a special existence of the human in the martial arts, I must now go on to present the existence of a purpose for the existence of the martial arts human. Namely, the existence of the martial arts human that I have presented until now is an existence that acts in order to realize the martial arts human image. It is that purpose for which the existence is acting. Therefore, I must now go on to develop a presentation concerning the martial arts human image-the teleology of the martial arts human in each nation and each era. I would like to affirm the martial arts human image that comes from the existence of the martial arts human, who exists with special aspects in the martial arts.

7

The Teleology of the Martial Arts Human

Until this point, I have contemplated the existential essence in the phenomena of all types of martial arts. I have shown clearly and confirmed that in every country in the world, every type of martial arts human exists in the world of each type of martial art. However, at the same time, this existence includes the purpose of the martial arts human, namely, the martial arts human image. It is not simply the existence of the martial arts human, but also an existence that tries to realize the ideal image that the martial arts human must attain. Above all, the practice of all types of martial arts that are being conducted in scholastic physical education and sports in every country in the world occurs for the sake of the realization of all types of the martial arts human image by all types of the martial arts human. Also, there is the necessity for physical education and sports studies research concerning all types of martial arts in every country in the world (such as physical education and sports studies philosophy, physical education and sports studies psychology, physical education and sports studies physiology, physical education and sports studies sociology, physical education and sports studies history, etc.) in order to plan the realization of the martial arts human image, in the practice of the martial arts or the applied practice where martial arts is dealt with, in physical education.

At this point I will go on to speculate about what kind of special ideal image is meant by the purpose of the martial arts human in all nations in the world or, more specifically, by the martial arts human image in all nations in the world.

The martial arts human image in all nations in the world is, of course, the purpose of the practice of the martial arts, but it is necessary to explain clearly what in reality this word directly refers to. It refers to the ideal image in which the actions of the martial arts human as an opponent in the practice of the martial art are existing together doing superior actions. The martial arts human image is the ideal image that is living and exists ideally from one era to the next era in every country in the world. This is determined by the research of the physical education and sports theory specialists (such as physical education and sports studies philosophers, physical education and sports studies psychologists, physical education and sports studies physiologists, physical education and sports studies sociologists, physical education I and sports studies historians, etc.) that are living in each era in every country in the world. The term *martial arts human image* refers directly to the ideal existence that adds weight, depth, size, and breadth to that acting existence.

According to the nature of the substance of the martial arts, human, there are really two different kinds of nature. Also, these two natures dynamically act together and form the firm martial arts human image. The fist is the part of the purpose that has a universal nature that is common, no matter what the time, no matter what the place, no matter what the country. For example, all of the superior actions of the movement human (oneself) and the movement human (opponent)–in other words, the attempt to realize the martial arts human image-even though there are differences between the histories, cultures, ideas, races, languages of the countries in the world, share a common universal nature.

The second is the concrete purpose of the martial arts human, which is variable depending on the time, society, nation, age, sex, and other variables that differ from country to country. In every country, there is originality in history, idem, culture, and national language. The martial arts human image of a certain era in each country of the world has the aspects of that era. Furthermore, from the point of view of age, the various types of martial arts human images for children are different from the various types of martial arts human images for old people. From the point of view of sex, the martial arts human images for males and females are different. The images of the martial arts human are not identical, due to the various human differences. Therefore, as opposed to the purpose of the universal substance of the martial arts human this points to the variable, concrete purpose of the martial arts human. The constitution of the teleology of the martial arts human relies on the support/being-supported relationship between these two sides, which is a relationship that acts dynamically and mutually to support each side. The martial arts human image of the former is the purpose of the martial arts human, while the martial arts human image of the latter is the goal of the martial arts human. The difference between these words clearly points to the difference between the universal purpose and the variable purpose. Therefore, the martial arts human image consists of the purpose substance as its core, and that which surrounds the purpose substance is the goal substance. The dynamic relationship between them assumes the character of abstract/concrete-concrete/abstract. Because of this, the martial arts human image possesses unifying qualities that transcend the realities of nationality, age, sex, etc. (time and space), but at the same time this teleology is also one that sees those realities as realities. This can be summarized in figure 12.

Next I would like to go on to explain the purpose of the martial arts human. Specifically, of what substance is the martial arts image itself constructed. I will explain this point.

The structure of the martial arts human image is made up of two types; a connotative structure and a denotative structure. These form the living, unified whole. There are the actions of all of the many element images, and as a whole they act ideally. If we broadly divide these various idealistic elements, they come from the connotative structure and the denotative structure. (Refer to figure 13.)

In physical education and sports, the martial arts human forms the special society of the martial arts. He works ideally in a unique way. At the same time, he is regulated in a unique way and exists ideally.

The Image of Connotative Structure

In the actions of the martial arts, human image, there is the image of connotative structure. This acts as the foundation for the generation of the image of denotative structure and thus is a vitally important area. The image of connotative structure itself is formed from the various element images that become the many different ideals. It is formed from the ideal of the image of life energy that comes from physical education and sports nutrition studies and physical education and sports hygiene, the ideal of the image of the body and the image of the mind (mind-body image) that come from physical education and sports philosophy, the ideal of the image of body strength, the image

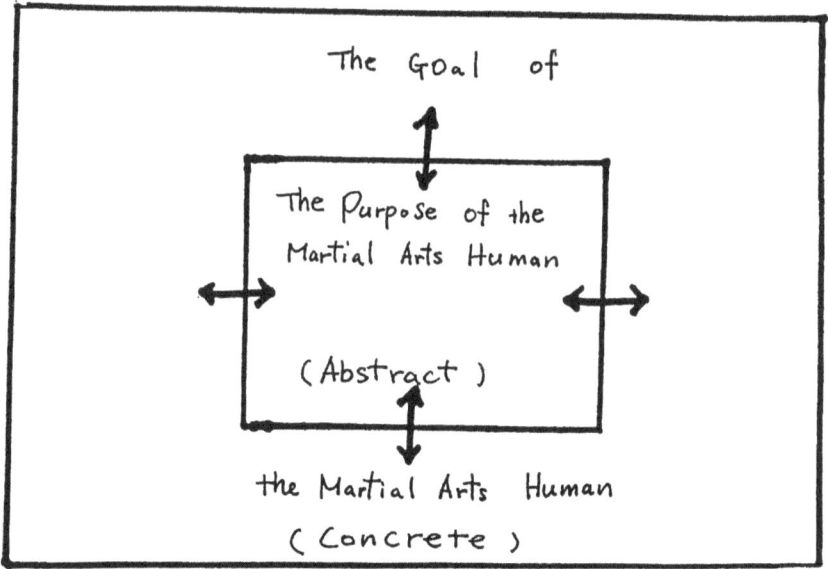

**Figure 12. Constitution of the martial arts human image
in each nation in the world**

of flexibility, the image of physique, and the image of physical condition (the image of health) that come from physical education and sports physiology, etc. The physical education and sports studies researchers of every country in the world will go on to prove the realistic existence of martial arts human. Relying on the leadership of this proof, the previous images of the connotative structure of the martial arts human will be concretely alive and acting ideal images. Then, in order that the physical education and sports studies researchers of every country in the world expand on the substance of the words of these various elements, and in order to promote understanding of these words as living things, the research of purpose will proceed. As a result, to the question: "Why are the educational ministries of every country in the world conducting and practicing all kinds of martial arts in scholastic physical education?" one will be able to provide a direct answer from the various fields of physical education and sports studies, namely, physical education and sports philosophy, physical education and sports psychology, physical education and sports physiology, physical education and sports

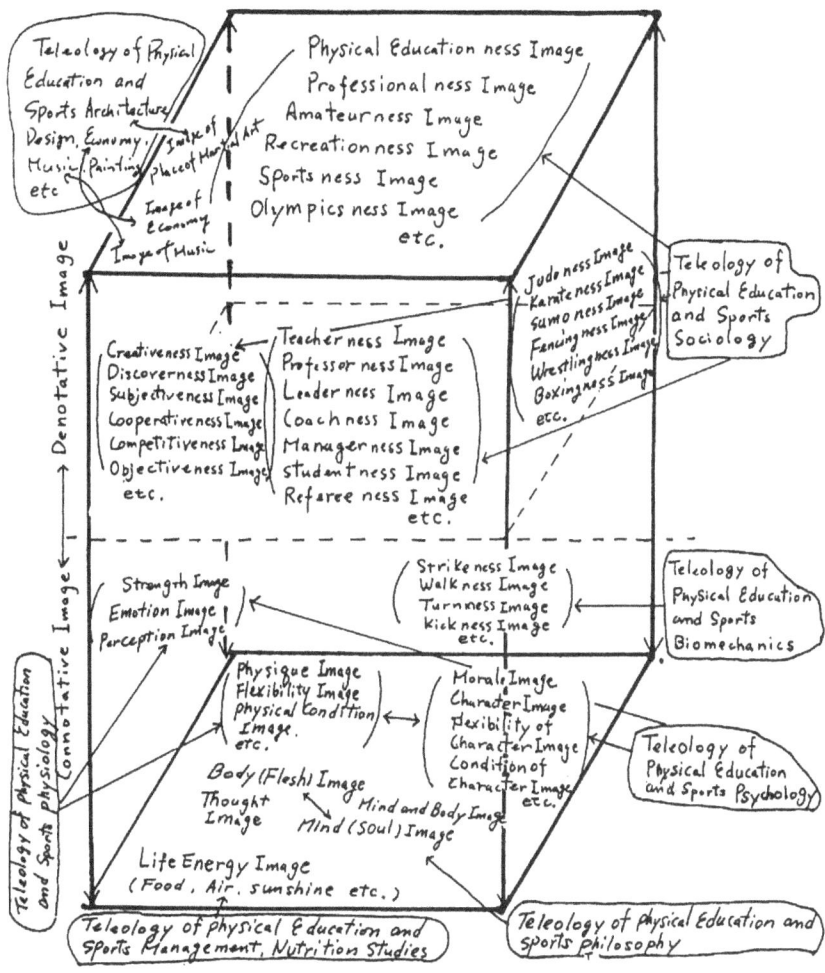

Figure 13. The martial arts human image in each nation in the world

sociology, physical education and sports history, etc. For example, from physical education and sports philosophy, all types of martial arts are practiced in scholastic physical education and sports in order to realize the image of the mind and body of all types of the martial arts human. The content of the image of the mind and body can be explained relying on the research of physical education and sports philosophers. Of course, the contents of the partial element images presented there all are ideal contents drawn from the proof of all of the specialist researchers in physical education and sports studies, and at the same time, in the space of the various elements in the image of connotative structure, they are doing superior actions.

Also, there are the various elements that do superior actions in the image of the denotative structure as well. For example, the image of body strength is formed by the superior inner actions of body strength itself, acting in superior actions in relation to the various elements, such as morale, flexibility, cooperativeness, competitiveness, physical condition, creativeness, etc.

As is shown above, the image of connotative structure in the martial arts human image is the entirety of the various elements of the connotative structure that have been amassed by the physical education and sports studies researchers in every country in the world and the physical education and sports studies research of every era. However, this image of connotative structure not only acts in the image of connotative structure but works in the image of denotative structure. So what kind of substance of ideal images makes up the image of the denotative structure of the denotative structure of martial arts human? I will go on to deal with this question.

The Image of Denotative Structure

In the action of the martial arts human image as a martial arts human image, there is an image of denotative structure. In the ideal image that is generated from the image of connotative structure, the origin of the formation of the image of denotative structure is included. Inside the denotative structure itself, which acts as the denotative structure, are the actions of the various element images.

Looking from the specialized point of view of the physical

education and sports sociologists and scholastic physical education and considering the existential direction of the martial arts human, if an inquiry is made to determine the ideal images of that existence, then, in the following way the idealistic elements of the denotative structure become visible. The image of sports-ness, the image of physical education-ness, the image of amateur-ness, the image of professionalness, the image of recreation-ness, the image of teacher-ness, the image of student-ness, the image of leader-ness, the image of manager-ness, the image of coach-ness, the image of director-ness, the image of follower-ness, the image of judo-ness, the image of fencing-ness, the image of boxing-ness, the image of creativeness, the image of cooperativeness, the image of competitiveness, the image of objective-ness, the image of discovery-ness, the image of subjectiveness, etc. From the above kinds of images of elements, the image of the denotative structure in the martial arts human image is formed. The various images of elements above are the various aspects of the martial arts human image, and they are things that have been culled from researchers in physical education and sports sociology and scholastic physical education. Then the images of the various elements in the denotative structure acts in a way that promotes the idealistic condition of the connotative structure, while at the same time they are the superior denotative elements that act in a way that promotes the idealistic condition of the elements in the image of the denotative structure. Therefore, each of the elements in the denotative structure itself is an element that is superior and acts ideally.

In the above manner, the martial arts human image itself is the purpose of the existence of the martial arts human in every country in the world. Therefore, this is limited by the existence of martial arts human, and in reality there is a purpose in straining to derive the martial arts human image from this existence. For example, in order to explain this martial arts human image as a martial arts human in reality, we can divide the martial arts human image into its various different types, such as the judo-ness image, the fencing image, the boxing image, the wrestling image, and so on. We can concretely express the goal of the martial arts human if we look, for instance, at the judo human from various points of view. From the point of view of school level, there are judo human images in the elementary school and the high school. From the point of view of sex, there are the male judo human image and the female judo human image. From the point of view of age, there are the ten-year-old judo human image and the forty-year-old judo human image. From the point of view of nationality, there are the judo human image as an American, the judo human image as a Japanese, the judo human image as a Russian, the judo human image as a Swede, the judo human image as an Australian, the judo human image as a Frenchman, the judo human image as a German, the judo human image as an Italian, and so on. In other words, because the existence of all types of the martial arts human in every country of the world is different, the purpose of the martial arts human can be materialized as different goals by the different nationalities, national languages, backgrounds of national histories, and other national differences. On the other hand, while the martial arts human image can make as its purpose the various unique martial arts human images of each country in the world, from a global, humanistic, common point of view, it can also present a purpose that is the martial arts human image as a world citizen provided that the existence of all types of the martial arts human practicing all kinds of martial art in all places around the world can be confirmed. This purpose can be erected as a common purpose of all types of the world citizen, or perhaps mankind, in the martial arts human image.

Above I have presented the purpose of the martial arts human or, more specifically, the substance of the martial arts human image (limited to only the important substance necessary in martial art theory), As a result, we have reached a point at which the following kinds of questions can be answered:

Question 1: Why are the educational ministries of every country in the world practicing all types of martial arts in scholastic physical education?

Answer: All types of martial arts are being practiced in scholastic physical education in every country in the world in order to realize all types of the martial arts human image as the specific humans of every country in the world.

Question 2: Why are the educational ministries of every country in the world offering classes on the theory concerning all types of martial arts in scholastic physical education?

Answer: This is so that in the scholastic physical education of every country in the world physical education teachers will show the peaceful practice of all types of martial arts to the students and explain the practice of all types of martial arts to the students and the students will understand them.

Question 3: Why are the physical education and sports researchers of every country in the world needed for conducting research in fields such as physical education and sports psychology, physical education and sports philosophy, physical education and sports physiology, physical education and sports history, physical education and sports sociology, etc. Furthermore, is it necessary in human society, the human nation, and the human world?

Answer: It is absolutely necessary for national formation of physical education and sports studies (including martial arts studies). This is so that the place of the martial arts in every country in the world will be realized. This research is the guarantee of the sound practice of martial arts in every country. Also, through this research we physical education and sports scholars can build the national theory of the martial arts in every country in the world that supports human nations and the human world.

Question 4: Why must a World Physical Education and Sports Academy be established?

Answer: Relying on the development of this type of research, the martial arts human image in every country in the world and the martial arts human image of each era of mankind will be constructed, thus developing the guarantee of peace within every country and in the world. Also, the academy will nurture physical education and sports researchers who will contribute to peace in every country and to world peace or will work as responsible professors in the future at college, university, and graduate schools that support the nation and world as a human society through a true theory of knowledge.

Question 5: Why must a physical education and sports academy be established in every country in the world?

Answer: Physical education and sports researchers (from all the fields) are necessary to conduct the national martial arts theory in every country and guarantee that the practice of martial arts in every country in the world is a peaceful practice. And through these efforts we are able to promise prosperity of nations and prosperity of mankind. (A ministry of education in every nation has to answer all questions concerning martial arts in public because of letting pupils practice some kinds of martial art performing from elementary school to graduate school. Instead of the ministry of education in all nations, we scholars of physical education and sports in all nations take responsibility for answering the questions concerning martial arts in public.)

Another question we can pose in order to recover our professional trust in all nations is: Why do we need doctors for physical education and sports studies? Why do we have to plan the doctoral programs in graduate school in all nations? What does this word professor in physical education and sports studies mean? More sharply, Why do we need professors for our physical education and sports studies? Does a professor mean a player of talk without responsibilities for actual physical education in colleges, universities, and graduate schools for the human nation, mankind, etc.?

In addition, any questions concerning the purpose of formation related to all types of martial arts in every country in the world can be answered from the teleology of the martial arts human. Also, from the purpose it is necessary to go on to develop support for peace in every country and world peace.

Furthermore, from the presentation of the ontology and teleology of martial arts human in every country in the world we must now go on to develop the methodology of the martial arts human in every country in the world, by which the existence of the martial arts human in every country in the world realizes the martial arts human image of every country in the world. This will deal with the method by which the existence of the martial arts human in every country in the world realizes the martial arts human image. The methodology will be organically connected to the ontology and the teleology and will have the unique quality of working together with them. This kind of undertaking will work through the realization of the establishment of universal martial arts theory, which unites all countries in the world and accepts differences between all countries in the world.

8

The Methodology of the
Martial Arts Human

The methodology of the martial arts human is an original theoretical area that deals with both the movement human and movement apparatus sides of the phenomena of all type martial arts. These two sides, which are referred to directly by the term *martial arts human*, can be said, depending on how they work together, to emphasize the movement apparatus as a martial arts human, only the ability required for the movement human (opponent) is required of the movement human as a martial arts human. On the other hand, if we emphasize the movement human as martial arts human, only the ability required for the movement human as martial arts human is required of the movement human (opponent). (It means that skillful movement is needed.) Therefore, achieving the required ability that is possible when both sides accept each other's demands is imperative. This type of method is the only advanced method by which the martial arts human image can be realized in each nation in the world. Toward that end, there are notably methodologies, one in relation to time (era, etc.) and one in relation to space (nation, etc.). The former considers the experience of becoming a martial arts human in terms of time, while the latter considers the experience of becoming a martial arts human in terms of space. Therefore, the method that realizes the martial arts human image must give the appropriate weight to experience in time and experience in space.

Theoretical Foundation and Ground for the
Formation of the Martial Arts Human Methodology

Before presenting the methodology of the martial arts human, it is necessary to fist make clear the reasons why it is possible to present such a methodology. In order to do this, we must look at the theoretical foundation and the ground for the methodology. The theoretical foundation for the formation of the methodology of the martial arts human relies on the movement- cultural, educational, and social ontologies of the martial arts human and the teleology of the martial arts human already presented. The ground for the formation of this methodology is the fact that in scholastic physical education in every country around the world martial arts is being practiced. The former is based on the development of the theory, while the latter comes from the practice of martial arts.

The Characteristics of the Methodology of the Martial Arts Human

There are two characteristics associated with the content of the methodology of the martial arts human. First, it is an unchangeable, universal, abstract methodology, applicable to any country at any time. Second, as country (space) and era (time) change, it is a concrete, realistic methodology that changes accordingly. The methodology of the martial arts human is constructed with the former at the core, while the latter surrounds it, both working together to preserve the relationship. More specifically, the former is the area of the methodology based on the common qualities of all countries and constructed by the physical education and sports researchers of every country in the world so that the practice of martial arts in scholastic physical education in every country in the world serves to realize the martial arts human image in each era. Meanwhile, the latter is the area of the methodology that has the quality of grasping the differences in the realistic aspects of the martial arts human, i.e., country, era, age, sex, school, etc., as differences in realistic aspects.

Elements of the Formation of the Contents of the Methodology of the Martial Arts Human

In regard to the formation of the methodology of the martial arts human, both the theoretical foundation and the practical ground have been presented already. However, I believe that the latter, the practical grounds, give an extraordinarily important reason for the formation of the methodology of the martial arts human. Namely, because of the existence of the practice of martial arts in physical education programs, the existence of the practice of martial art in society, and the existence of physical education teachers, mentors, pupils and students who play a function in society, the need for the methodology of the martial arts human becomes apparent.

In that case, physical education teachers and mentors are those who lead students to become martial arts humans and realize the martial arts human image, while students and followers who receive all forms of martial arts education are those who look toward becoming all forms of martial arts human and realizing all forms of the martial arts human image. Therefore, the human relationship between the teachers and mentors, and students and followers in the phenomenon of martial arts will all become the martial arts human and realize the martial arts human image. It is a mutual relationship that exists to realize the martial arts human image.

Those fostering the martial arts human have experience in the past of fully (deeply and widely) becoming a martial arts I human in order to realize the martial arts human image. They are those who possess the leadership qualifications to be able to realize the martial arts human image. On the other hand, those becoming martial arts humans must receive leadership in order to realize the martial arts human image. They are those of whom study skills are demanded.

With the relationship between physical education teachers, who try to realize the martial arts human image and foster students as martial arts humans, who study while looking toward becoming martial arts humans realizing the martial arts human image as the ground, the various structural elements of the methodology of the various kinds of martial arts human are formed. Specifically, these elements include study, leadership, evaluation curriculum, educational resources, study ability, study processes, leadership ability, skills, etc. Classifying these elements into large groups, we may divide them into study, leadership, and educational resources. The terms *skill, study ability, study process,* etc., are technical terms connected with the student or follower becoming a martial arts human and trying to realize the martial arts human image and therefore are study terms. The terms *leadership ability, evaluation, curriculum,* etc., are all terms connected with the teachers and mentors trying to realize the martial art human image and turn their students into martial arts humans and are therefore leadership terms. Finally, what brings the leadership and study together at the place of the martial arts are the educational resources. The structural elements of the methodology of the martial arts human are systematized in the manner described in the figure below.

Study. This is the state of those becoming martial arts humans in which they learn all of the various things they must learn from those helping them to become martial arts humans in order to realize the martial arts human image.

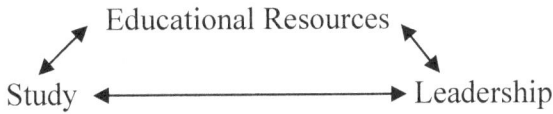

Figure 14. The structural elements of the methodology of the martial arts human in each nation in the world

Also, we will call students those who, under the supervision of those fostering the martial arts human, strive to learn that which they need to become martial arts humans. Furthermore, study ability is ability that students possess to learn all the constructive knowledge required in order to become martial arts humans and realize the martial arts human image. Skill is a part of study ability and is the condition of the mastery of the necessary techniques required to become a martial arts human and realize the martial arts human image. Also, study process is the process by which, under the leadership of those fostering the martial arts human, those becoming martial arts humans learn all of the relevant knowledge.

Leadership. This is defined as the ability to lead those who will become martial arts humans on the part of those who will foster their becoming martial arts humans by giving them all the various knowledge they will need toward the goal of realizing the martial arts human image. Leadership ability is the ability of those fostering martial arts humans, with the goal of realizing the martial arts human image, to fully develop those becoming martial arts humans (students). The leadership process is the process by which those fostering martial arts human, with the goal of realizing the martial arts human image, lead those becoming martial arts humans. Furthermore, evaluation is the process by which those fostering martial arts humans decide what level those becoming martial arts humans have reached and how far they have advanced in approaching the realization of the martial arts human image. Curriculum is the study route through which those fostering martial arts human lead those becoming martial arts humans in order to realize the martial arts human image.

Educational Resources. We collectively use this term to refer to all materials those fostering martial arts humans use to lead those becoming martial arts humans to realize the martial arts human image, along with all study materials used by those becoming martial arts humans aiming to realize the martial arts human image. Therefore, the educational resources lay the role of intermediaries in the formation of the leadership and study of the martial arts human and are necessary methodological elements in the realization of the martial arts human image. The educational resources include natural educational resources and man-made educational resources. The former are sunshine, air, weather (clear, rainy, snowy, cloudy), air pressure (wind), water (water in a pool), earth (ground), etc. The latter include gymnasiums, lighting, cloth, tools, shoes, stage, etc. Therefore, in the broad sense of the term, *educational resources* refers to the combination of natural educational resources and man-made educational resources but, when taken in the narrow sense of the term refers mostly to man-made educational resources.

The Construction Method of the Methodology of the Martial Arts Human as National Theory in Every Nation in the World

It is imperative that we use the terminology of the structural elements of the methodology of the martial arts human, namely, *study (skill, study process, etc.) leadership (evaluation, curriculum, leadership process, leadership ability,* etc.), and *educational resources* in order to realize the martial arts human image. However, it is also necessary to answer the question of how the content of these elements can be given shape.

I will now present these kinds of problems related to the construction of the methodology of the martial arts human. From the standpoint of those dealing with fundamental theory of physical education studies, it is possible to construct a methodology that answers these kinds of questions. The methodology of the martial arts human should use the original specialized vocabulary from each specialized area of physical education, and consider study, leadership, educational resources, etc. We can create a separate methodology from each field of physical education that serves to realize every partial image of the martial arts human in each era and each nation that emerges from that field. In regard to the methodology of the martial arts human from physical education physiology, for instance, while considering study, leadership, and educational resources we can construct an original methodology, using the specialized terms of physiology, such as *strength, physique, health*, and *flexibility*, that serve to realize the strength image, the physique image, the health image, and the flexibility image of the martial arts human.

Likewise, in regard to the methodology of the martial arts human from physical education psychology, while considering study, leadership, and educational resources we can construct an original methodology, using the specialized terms of psychology, such as *character, morale, mental health, flexibility*, etc., that serve to realize the character image, the morale image, the mental health image, and the flexibility image of the martial arts human. In regard to the methodology of the martial arts human from the physical education philosophy, while considering study, leadership, and educational resources we can construct an original methodology, using the specialized terms of philosophy, such as *mind, body, mind-body relationship, soul, flesh*, etc., that serve to realize the mind image, the body image, the mind-body relationship image, the soul image, the flesh image, etc., of the martial arts human. In regard to the methodology of the martial arts human from physical education educational science, while considering study, leadership, and educational resources we can construct an original methodology, using the specialized terms of educational science, such as *creativity, subjectivity, objectivity, cooperation, competition*, etc., that serve to realize the creativity image, the subjectivity image, the objectivity image, the cooperation image, and the competition image of the martial arts human. In regard to the methodology of the martial arts human from physical education sociology, while considering study, leadership, and educational resources we can construct an original methodology as a national theory, using the specialized terms of sociology, such as *performer, amateur, professional, sports, physical education*, etc., that serve to realize the performer image, the amateur image, the physical education image, the sports image, and the martial arts image of the martial arts human. In regard to the methodology of the martial arts human from physical education and sports biomechanics, while considering study, leadership, and educational resources we can construct an original methodology as a national theory, using the specialized terms of biomechanics, such as *grasp, run, catch, walk, stand, hang, turn*, etc., that serve to realize the grasping image, the running image, the catching image, the walking image, the standing image, etc., of the martial arts human. Moreover, the construction of the original methodology of the martial arts human for each of these specialized fields of physical education must be living, changing entities, taking into account the realistic existence of things such as nationality, race, age, sex, etc., to always be the best methodology for physical education researchers at the present time. Therefore, research specialists in each field of physical education must, while referring to the knowledge in physical education history for advice, construct separate methodologies as national theories responsible for each specialized field.

In the preceding manner, it is possible to construct a methodology of the martial arts human for every country in the world. Thus we are able to form a national methodology of martial arts study in each country in the world and in each era by each national language.

Part III

Theory of International Skating Studies for the Achievement of Peace

1

A Word from the Author

The term *skating human (ice human)* is a symbolic term that works toward national peace and world peace. We, the world's physical education and sports scholars, must regard this word as dearly as our own lives. This is because without the existence of the skating human, none of the language concerning skating and research concerning skating could be formed. The existence of the skating human builds and determines it all. The existence of skating humans makes many national languages possible. However, the national languages are not able to make the skating human exist in all nations. The skating human speaks American English, Japanese, German, French, Italian, Korean, British English, Spanish, Chinese, etc., in fact. The skating humans in China speak Chinese. The skating humans in Russia speak Russian. The skating humans in the United States speak American English. The skating humans also create other words like sound (noisy or nice), imitation sound, and onomatopoeic words in the phenomenon of skating. All national languages in the phenomenon of skating are a proof of the existence of the skating human in each nation. The term *skating human* will be the universal language of the world's physical education and sports scholars as long as the phenomenon of skating continues in all the nations. It is a specialized term, even a holy term.

I present this book for the benefit of all the physical education and sports scholars of each of the world's nations alike.

2

Establishing the Hypothesis for Creating Skating Studies

The following questions are the fundamental motives for attempting to create the theory of international skating studies for the achievement of peace (the principle of physical education and sports studies and research for all nations in the world):

1. Why, in the scholastic physical education programs of the education ministries of each country in the world, are teachers or professors using any types of skating as an educational resource to lead students?
2. Why are the physical education and sports researchers of each country in the world conducting research concerning any types of skating?
3. Why are physical education teachers and physical education and sports researchers and professors of every country in the world conducting classes, lectures, and symposia in schools, colleges, universities, and graduate schools, concerning the theory of any types of skating?
4. Why does the IOC adopt any types of skating in the Olympics?
5. Why does the research concerning skating studies belong to the physical education and sports studies?
6. Why is the research concerning skating studies worthy of a doctorate or master's degree in physical education and sports studies?
7. Why do we need physical education faculties in colleges, universities, and graduate schools in the nation and the world?
8. Why do we need physical education and sports scholars and professors who provide lectures for the students in public and to employ them in public?
9. Why do we need physical education and sports studies, including

skating study, in all nations in the world? What about the social necessity for public skating study?

We physical education and sports scholars ask the questions above in order to restore public, social, national, and world trust in profession. This means that we physical education and sports scholars have social, national, and world problems. It also questions what education in all schools, from elementary school to graduate school, in all nations in the world is in reality and why the education in all nations in the world is needed for development of the human nation and human world. I ask those questions when I look seriously at the current situation of physical education research and studies. There are very poor situations. I must stand up for new generations of all nations in public.

Currently there is no theory (principle) in the world's physical education and sports research that can answer these fundamental questions of skating research. This is the most important problem that I have to take responsibility for as a physical education scholar in public. Therefore, I try to think that I undertook the problem and tried to solve the problem and tried to build the theories by which I could answer all of the questions. The motive that I have in trying to formulate the theory for studies of skating is mentioned above.

Here, in order to ask myself and answer the questions. "What are all types of skating?" and, more generally, "What is skating?" I have formed the following hypothesis: "When a human skates is when a human becomes a skating human. (When a human skates is not when a human becomes a human.)" As a reason for the formation of the hypothesis, I believe that to skate is to skate, and to skate is not not skating. To do is to become.

This new term (which will become a specialized term used among physical education and sports scholars) has been created in order to convert terms such as *skating* and terms included in it (*figure skating, speed skating, bobsled*, etc.) into moving, living words. Also, the world's physical education teachers take their responsibilities from the social reality of skating being taught by sports leaders to sports students and followers.

Also in this book I have used the word *movement human*. When we perceive the phenomenon of skating, we see people moving on ice. In order to express the existence of the moving human being (apart from the technique one may have in one's arms and legs) in one noun phrase, we say "movement human." This term refers to the entire existence of the human (individual) and some other (another person or something else) dynamically working together in both a passive and active relationship.

The term *skating human* is used, to represent collectively all of the various types of skating, such as women's figure skating human, bobsled human, 1,000-meter speed-skating human, men's figure-skating human, 500-meter speed-skating human, etc. Each of these terms refers directly to the existence of the acting relationship between human and ice in each type of skating. It is this relationship, too, that gives life to and maintains the socially significant term *skating*.

Next I would like to explain in detail what is directly indicated by the term *skating human*. The object to which the words *skating human* refers is the entirety of the acting relationship between a movement human as skating human and a movement ice as skating human in the phenomenon of the skating or in the phenomenon in which skating is dealt with. In the world of skating, the movement human as skating human and movement ice as skating human together make up the skating human. In this situation, the movement human is a movement human related to a movement human as skating human and the movement ice as skating human is a movement human as skating human related to movement ice as skating human. Therefore, the two share a common point that conned them. Specifically, this common point is the existential form in which the skating humans act together in mutual independence and in certain aspects move in a uniform motion. However, if we look objectively at them, we can divide the skating human into a skating human as a movement human and a skating human as a movement ice.

Therefore, in presenting the theory, in order to refer directly to both the skating human as a movement human and the skating human as a movement ice, we will use the term *skating human* for simplification. Only when we wish to make an explicit distinction between the two sides will we use the expressions *skating human as a movement human* and *skating human as a movement ice*. Therefore, the expression *skating human* refers to both the movement human as skating human and movement human as the skating human sides of the skating.

There were many reasons for the creation of the special term *skating human*, but the most important of these was the need to distinguish the general human existence from the existence experienced in the special world in which skating is dealt with in physical education and sports studies and to make this special independence clear. In addition, this term serves to help construct national theories (skating studies) to explain the unique practice of skating.

The next matter with which we must concern ourselves is the development of all types of skating phenomena and phenomena that involve the applied exercises of skating in every country in the world. Specifically, in what form does this living phenomenon appear to our eyes? In other words, which actions in the living phenomenon of skating are essential and which are nonessential? Understanding this distinction and synthesis will lead to a clear insight into this living phenomenon of skating.

In order to answer these questions, I will examine the living phenomenon of the skating itself, relying on intuitive analysis and the integrated judgment method. As was stated in the hypothesis, the essence of the existence of the living phenomenon of the skating and the phenomenon in which the applied exercises of skating is dealt with and the nonessence of that existence (auxiliary actions to the existential essence) are manifested in the various aspects of the skating human, such as the track-and-field human, the ball human, the flying human, the dance human, etc. Please see figure 15 for an explanation of this idea. There are, in other words, all the essential structural elements that form the living phenomenon of the skating.

If we analyze the primary factors that form the movement relying on our perceptions of the skating phenomenon and then integrate these back together, we can come to understand the movement itself. For example, if we look at the action of the skating human, we see that he acts on the ground, the air, the image, the ball, the human, etc., in reality, to form the living phenomenon of skating. The instant the skating human acts in relation to ground without ice (in the case of

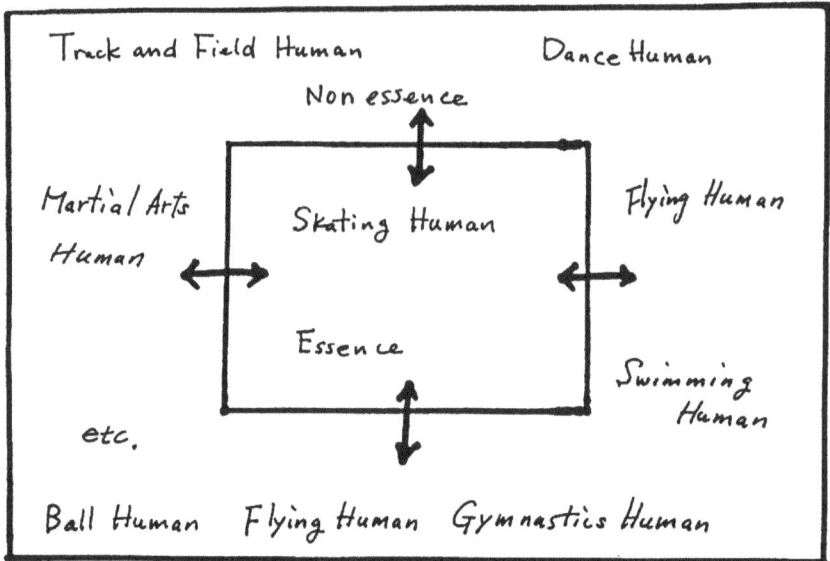

Figure 15. Formation elements of the living phenomenon of skating human in each nation in the world

skate training) he begins to exist as a track-and-field human. In the instant the skating human acts momentarily in relation to another image, he begins to exist as a dance human. Furthermore, in the instant the skating human acts momentarily in the air, he begins to exist as a flying human. There are the auxiliary actions in the living phenomenon of the skating that create motion and that act indirectly on the movement of the skating human.

In order to determine if figure 15 is true or false, let us try to return to the living phenomenon (fact) of each type of skating. For instance, I explain the living phenomenon of figure-skating human in the skating using a graph. We can say that in the actions of the figure-skating human, the figure-skating human appears as the existential essence. At the same time, the phenomenon appears as a composition of transient aspects of the nonessential, such as the dance human (he may be skating momentarily with some image), the track-and-field human Ole may perform skating with acting on the ground or the artificial ground), the flying human (he may perform skating with acting in the air), etc. The phenomenon of skating human is, most importantly, the actions of the skating human as ice movement on which the movement human becomes skating human. I can explain concrete matters of actual skating with figure 15. That means figure 15 is true. So we need many kinds of special terms in order to construct national skating studies. If the figure skating is performed outdoors the figure-skating human may act momentarily in rain and water (like swimming human). The determining factors affect the valuation of the skating, but above all, it is determined by the action of the skating human. Therefore, the skating human in the phenomenon of the skating is essential existence. Why? I explain it as evidence of the existence of the skating human, because existence of the skating human creates all of the following things: national languages, special terms of skating, actual sounds of phenomenon of skating, etc. The actions of the skating human mean movement ice as skating human for the sake of doing skating and movement human as skating human for the sake of doing skating.

Therefore, it is possible to say that all of the living phenomena of the various types of skating can be found in every country in the world, being formed by a mixture of the characteristics of the living phenomena of martial arts human, track-and-field human, flying human, dance human, etc. Most important, all are formed from the existential essence of the skating human, namely, the living actions of the skating human that determine the process and result of the skating. As evidence for them, we can say that the points scored in a skating competition, which depend upon the actions of the skating human in skating, provide dynamic variations in the aspects of the phenomenon and the result of skating is determined by them. They also produce a lot of words (specific terms) in relation to the skating in national languages and nonwords like sounds and imitation sounds in the phenomenon of skating. Therefore, the action of the skating human determines everything in the phenomenon of skating.

I would like to put forth this idea in the form of a hypothesis: that the phenomenon of skating is the mutual actions of specific humans, that is, skating human as a movement human and skating human as a movement ice, namely, the skating human. However, in order to do this I must provide some clear evidence that is able to confirm that this is the existential essence of the phenomenon of skating. This would be the factual grounds for the formation of these words. In order to speak scientifically about the phenomenon of the movement human as skating human and the phenomenon in which movement ice as skating ice is dealt with, we must make this existential essence that will be the object of the analysis very clear. In other words, it is necessary to confirm whether or not the term *skating human* is a term that possesses realistic qualities in the phenomenon of skating.

Thus I would begin to think that I could incorporate this method into an ontology of the skating human. In other words, using the term *skating human*, I will explain in detail the reality of skating. Thus, should it be possible to prove this hypothesis, the skating human would be the existential essence in the phenomenon of skating and *skating human* would become specialized terminology whose use would be required any time skating research is being conducted. Furthermore, we would begin down the road toward the construction of a theory of skating studies dealing with the entirety of practice and theory. It would be possible to advance the theory by means of a teleology and a methodology and, finally, to form skating theory (in a world united and different). A distinction would be made between the aspects of skating studies that affect the daily lives of people and those special areas that the skating human experiences in the skating studies and practices. When names are given to these boundaries, skating studies will begin to be formed.

I have ascertained that the existence of the skating human can be grasped as three aspects, and in this way I hope to make this existence clear. Specifically, the movement-cultural existence of the skating human, the educational existence of the skating human, and the social existence of the skating human. These all point to the fact that in every country in the world the skating human exists in many ways and forms a special world. I will begin my undertaking of this from my understanding of the existence of this skating human the skating human that exists in every country in the world.

3

The Movement-Cultural Ontology
of the Skating Human (or Ice Human)

The skating human lives in the movement culture and the skating human exists possessing movement-cultural aspects in all nations in the world. This comes from a connotative structure and a denotative structure. Together they maintain independent functions while living and existing as a whole.

The Connotative Structure

The skating human as a movement human is organically constructed with a head, a torso, hands, and feet. Internally, he is partially muscles, bones, organs, a brain, etc., which all rely on blood for their actions. However, the skating human as movement human is actually made of many materials, such as a certain amount of air, and various other objects, all of which will be acted upon by the existing life energy. These are based on factors of nature, which include gravity, temperature, climate, sunshine, rain, snow, etc., and Micial factors, which include gymnasiums and arenas, rinks, lighting, etc., and they act on individual or group behavior and skill. However, these factors act together with factors dependent on the skating human as a movement human himself, such as perception, thought, emotion, etc. Therefore, the skating human as a movement human exists as a complex synthesis of the various factors that make up each specific human.

There are other aspects of the skating human as an object movement, including men's figure-skating human, men's freestyle-skating human, speed-skating human, 1,000-meter women's skating human, bobsled human, luge human, ice-dance human (essentially, this human belongs to dance human, so this human is exceptional in the categories of the principle), etc. Therefore, this term *skating human* means specific human existence and ice existence for skating in the phenomenon of skating.

As individual actions, the two sides (the skating human as a movement human and the skating human as a movement ice) approach each other, come into contact, and separate from one another. These actions consist of various types, such as pushing, touching, grasping, kicking, punching, jumping, striking, holding, thrusting, sliding, etc.

As group actions, the two sides (the skating human as a movement human and the skating human as a movement ice) approach each other, come into contact, and separate from one another. These group actions consist of various types, such as yelling, using signals, watching, etc.

The actions of individual and group technical skills are based on the actions of eyes, ears, tongue, skin, etc., of the skating human as a movement human and the actions of bones, bowels, and organs such as the heart, lungs, etc. Finally, the actions of thought, emotion, etc., also contribute. In other words, while the sensation/thought/emotion system's part have independent functions, they are organically and dynamically related and participate in the skilled actions of the skating human as a movement human. In making value judgments about skilled actions, such as good/bad, achieved/not achieved, the skating human as a movement human relies greatly on the actions of the sensation/thought/emotion system. The decisions and conflicts are: "my head hurts, but I have to keep performing hard," "I'm tired, so I'll quit soon." "I challenge the ice as a 1,000-meter skating human, so I must do my best," "my hands hurt, but I have to try harder," "my teacher sees my figure-skating performance, so I must try to do my best," etc. Those phrases point to the dynamic actions of the skating human of sensation/thought/emotion, sensation/emotion, sensation/thought, thought/sensation, emotion/sensation, emotion/thought/sensation, and so on (figure 16).

The Denotative Structure

The skating human as a movement human appears in various movement-cultural aspects in all nations in the world. If we were to classify these movement-cultural aspects, we could classify them in

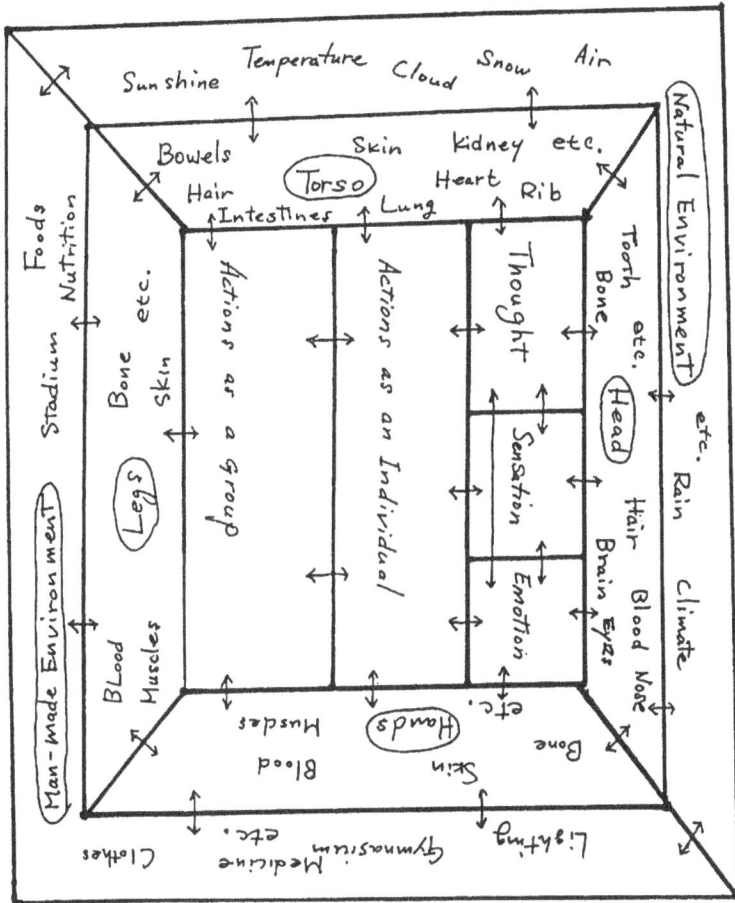

Figure 16. The many kinds of action of the connotative structure of the skating human in each nation in the world

the following four types, because basic forms of all movement human are composed by actions approaching someone and some substance (including water, image, air, ball, snow, etc.), touching actions to someone, and some substances, and separating actions to someone, and some substances, in fact. When we watch all actions of the movement human we can confirm three kinds of characterized actions through existence of the movement human in physical education and sports practices.

The first type includes a kind of skating event in which either the movement human as skating human just approaches the movement ice as skating human or the movement ice as skating human just approaches the movement human as skating human. There is no skating human now as movement human like this type nowadays. However, this kind of skating event might be introduced by some skating specialists in the future.

The second type includes skating events in which the action of the movement human (as the skating human) and the movement ice (as the skating human) are mutually disjunctive and conjunctive, such as luge human as movement human, figure-skating human as movement human, speed-skating human as movement human, ice-dance human as movement human, etc.

While both type 1 and type 2 deal with individualistic movement-cultural properties, the following type 3 and type 4 deal with movement-cultural properties that are oriented by the group, more than two people, from the movement human (as skating human).

The third type includes skating events in which the actions of the group of skating humans as movement humans attempt to a approach the other group of skating humans as movement ice or separate from the other group of skating humans as movement ice. Today skating of this type has the appearance of the speed-skating relay in reality, but there is the possibility of adding another speed-skating human as movement human in a competition among groups in future.

The fourth type of skating human in the phenomenon of skating is the skating human in which the skating human as a movement human in the group and skating human as movement human in the group repeat actions of mutual approach, separation, and contact. With the skating human as a group event, for example, there is possibly a speed-skating relay of humans as movement humans in the group, bobsled humans in group in a competition, among more than two groups that belong to this fourth type.

In this manner, it is possible to classify the movement-cultural existence of every skating phenomenon based on the substance and type of actions of the skating human. (Refer to figure 17.) However, each skating human as a movement human exists in a manner that presents unique aspects. The skating human as movement human exists with unique aspects not found in skating human as movement human. (The bobsled human as movement human is absolutely the bobsled human as movement human.) The bobsled human as movement human exists with unique aspects not found in speed-skating relay human as movement human. (The speed-skating relay human is absolutely speed- skating relay human as movement human in fact.) Therefore, each type of skating human appears in his own unique movement-cultural aspects.

Speed Skating-ness
(the Speed-Skating Human as Movement Human)

The speed-skating human as a movement human exists in aspects of speed skating. For example, there is either a direct or indirect relation to the apparatus of speed skates, the rules of speed skating, the facilities of speed skating, the terminology of speed skating, etc. The appearance of the speed-skating human as a movement human forms the unique world of speed skating.

Luge-ness (the Luge Human as Movement Human)

The luge human as a movement human exists in aspects of luging. For example, there is either a direct of indirect relation to the apparatus of luge, the rules of luge, the facilities of luge, the terminology of luge, etc. The appearance of the luge human forms the unique world of luge.

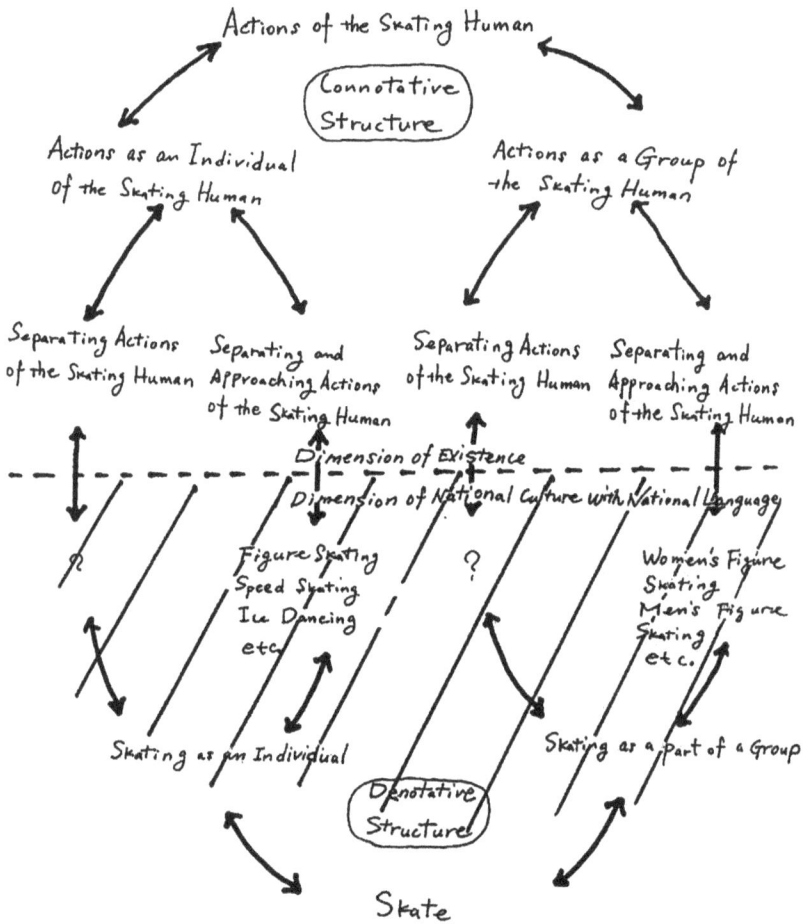

Actions of the Skating Human

Connotative Structure

Actions as an Individual of the Skating Human

Actions as a Group of the Skating Human

Separating Actions of the Skating Human

Separating and Approaching Actions of the Skating Human

Separating Actions of the Skating Human

Separating and Approaching Actions of the Skating Human

Dimension of Existence

Dimension of National Culture with National Language

?

Figure Skating
Speed Skating
Ice Dancing
etc.

?

Women's Figure Skating
Men's Figure Skating
etc.

Skating as an Individual

Denotative Structure

Skating as a Part of a Group

Skate

Figure 17. The movement-cultural existence of the
skating human in each nation in the world

82

Bobsled-ness (the Bobsled Human as a Movement Human)

The bobsled human as a movement human exists in aspects of bobsledding. For example, there is either a direct or indirect relation to the apparatus of bobsledding, the rules of bobsledding, the terminology of bobsledding, the facilities of bobsledding, etc. The appearance of the bobsled human as a movement human forms the unique world of bobsledding.

Women's Figure Skating-ness
(the Women's Figure-Skating Human as a Movement Human)

The figure-skating human as a movement human exists in aspects of figure skating as a woman. For example, there is either a direct or indirect relation to the apparatus of figure skating, the rules of figure skating, the facilities of figure skating, the terminology of figure skating, etc. The appearance of the figure-skating human forms the unique world of figure skating.

As there are several skating events that have been introduced, as mentioned above, the number of skating events may increase in the future, as skating events we have never seen emerge in this way, the skating human as a movement human exists in all the various movement-cultural aspects in every country in the world, in the United States as Americans, in Russia as Russians, in France as Frenchmen, in England as Englishmen, and in China as Chinese. The skating human exists in these various movement-cultural aspects. Each skating human exists to speak each national language in each nation on the earth, fact.

4

The Educational Existence of the
Skating Human(or Ice Human)

In the special society of physical education in every country in the world, the skating human as a movement human exists, possessing an aspect of physical education. Every type of skating is evaluated educationally. Certainly, opinions are formed about whether a skating human builds a certain strength, develops character, fosters mental growth, fosters creativity, etc. The educational existence of the skating human as a movement human comes from a connotative structure and a denotative structure. Each works based on an independent structure, and as a whole they exist educationally.

The Connotative Structure

In order to make clear the actions of the skating human, we will analyze them and use integrated judgment, by looking both from the social actions of the skating human toward the living energy and from the living energy toward the social actions of the skating human. In this manner, we can grasp fully the entire substance of the actions of the skating human. We have some factors that are expressed, such as body strength, flexibility, etc., while in contrast, some factors are expressive, such as the mind, soul, character, personality, condition of character, morale, flexibility, etc. These factors work in a living, separate manner, and at the same time the actions of the skating human are in the integration of all of these living elements. By using these words to inquire about the nature of the actions of the skating human, we can elucidate the concept of the skating human. Therefore, these words refer to the various partial factors that make these words is based upon the supply and demand of living energy produced by the unification (actions of digestion, actions of oxidation) that takes place inside the individual of the mutually conflicting elements of air and food and the skating human. In other words, the source is the transformation of the various elements, such as body, body strength, flexibility of body, physique, physical condition, mind, soul, morale, flexibility of mind, personality, condition of character, etc., into a living entity. Therefore, the words *body, body strength, flexibility of body, physique, physical condition, mind, soul, morale, flexibility of mind, personality, condition of character*, etc., are all living words and are words that have come to refer to reality.

On the other hand, we have said that the action of the skating human is formed from a synthesis of the various types of actions of the skating human expressed as mind, body, soul, physique, physical condition, body strength, flexibility of body, condition of character, morale, and flexibility of mind. It should be noted that in our analysis of the actions of the skating human we said that there is both a movement human and a movement ice side of the skating human, with mutually different objects. Since this is the case, it may not be appropriate to use the same type of language to explain both. However, based on the common point of view that both share as the skating human, we will use the same language to explain them.

The analysis and synthesis of these two sides, the skating human as a movement human and the skating human as a movement ice, are shown in figure 18 and figure 19.

Also making up the actions of the skating human are skilled actions, which express technique. However, if we analyze these skilled actions, we can see that they are made up of actions of the conduct of the skating human and the substance of the kind of technique being expressed. In other words, the actions of the conduct of the skating human, together with the substance of the technique, make up the reality of the skilled action of the skating human and exist united in reality. These exist in a relationship that is mutually life-giving and enlivened, creating the phenomenon of the skilled existence of the skating human.

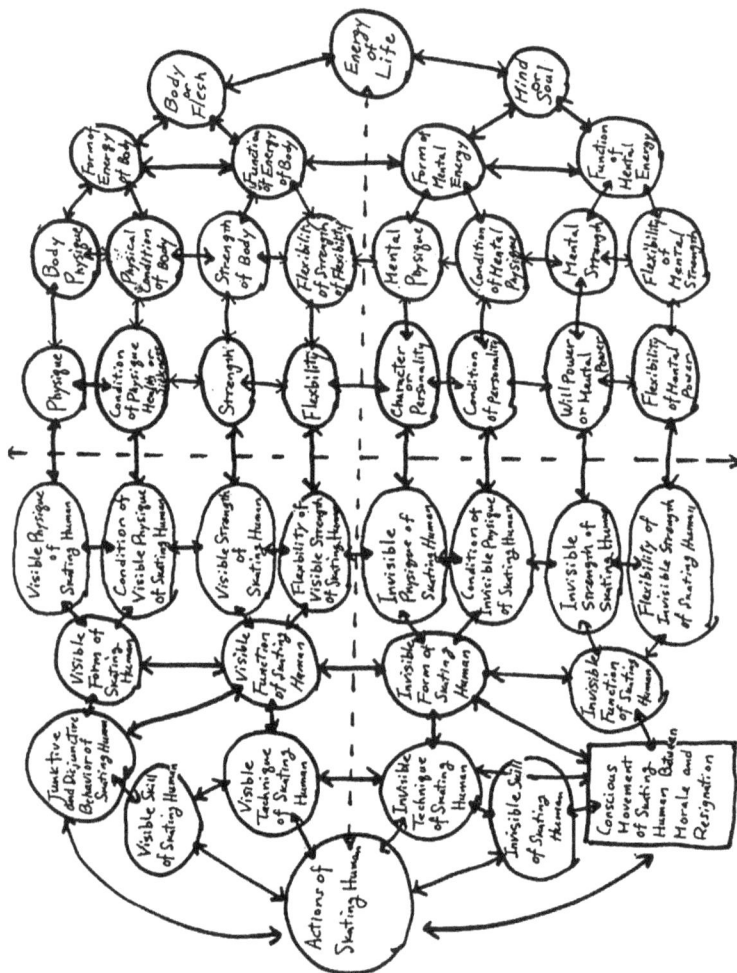

Figure 18. Action types of the skating human in each nation in the world

The types of skilled actions of skating human

The types of life energy of skating human

86

I The visible Physique of the Skating Human

   Movement Human : Size, Weigh, Color, Shape, Height, etc.

   Movement Ice : Depth, Shape, Weigh, Color, Size etc

II The Substance of the visible Physique of the Skating Human

   Movement Human : Quality of the visible Physique of the Movement Human,
                    Visible Amount of Movement Human, (Illness or Health?)

   Movement Ice : Quality of Movement Ice, Visible Condition of Movement Ice
                  (Support of Illness or Support of Health?)

III The Visible Physical Function of the Skating Human

   Movement Human : Endurance and Speed of Movement Human (time) and
                    Movement Sphere and Speed of Movement Human (Space)

   Movement Ice : Endurance and Speed of Movement Ice (Time) and
                  Movement Sphere and Speed of Movement Ice (Space)

IV The visible Condition of the Function of the Skating Human

   Movement Human : The Effective physical Ability and Flexibility of the Skating Human
                    in Response to the Skating Phenomenon

   Movement Ice : The Effective physical Ability and Flexibility of the Skating Human
                  in Response to the Skating Phenomenon

- -

   The Invisible Physique of the Skating Human

V Movement Human : Invisible Physique of the Skating Human
                    (Mental Physique, Mental Impression, etc.)

   Movement Ice : Invisible Physique of the Skating Human
                  (Support of Mental Impression, Support of Mental Physique, etc)

   The Substance of the Invisible Physique of the Skating Human

VI Movement Human : Condition of the Invisible Physique of the Skating Human
                     (Mental Illness or Mental Health?)

   Movement Ice : Condition of the Invisible Physique of the Skating Human
                  (Support of Mental Illness or Support of Mental Health?)

   The Function of the Invisible Physique of the Skating Human.

VII Movement Human : Function of the Invisible Physique of the Skating Human
                      (Mental Power, Mental Endurance, etc.)

   Movement Ice : Function of the Invisible Physique of the Skating Human
                  (Support of Mental Power, Support of Mental power, etc.)

   The Condition of the Invisible Physical Function of the Skating Human

VIII Movement Human : Condition of the Invisible Physical Function of the Skating Human
                       (Mental Flexibility, Mental Adjustable Ability, etc.)

   Movement Ice : Condition of the Invisible Physical Function of the Skating Human
                  (Support of Mental Flexibility, Support of Mental Adjustable Ability
                  etc.)

**Figure 19. The types and contents of the actions of the
skating human in each nation**

The Denotative Structure

In regard to the denotative structure of the educational existence of the skating human, I have attempted some analytical speculation that will explain it, as shown in figure 20.

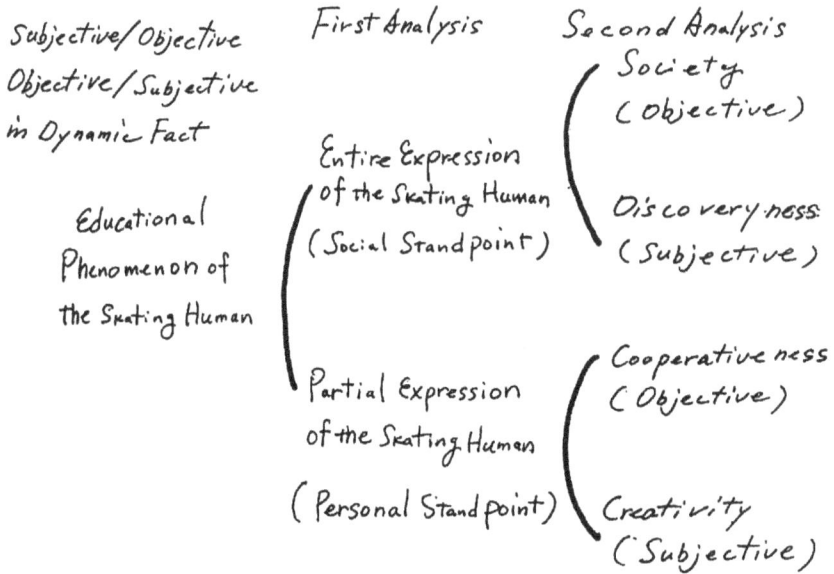

Subjective/Objective   First Analysis   Second Analysis
Objective/Subjective   Society
in Dynamic Fact   (Objective)

                        Entire Expression
Educational   of the Skating Human
Phenomenon of   (Social Standpoint)   Discovery ness
the Skating Human   (Subjective)

                                          Cooperative ness
                                          (Objective)
                        Partial Expression
                        of the Skating Human
                        (Personal Standpoint)   Creativity
                                               (Subjective)

Figure 20. The educational existence of the skating human in each nation in the world

Here I will explain each of the educational elements of the skating human dealt with in the second analysis of the educational phenomenon of the skating human.

Society

The skating human functions in the special society of skating. However, in order to create this special society, the skating human must work by accepting and approving all of the factors. Specifically, the skating human as a movement human that takes on the special social role of player acts both socially and morally. The skating human as a movement human acts in participation with the special humans

88

that take on the social roles of judges, teachers, leaders, etc., and even with things that are set up for the purpose of becoming a skating human as a movement human, such as unique facilities, equipment, rules, etc. In this manner, the phenomenon of the skating occurs when, as the skating human as a movement human is enlarged from some person to some thing and from some thing to some person, it acts both socially and morally. However, while the society of the skating human as a movement human provides the nature of a special society, in order that skating occur in general society, it exists in the twofold relationship with general society and the special society of the skating.

Discovery-ness

The skating human as a movement human acts creatively. At the same time, a skating human as a movement snow also acts creatively. In the actions of the skating human, there are situations in which new technical content or form, no similar example to which existed in the past, are added. These new techniques are conceptualized and given special names. This itself points to the discovery-ness of the skating human. For example, names in the skating events themselves point to the discovery-ness of the skating human. For example, we are able to find in it so many things from Olympic skating. The original words for skating that the Olympics had made were in proof of discovery-ness of skating human. There is a certain manner in which the Olympics brought about the birth of the new skating. In this way, there are situations in which a new skating human given movement-cultural existence in history is formed. The discovery-ness of the skating human consists of both the creative and historical expansion aspects of these actions.

Cooperativeness

In the phenomenon of skating, there are many cases in which the skating human acts in a group. In these cases, cooperative intentions are demanded of the skating human. This cooperativeness depends on the mutual relationship between acting skating humans that have taken on the social role of the player (athlete), and therefore this is a social action. There is a cooperativeness (or competition), from a unified standpoint and cooperativeness from a different standpoint. For example, the general factors of the school associated with the individual skating human: the religion, age, sex, etc., may be identical or different. Also, the various factors of the special standpoint of the skating such as skill level of the skating human, the player (athlete) or competitor role, companions, etc., may be identical or different.

In this way, the actions of the cooperativeness of the skating human exist as the nature of the identities and differences of the special things limited only to the skating. So if we try to limit it to only the cooperativeness in the special society of the skating human the cooperativeness of identity recognition of the skating human is based on the recognition of technical standpoint and the cooperativeness of difference recognition is based on the recognition of existential standpoint.

Creativity

The skating human, in the living, always-changing space of skating, acts while at every moment being faced with the problem: "In what way should I best handle skating human as ice movement?" The skating human as movement human, who has been acted on by a skating human as an ice movement, is a concrete expression of the skill of the skating human as a movement human himself. It is something that indicates the level of skill. Therefore, the skating human as movement human demands skill from the skating human as a movement ice, and conversely, the skating human as a movement human exists while demanding skill from a skating human as an ice movement. Through the skill demands of these two sides, the skating human creates. For example, a skating human is an ice movement that is thrown by the skating human as a movement human, which has taken the social role of skating human as an athlete or performer and a skill. Then the skating human as a movement human tries to face this ice movement and, through the skating human of an ice movement as an extension of the individual's body, tries to respond to the skilled action of the skating human as an ice movement. As a result, the excellent performance as a skating human, tools, special terms of skating, and so forth, will be created.

The creativity of the skating human can be seen in the creativity of the partial cause/effect action of playing and the action of going inside and the action of doing well and the action of failure. Through this partial cause/effect process, the action of winning, the action of losing, and the action of a draw are created. Creativity can be seen in the partial cause/effect process, the action of winning, the action of losing, and the action of a draw are created. Creativity can be seen in the partial cause/effect actions in the entire process of the skating, from start to finish. Furthermore, the creativity generates the subjective emotions of happiness, vexation, anger, and sorrow at every instant in the skating human as a movement human and the skating human as an ice movement, in the special living space of the skating, acting creatively in an original way. These actions bring about a reformation of the self-consciousness of the possibilities of ability in the skating human who has taken on the special role of performer. In this special society, it gives meaning to life.

In this way, the skating human exists educationally. At the same time, he exists as the educational being in scholastic physical education in every country in the world and is an expression of every country in the world (each national language) by his existence.

5

The Social Ontology of the
Skating Human (or Ice Human)

The skating human exists within general society. There he exists in each nation while possessing an aspect of social existence in which he lives trying to enact original plans. For example, from the factual phenomenon of the skating all kinds of words have been derived, such as *physical education, recreation*, etc. On the other hand, in social actions of the skating human there are various kinds of sociological terms that have been created, such as *fair, unfair, cooperative*, etc. This can be said to be implicit proof that the skating human exists socially concerning the social existence of the skating human. In order to grasp his factual living state as a living state, I will divide this into a connotative structure and a denotative structure and explain each. Therefore, the social existence of the skating human is the entirety of the independent actions of connotative structure and denotative structure.

The Connotative Structure

Let us consider the basic aspects of the actions of the skating human. In the case of the individual, it is the actions of mutual separation/contact within the skating human. In the case of the group, it is the actions of mutual separation/contact among many skating humans. In other words, the basic principle is the entirety of the motion that occurs when the skating human as a movement ice and the skating human as a movement human mutually separate, approach, and contact.

If we apply this fact to each kind of the entire phenomenon of the skating, it will be understood easily. This is shown in figure 21.

In other words in order to grasp this dynamic separation/contact relationship between the skating humans, one must begin by looking objectively from the action of the body of the skating human. Meanwhile, there are also the actions of the mind of the skating human, namely, the separation/contact movement of consciousness. Those actions come from the fact that when dealing with the apparatus, the skating human as a movement human recognizes a skating human as movement ice by the action of unconscious-conscious. The strength, or perhaps weakness, of the actions of the consciousness of the skating human as a movement human is located in the polarized structure of the morale and resignation of the consciousness. The strength or weakness depends throughout on the manner in which the consciousness moves between those polarizations (figure 22).

As the skating human as a movement human lives, breathes, and goes to a skating human as a movement ice and as a skating human as a movement ice lives, breathes, and goes to the skating human as a movement human, the morale strengthens the consciousness. In other words, the morale strengthens the unified perception of both sides of the skating human, the skating human as a movement human and the skating human as a movement ice. It also promotes the manifestation of living as a skating human. For example, in a hotly contested skating event, the performer himself and each action that the performer takes come to be perceived as a unified dimension.

Because the morale is a living thing, it promotes flattering aspects, but since it is caused through the consciousness's condition of resignation, it moves to the resignation, which is a different kind of element. Primarily, the morale of the skating human is in the dimension of time, which has a passive nature and has some bad points, but in the dimension of space it has an active nature. The morale possesses these kinds of properties.

However, the resignation of the skating human is the condition of the consciousness of the preparatory steps for displaying the consciousness of morale. Therefore, the resignation of the skating human, in relation to the morale, is an element of denial, but on the other hand, it provides a kind of quality that serves to support morale as well. In the realm of space the resignation of the skating human is weak and passive, but in the realm of time it is strong and active.

The connotative structure of the social existence of the skating

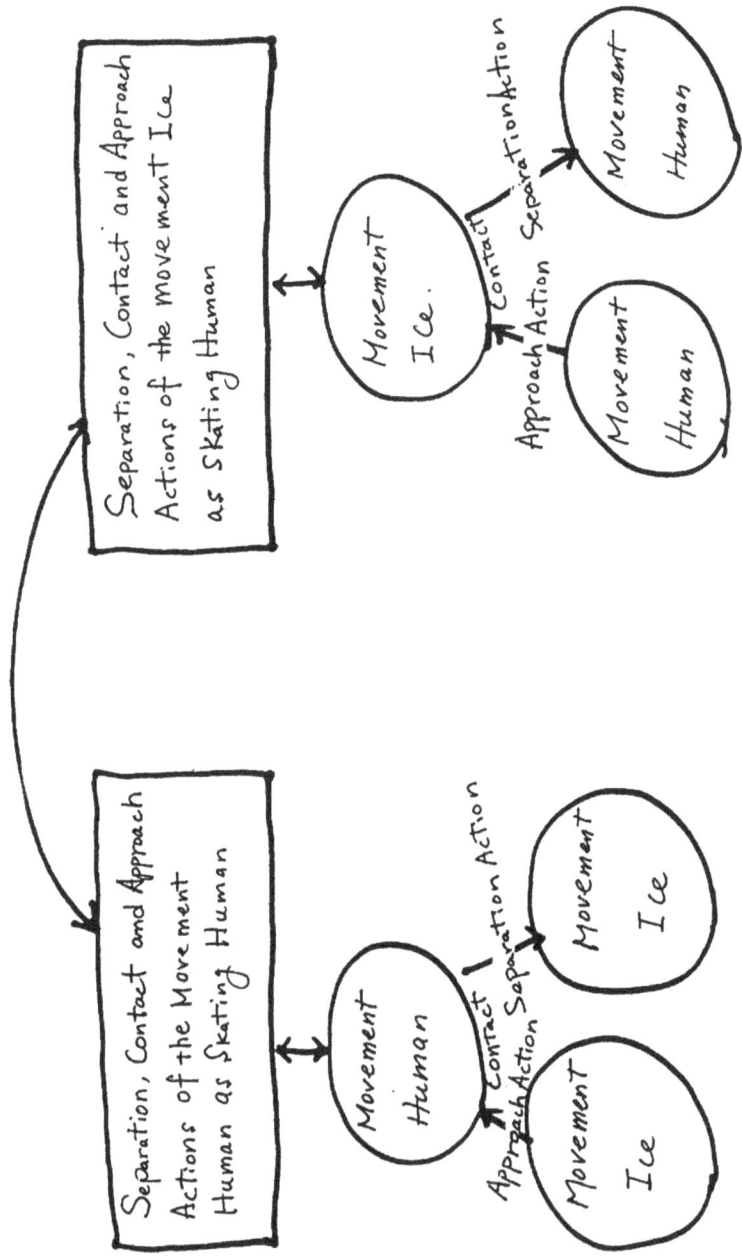

Figure 21. Separation, contact and approach actions of skating human in each nation in the world

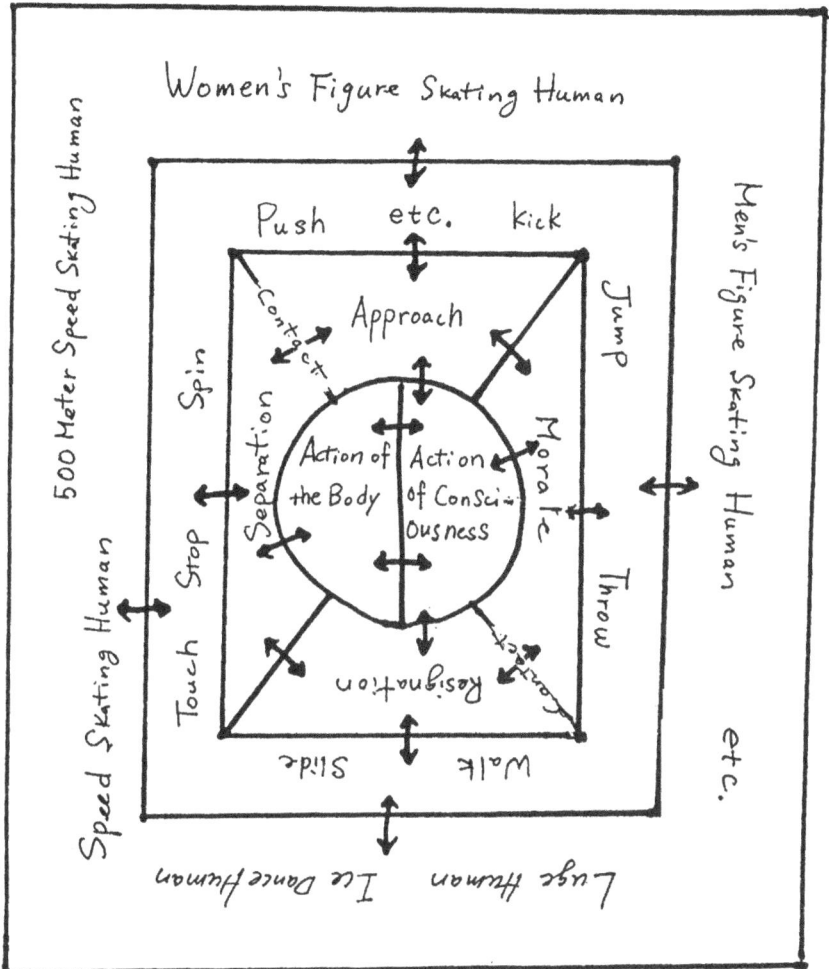

Figure 22. Relation between existence of the skating human and the words of languages connecting phenomenon of the skating human in each nation in the world

human presents the mutual actions of separation/contact between the skating humans. Objectively the body acts by the separation/contact actions, and at the same time subjectively the mind acts by the separation/contact action. Together they act as a whole. Within these actions, the changes in consciousness are acting, namely by presenting the aspects of morale and resignation.

Concerning the actions of the skating human, we use many different expressions to indicate them. These different expressions all rely on the aspects of the actions of the skating human. (Refer to figure 23.)

For example, in order to create sentences for classifications within the types of skating human, such as the action of the skating human, one would proceed in the following way. The figure-skating human as a movement human jumps (action of skater), at the same time, the skating human as an ice movement is jumped (action of ice for skating). The speed-skating human as movement human pushes; at the same time, the speed-skating human as an ice movement is pushed.

In the above manner, the actions of the connotative structure of the skating human themselves act in an original way. At the same time, they also act with aspects of the denotative structure.

The Denotative Structure

In the following way, I have analyzed and gained insight into the denotative elements of the social existence of the skating human, and I have attempted to extract the denotative elements themselves. (See figure 24.)

Using figure 24, I will explain each of the social factors of the skating human listed in the second analysis.

Recreation-ness/Competitiveness

First there is recreation-ness, in which the skating human amuses himself with entertaining skating, such as when a group of coworkers or a family enjoys skating. There is also competitiveness, which includes tension of the kind of seriousness such as when competitive leagues are commissioned by the sponsorship of all kinds of

Names of Actions of the Skating Human as Movement Ice

Names of Actions of the Skating Human as Movement Human

$$\left(\begin{array}{l} \text{being pushed} \\ \text{being moved} \\ \text{being bounced} \\ \text{being crept} \\ \text{being rolled} \\ \text{being jumped} \\ \text{being grasped} \\ \text{being touched} \\ \text{being slided} \\ \qquad \text{etc.} \end{array} \right) \text{and} \left(\begin{array}{l} \text{pushing} \\ \text{moving} \\ \text{bouncing} \\ \text{creeping} \\ \text{rolling} \\ \text{jumping} \\ \text{grasping} \\ \text{touching} \\ \text{sliding} \\ \qquad \text{etc.} \end{array} \right)$$

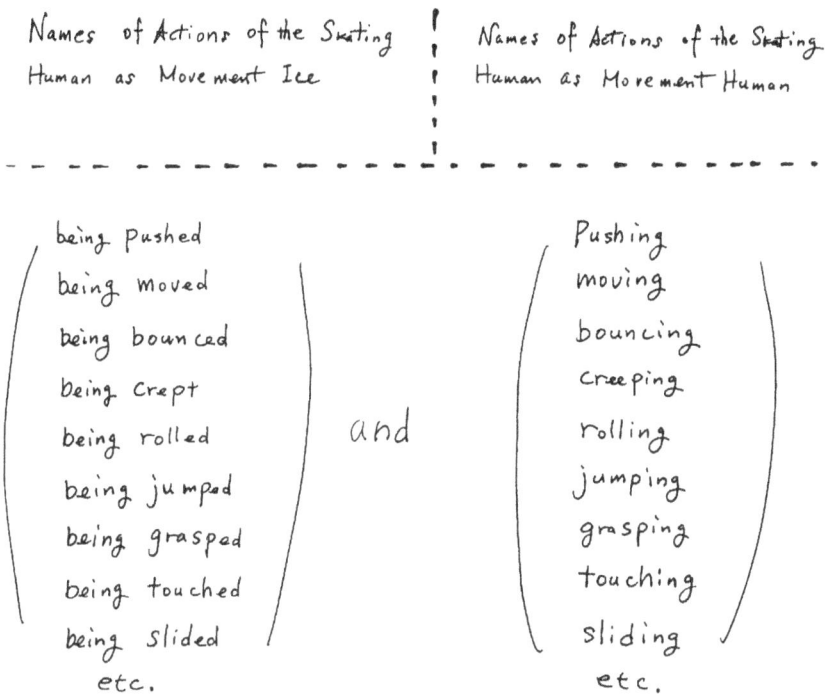

Figure 23. Natural expressions related to the actions of the skating human in each nation in the world

competitive groups. The recreation-ness of the skating human fosters a place for the meeting of the hearts of the skating humans as an ice movement and the skating human as a movement human and the skiing human as an ice movement. It is a softening aspect that encourages mutual understanding.

Then there is competitiveness, which is the aspect of the skating human where, within the rules of competition, a skating human as an ice movement or perhaps a skating human as a movement human and a skating human as a nice movement act with bravery and valorous determination. The greater the scale of the competitive league, the more the spirit intensifies, and the competitiveness of the skating human appears more conspicuous. For instance, this is the case in all the types of skating in international leagues, etc.

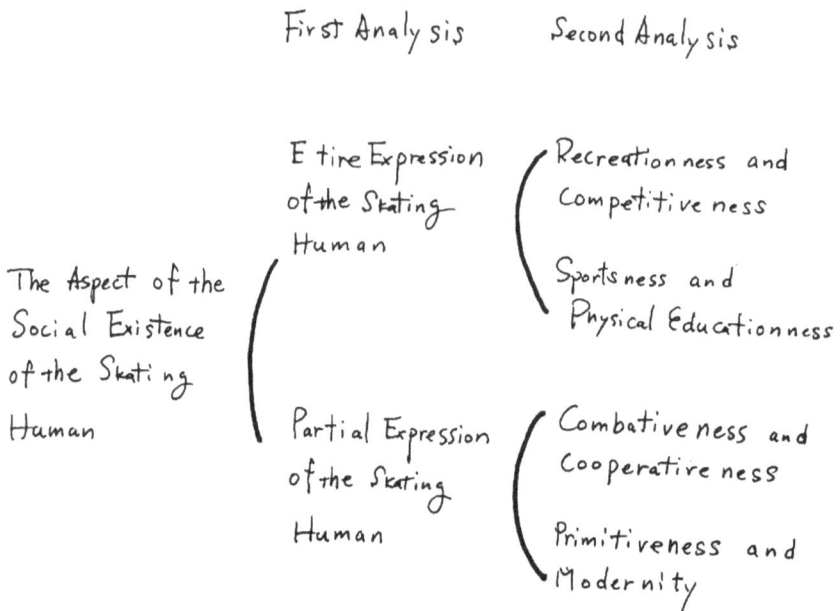

First Analysis   Second Analysis

The Aspect of the
Social Existence
of the Skating
Human

Entire Expression
of the Skating
Human

Recreation-ness and
Competitive-ness

Sports-ness and
Physical Education-ness

Partial Expression
of the Skating
Human

Combative-ness and
Cooperative-ness

Primitiveness and
Modernity

Figure 24. The social existence of the skating human in each nation in the world

Sports-ness/Physical Education-ness

In the phenomenon of skating, based on the fundamental structure of the teacher and pupil, the educational environment and content are given in the school's gym or a corresponding place.

This is the physical education-ness of the skating human performing in each skating event. The physical education-ness of the skating human is an educational phenomenon that depends on the sum total of the teacher and pupil, This is an aspect of the special society called school and an aspect of the actions of the skating humans as teacher (or professor) and students (as they are driven by sociological terms) that comes from a regionally narrow scope. The student who is recognized by the school side, perhaps specially selected, from nursery school through elementary, junior high, and high school, will be acting the role of the physical education-ness of the skating human. On the other hand, the phenomenon of skating in general society is an expression of the sports-ness of the skating human. We can see the sports-ness of the skating human because the sphere of skating belongs to sports. It is of course possible to make skating belong in the realm of sports. If it were so, the sports-ness of skating human would be the aspect of the skating human in which, in the social phenomenon that relies on the sum total of leaders and followers, a wide range of many kinds of skating would be developed with no relevance to sex, age, or occupation. Furthermore, there are the phenomena of figure skating, speed skating, ice hockey, etc. All of these are expressions of the sports-ness of the skating human.

Combativeness/Cooperativeness

In the actions of the skating human, there are the elements of the contrasting actions of combativeness and cooperativeness. The action of an individual skating human as a movement human on a team of skating humans is an expression of cooperativeness. This action of the play between companion skating human creates a oneness of the team/individual and builds many conscious states. It conspicuously expresses the cooperativeness of the skating human. This aspect can also be seen in the phenomenon where a group does skating, whereas actions of the skating human, the skilled actions of the skating human as an individual, are sublimated to the skilled actions of the skating human as a group. Namely, when there is a lack in the skilled actions of one skating human as a movement human, it is compensated for by the skilled actions of some other skating human as a movement human as an individual. In addition, there is also the aspect in which in order for one skating human as a movement human as an individual to perform skilled actions, some different skating human as a movement human as an individual tries to give assistance. In these forms, this aspect appears.

In contrast to this, there are also times when, with a severe attitude toward other skating humans, the skating human as an individual feels other skating humans are rivals or opponents. This is an expression of the combativeness of the skating human. It is most conspicuous in the setting of vehement competition between skating humans. Combativeness can be seen in every phenomenon of the skating and every phenomenon in which the skating human as movement ice-covered ground is dealt with. It is the moment when the skilled actions of the skating human as movement ice and they feel them as rivals. It also can be the movement of rivals that appears between the skilled actions of skating humans of a group.

Primitiveness/Modernity

In skating, there is the primitiveness of the skating human, in which the skating human directly engages the other skating human in movement ice contact. In skating such as each play on ice along children, play on ice among adults, etc. (barefoot, uncovered palms of hands, etc.), there is momentary direct contact with the ice movement as skating human in the actions toward the skating human as a movement human that has taken on the role of performer, such as the situations of hand grabbing, touching, kicking, etc. Therefore, the primitiveness of the skating human involves giving a direct impact to the body of the skating human, but the opportunities to handle the skating human as ice movement are relatively frequent. (There is no skating event with such primitiveness of the skating human now.)

On the other hand, there is an aspect of modernity of the skating human in which in the relation between skating human (human side) the skating human (ice side) acts by using equipment, uniforms, shoes, music, etc., in figure skating, speed skating, ice hockey, ice dance, etc., by getting specific uniforms, skates, skating boots, skating gloves, etc., in skating events that conspicuously express the modernity of the skating human. In the modernity of the skating human, the impact of the ice received by the body of the skating human as a movement human is small. The handling of the ice is relatively rare, and the freedom of the skating movement is limited.

Moreover, to say that here in the denotative structure we have come up with a comprehensive list of all of the words that refer to the social existence of skating human would be added. I have aimed only for a coordinated understanding of the social existence of the skating human and understanding of it as a living existence. Furthermore, if we look at the all too various elements of the social existence of the skating human, such as the amateurness or professionalness (there is not at present) of the skating human, the fair play-ness of the skating human, and the playfulness of the skating human we can see that these elements are vital elements that act to stir up the social aspects of the skating human. In this manner, in every country in the world, the skating human expresses the originality of each country and carries on a social existence. In the stream of time of past-present-future, this existence lives in the present as realistic beings and this existence is variable and alive.

6

Generalizations from the Ontology of the Skating Human (or Ice Human)

Up to this point, the three existences of the skating human, namely, the movement-cultural, the educational, and social existence, have been explained clearly. *Skating human*, when taken as in the hypothesis, is language that refers to the existential essence of the phenomenon of skating and the phenomena in which ice is dealt with. In other words, we have confirmed the fact that the words *skating human* are alive and exist, forming the special expanding world of skating and dealing with images for skating in every country in the world. We have also confirmed the fact that these words refer directly to a special kind of human. Skating humans exist as the expression of each country (national language) in the world, in the United States as Americans, in Russia as Russians, in China as Chinese, in Japan as Japanese, in Sweden as Swedes, etc. The skating human speaks American English, Chinese, Korean, German, British English, Italian, French, Spanish, etc., in the phenomena of skating. In the present of the ever-flowing stream of past-present-future, with living and variable aspects, he exists and lives.

Now, as a result of the clear evidence of the existential essence of the skating and the clear evidence of the existence of the skating human in the phenomenon of skating, the following kinds of questions can be answered:

Question 1: What is the phenomenon of skating?
Answer: The phenomenon of skating is the phenomenon in which a human and ice become skating human through doing the skating. It is a special world in which the skating human performs (or acts).

Question 2: What does it mean to skate?
Answer: This is an action by which human and ice became a skating

human that can be divided into, on the one hand, a skating human as movement human and, on the other hand, a skating human as ice movement for skating.

For example (more concreteness):

Question 1: What is figure skating?
Answer: Figure skating is a practice by which human and ice become a figure-skating human.

Question 2: What does it mean to do figure skating?
Answer: This means becoming a figure-skating human, who can be divided into a movement human as a skating human and a movement ice as a skating human.

Question 3: What does it mean in physical education to skate?
Answer: This is the conduct in which the human and ice become the skating human (as movement human and movement ice) and both of these are physical education-ized and try to become physical education-ized.

Question 4: What does it mean in sports to skate?
Answer: This is the conduct in which the human and ice become skating human in both sides, and both of these are sports-ized and try to become sports-ized.

Any other questions concerning the phenomenon of skating itself can be answered from the educational, social, and movement-cultural ontologies previously presented.

Furthermore, this skating human encompasses every type of skating human. Namely, it is the existence of luge human, the existence of speed-skating human, the existence of ice-dance human, the existence of ice-hockey human, etc. Also, depending on the differences in sex, age, race, school, occupation, etc., the above specific humans in phenomena of skating exist as different expressions.

In the above manner, through the movement of speculation, the establishment of the ontology of the skating human, from both an abstract standpoint to a concrete standpoint, from the existence to being and from being to existence, became possible. Here we can generalize this system as the ontology of the skating human.

Finally, while I have referred to the existence of the skating human as a special existence of the human in skating, I must now go on to present the existence of a purpose in the existence of the skating human. Namely, the existence of the skating human I have presented until now is an existence that acts in order to realize the skating human image. It is that purpose for which the existence is acting. Therefore, I must now go on to develop a presentation concerning the skating human image-the teleology of the skating human in each nation and each era. I would like to affirm the skating human image that comes from the existence of the skating human, who exists with special aspects in skating.

7

The Teleology of the Skating Human
(or Ice Human)

Until this point, I have contemplated the existential essence in the phenomena of all types of skating. I have shown clearly and confirmed that in every country in the world, every type of skating human exists in the world of each type of skating. However, at the same time, this existence includes the purpose of the skating human, namely, the skating human image. It is not simply the existence of the skating human, but also an existence that tries to realize the ideal image that the skating human must attain. Above all, the practice of all types of skating that is being conducted in scholastic physical education and sports in every country in the world is for the sake of the realization of all types of the skating human image by all types of the skating human. Also, there is the necessity for physical education and sports studies research concerning all types of skating in every country in the world (such as physical education and sports studies philosophy, physical education and sports studies psychology, physical education and sports studies physiology, physical education and sports studies sociology, physical education and sports studies history, etc.) in order to plan the realization of the skating human image, in the practice of the skating or the applied practice where skating is dealt with, in physical education.

At this point I will go on to speculate about what kind of special ideal image is meant by the purpose of the skating human in all nations in the world or, more specifically, by the skating human image in all nations in the world.

The skating human image in all nations in the world is, of course, the purpose of the practice of the skating, but it is necessary to explain clearly what, in reality, it is that this word directly refers to. It refers to the ideal image in which the actions of the skating human as a movement human and the actions of the skating human as movement ice in the practice of the skating are existing together doing superior actions. The skating human image is the ideal image that is living and exists ideally from one era to the next era in every country in the world. This is determined by the research of the physical education and sports theory specialists (such as physical education and sports studies philosophers, physical education and sports studies psychologists, physical education and sports studies physiologists, physical education and sports studies sociologists, physical education and sports studies historians, etc.) that are living in each era in every country in the world. The term *skating human image* refers directly to the ideal existence that adds weight, depth, size, and breadth to that acting existence.

In the nature of the substance of the skating human there are really two different kinds of nature. Also, these two natures dynamically act together and form the firm skating human image. The first is the part of the purpose that has a universal nature that is common to any time, to any place, and to any country. For example, all of the superior actions of the movement human as skating human and the movement ice as skating human–in other words, the attempt to realize the skating human image–even though there are differences between the histories, cultures, ideas, races, languages of the countries in the world, share a common universal nature.

The second is the concrete purpose of the skating human, which varies depending on the time, society, nation, age, sex, and other variables from country to country. In every country, there is originality in history, ideas, culture, and national language. The skating human image of a certain era in each country of the world has the aspects of that era. Furthermore, from the point of view of age, the various types of skating human images for children are different from the various types of skating human images for old people. From the point of view of sex, the skating human images for males and females are different. The images of the skating human are not identical, due to the various differences. Therefore, as opposed to the purpose of the universal substance of the skating human, this points to the variable, concrete purpose of the skating human. The constitution of the teleology of the skating human relies on the support/being-supported relationship between these two sides, which is a relationship that acts dynamically and mutually to support each side. The skating human image of the former is the purpose of the skating human, while the skating human image of the latter is the goal of the skating human. The difference between these clearly points to the difference between the universal purpose and the variable purpose. Therefore, the skating human image consists of the purpose of substance as its core, and that which surrounds the purpose substance is the goal substance. The dynamic relationship between them assumes the character of abstract/concrete–concrete/abstract. Because of this, the skating human image possesses unifying qualities that transcend the realities of nationality, age, sex, etc. (time and space), but at the same time, this teleology is also one that sees those realities as realities. This is summarized in figure 25.

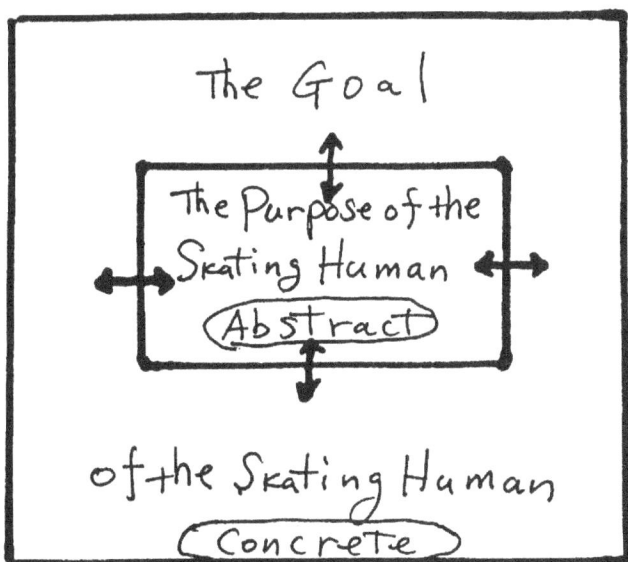

Figure 25. Constitution of the skating human image in each nation in the world

Next I would like to go on to explain the purpose of the skating human. Specifically, of what substance is the skating image itself constructed? I will explain this point.

The structure of the skating human image is made up of two types of structure: a connotative structure and a denotative structure. These form the living, unified whole. There are the actions of all of the many element images, and as a whole they act ideally. If we broadly divide these various idealistic elements, they come from the connotative structure and denotative structure. (Refer to figure 26.)

In physical education and sports, the skating human forms the special society of the skating in general society. He works ideally in a unique way. At the same time, skating is regulated in a unique way and exists ideally in general society.

The Image of Connotative Structure

In the actions of the skating human image, there is the image of connotative structure. This acts as the foundation of the generation of the image of denotative structure and thus is a vitally important area. The image of connotative structure itself is formed from the various element images that become the many different ideals. It is formed from the ideal of the image of life energy that comes from physical education and sports nutrition studies and physical education and sports hygiene, the ideal of the image of the body and the image of the mind (mind-body image) that come from physical education and sports philosophy, the ideal of the image of body strength, the image of flexibility, the image of physique, and the image of physical condition (the image of health) that come from physical education and sports physiology, etc. The physical education and sports studies researchers of every country in the world will go on to prove the realistic existence of the skating human. Relying on the leadership to provide this proof, the previous images of the connotative structure of the skating human will be concretely alive and acting ideal images. Then, in order that the physical education and sports studies researchers of every country in the world expand on the substance of the words of these various elements, and in order to promote understanding of these words as living things, the research of purpose will proceed. As a result, to the question: "Why are the educational ministries of every country in the world conducting and practicing all kinds of skating in scholastic physical education?" one will be able to provide a direct answer from the various fields of physical education and sports studies, namely, physical education and sports philosophy, physical education and sports psychology, physical education and sports physiology, physical

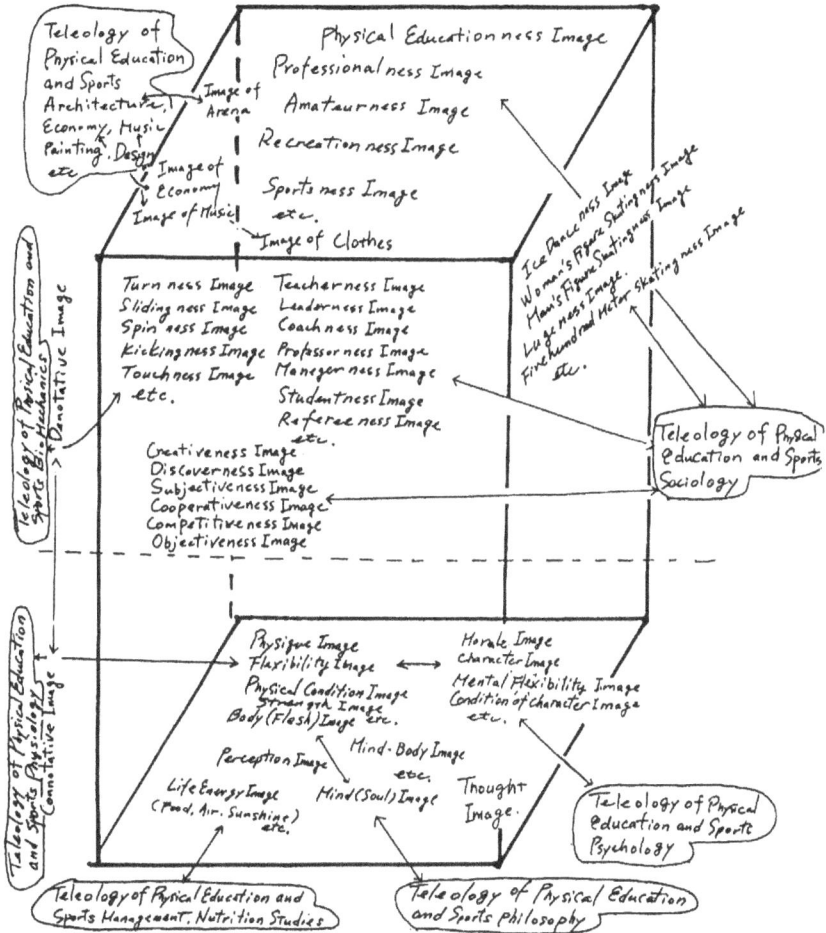

Figure 26. The skating human image in each nation in the world

education and sports sociology, physical education and sports history, etc. For example, according to physical education and sports philosophy, all types of skating are practiced in scholastic physical education and sports in order to realize the image of the mind and body of all types of the skating human. The content of the image of the mind and body can be explained relying on the research of physical education and sports philosophers. Of course, the content of the partial element images presented there all is ideal content drawn from the proof of all of the specialist researchers in physical education and sports studies, and at the same time, in the space of the various elements in the image of connotative structure, they are things that are doing superior actions.

Also, there are the various elements that do superior actions in the image of denotative structure as well. For example, the image of body strength is the superior inner actions of body strength itself, acting in superior actions in relation to the various elements, such as morale, flexibility, cooperativeness, competitiveness, physical condition, creativeness, etc.

As was shown previously, the image of the connotative structure in the skating human image is the entirety of the various elements of the connotative structure that have been amassed by the physical education and sports studies researchers in every country in the world and the physical education and sports studies research in each era. However, this image of connotative structure not only acts in the image of connotative structure but works in the image of denotative structure. So what kind of substance of ideal images makes up the image of denotative structure of skating human? I will now go on to deal with this question.

The Image of Denotative Structure

In the actions of the skating human image there is an image of denotative structure. In the ideal image that is generated from the image of connotative structure, the origin of the formation of the image of denotative structure is included. Inside the denotative structure itself, which acts as the denotative structure, are the actions of the various element images.

Looking from the specialized point of view of the physical education and sports sociologists and scholastic physical education and considering the existential direction of the skating human, if an inquiry is made to determine the ideal images of that existence, then in the following way the idealistic elements of the denotative structure become visible: the image of sports-ness, the image of physical education-ness, the image of amateurness, the image of professionalness, the image of recreation-ness, the image of teacher-ness, the image of student-ness, the image of leader-ness, the image of manager-ness, the image of coach-ness, the image of director-ness, the image of follower-ness, the image of women's figure skating-ness, the image of speed skating-ness, the image of relay-ness, the image of women's 1,000-meter skating-ness, the image of men's figure skating-ness, the image of luge-ness, the image of bobsled-ness, the image of ice hockey-ness (essentially ice hockey belongs to ball games, so it is exceptional in being categorized in skating study), the image of creativeness, the image of cooperativeness, the image of competitive-ness, the image of objectiveness, the image of discovery-ness, the image of subjectiveness, etc. From the above kinds of images of elements, the image of the denotative structure in the skating human image is formed. The above various images of elements above are the various aspects of the skating human image, and they are things that have been called from researchers in physical education and sports sociology and scholastic physical education. Then the images of the various elements in the denotative structure act in a way that promotes the idealistic condition of the connotative structure, while at the same time they are the superior denotative elements that act in a way that promotes the idealistic condition of the elements in the image of the denotative structure. Therefore, each of the elements in the denotative structure itself is an element that is superior and acts ideally.

In the preceding manner, the skating human image itself is the purpose of the existence of the skating human in every country in the world. Therefore, this is limited by the existence of the skating human, and, in reality, there is a purpose in straining to derive the skating human image from this existence. For example, in order to explain this skating human image as a skating human image in reality, we can divide the skating human image into its various different types, such as the women's figure skating image, the men's figure skating image, the speed skating image, the bobsled image, the luge image, and so on. We can express concretely the goal of the skating human if we look, for instance, at figure skating human from various points of view. From the point of view of the school level, there are figure-skating human images in the elementary school and the high school. From the point of view of sex, there are the men's figure-skating human image and the women's figure-skating human image. From the point of view of age, there are the ten-year-old figure-skating human image and the forty-year-old figure-skating human image. From the point of view of nationality, there are the figure- skating human image as an American, the figure-skating human image as a Japanese, the figure-skating human image as a Russian, the figure-skating human image as a Swede, the figure- skating human image as an Australian, the figure-skating human image as a Frenchman, the figure-skating human image as a German, the figure-skating human image as an Italian, and so on. In other words, because the existence of all types of the figure-skating human in every country of the world is different, the purpose of the figure-skating human can be materialized as different goals by the different nationalities, different national languages, backgrounds of national histories, and other national differences. On the other hand, while the skating human image can make as its purpose the various unique human images of each country in the world, from a global, humanistic, common point of view, it can also present a purpose that is the skating human image as a world citizen. Provided that the existence of all types of the skating human practicing all kinds of skating in all places around the world can be confirmed, this purpose can be erected as a common purpose of all types of the world citizen, or perhaps mankind, skating human image.

Above I have presented the purpose of the skating human or, more specifically, the substance of the skating human image (limited to only the important substance necessary in skating theory). As a result, we have reached a point at which the following kinds of questions can be answered:

Question 1: Why are the educational ministries of every country in the world practicing all types of skating in scholastic physical education?

Answer: All types of skating are being practiced in scholastic physical education in every country in the world in order to realize all types of the skating human image as the specific humans of every country in the world.

Question 2: Why are the educational ministries of every country in the world offering classes on the theory concerning all types of skating in scholastic physical education?
Answer: This is so that in the scholastic physical education of every country in the world physical education teachers will show the peaceful practice of all types of skating to the students and explain the practice of all types of skating to the students and the students will understand them.

Question 3: Why are the physical education and sports researchers of every country in the world needed for conducting research in fields such as physical education and sports psychology, physical education and sports philosophy, physical education and sports physiology, physical education and sports history, physical education and sports sociology, etc.? Furthermore, is this necessary in human society, the human nation, and the human world?
Answer: It is absolutely necessary for national formation of physical education and sports studies (including skating study). This is so that the place of skating in every country in the world will be realized. This research is the guarantee of the sound practice of skating in every country Also, through this research we, all physical education and sports scholars, can build the national theory of skating in every country in the world that supports human nations and the human world.

Question 4: Why must a World Physical Education and Sports Academy be established?
Answer: Relying on the development of this type of research, the skating human image in every country in the world and the skating human image of each era of mankind will be constructed, thus developing the guarantee of peace in every country and world peace.

Also, the academy will nurture physical education and sports researchers who will contribute to peace in every country and to world peace or will work as responsible professors in the future at colleges, universities, and graduate schools that support nations and the world as a human society through their true theory of knowledge.

Question 5: Why must a Physical Education and Sports Academy be established in every country in the world?
Answer: Physical education and sports researchers (from all the fields) are necessary to construct the national skating theory in every country and to guarantee that the practice of skating in every country in the world is a peaceful practice. And through these efforts we will be able to promise prosperity of nations and prosperity of mankind.

The ministry of education in every nation has to answer all questions concerning skating in public because of letting pupils practice some kinds of skating performed from elementary school to graduate school. Instead of the ministries of education in all nations, we scholars of physical education and sports in all nations must take responsibility for answering the questions concerning skating in public.

Other questions we can pose in order to recover trust of us as professionals in all nations are: Why do we need doctors for physical education and sports studies? Why do we have to plan the doctoral programs in graduate schools in all nations? What does this term *professor of physical education and sports studies* mean? More important, why do we need professors for our physical education and sports studies? Does *professor* mean a player of talk without responsibilities for actual physical education and sports practices? Why do we need faculties of physical education in colleges, universities, and graduate schools for the human nation, mankind, etc.?

In addition, any questions concerning the purpose of formation related to all types of skating in every country in the world can be answered from the teleology of the skating human. Also, through the purpose it is necessary to go on to develop support for peace in every country and world peace.

Furthermore, from the presentation of the ontology and teleology of the skating human in every country in the world, we must now go on to develop the methodology of the skating human in every country in the world by which the existence of the skating human in every country in the world realizes the skating human image of every country in the world. This will deal with the method by which the existence of the skating human in every country in the world realizes the skating human image. The methodology will be organically connected to the ontology and the teleology and will have the unique quality of working together with them. This kind of undertaking will work through the realization of the establishment of universal skating theory, which unites all countries in the world and accepts differences between all countries in the world.

8

The Methodology of the Skating Human
(or Ice Human)

The methodology of the skating human is an original theoretical area that deals with both the movement human and the movement ice sides of the phenomenon of all types of skating. These two sides, which are referred to directly by the term *skating human*, can be said, depending on how they work together, to emphasize the movement ice as a skating human, only the ability (or possibility) required for the movement ice as a skating human is required of the movement human as a skating human. (It means qualified ice for skater in sociological expression.) On the other hand, if we emphasize the movement human as skating human, only the ability required for the movement human as skating human is required of the movement human as skating human. (It means that skillful movement of skater is needed.) Therefore, achieving the required ability that is possible when both sides accept each other's demands is imperative. This type of method is the only advanced method by which the skating human image can be realized in each nation in the world. Toward that end, there are notably two methodologies: one in relation to time (era, etc.) and one in relation to space (nation, etc.). The former considers the experience of becoming a skating human in terms of time, while the latter considers the experience of becoming a skating human in terms of space. Therefore, the method that realizes the skating human image must give the appropriate weight to experience in time and experience in space.

Theoretical Foundation and Ground for the Formation of the Skating Human Methodology

Before presenting the methodology of the skating human, it is necessary to first make clear the reasons why it is possible to present such a methodology. In order to do this, we must look at the theoretical foundation and the ground for the methodology. The theoretical foundation for the formation of the methodology of the skating human relies on the educational, social, and movement-cultural ontologies of the skating human and the teleology of the skating human already presented. The ground for the formation of this methodology is the fact that in scholastic physical education in every country around the world skating is being practiced. The former is based on the development of the theory, while the latter comes from the practice of skating.

The Characteristics of the Methodology of the Skating Human

There are two characteristics associated with the content of the methodology of the skating human. First, it is an unchangeable, universal, abstract methodology, applicable to any country at any time. Second, as countries (space) and eras (time) change, it is a concrete, realistic methodology that changes accordingly. The methodology of the skating human is constructed with the former at the core, while the latter surrounds it, both working together to preserve the relationship. More specifically, the former is the area of the methodology based on the common qualities of all countries and constructed by the physical education and sports researchers of every country in the world so that the practice of skating in scholastic physical education in every country in the world serves to realize the skating human image in each era. Meanwhile, the latter is the area of the methodology that has the quality of grasping the differences in the realistic aspects of the skating human, i.e., country, era, age, sex, school, etc., as differences in realistic aspects.

Elements of the Formation of the Contents of the Methodology of the Skating Human

In regard to the formation of the methodology of the skating human, both the theoretical foundation and the practical ground have been presented already. However, I believe that the latter, the practical ground, gives an extraordinarily important reason for the formation of the methodology of the skating human. Namely, because of the existence of the practice of skating in physical education programs, the existence of the practice of skating in society, and the existence of physical education teachers, mentors, and pupils who play a function in society, the need for the methodology of the skating human becomes apparent.

In that case, physical education teachers and mentors are those who lead students to become skating humans and realize the skating human image, while students and followers who receive all forms of skating education are those who look toward becoming all forms of skating humans and realizing all forms of the skating human image. Therefore, the human relationship of the teachers and mentors and students and followers in the phenomenon of skating will all become the skating human and realize the skating human image. These are mutual relationships that exist to realize the skating human image.

Those fostering the skating human have experience in the past of fully (deeply and widely) becoming a skating human in order to realize the skating human image. They are those who possess the leadership qualifications to be able to realize the skating human image. On the other hand, those becoming skating humans must receive leadership in order to realize the skating human image. They are those of whom study skills are demanded.

With the relationship between physical education teachers, who try to realize the skating human image and foster skating humans, and students, who study while looking toward becoming skating humans and realizing the skating human image, as the ground, the various structural elements of the methodology of the various kinds of skating humans are formed. Specifically, these elements include study, leadership, evaluation, curriculum, educational resources, study ability, study processes, leadership ability, skill, etc. Classifying these elements into age groups, we may divide them into study, leadership, and educational resources. The terms *skill, study, ability, study process*, etc. are technical terms connected with the student or follower becoming a skating human and trying to realize the skating human image and are therefore study terms. The terms *leadership ability, evaluation, curriculum*, etc., are all terms connected with the teachers and mentors trying to realize the skating human image and turn their students into skating humans and are therefore leadership terms. Finally, that which brings the leadership and study together at the place of the skating is the educational resources. The structural elements of the methodology of the skating human are systematized in the manner described in figure 27.

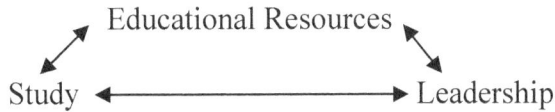

Figure 27. The structural elements of the methodology of the skating human in each nation in the world

Study. This is the state of those becoming skating humans in which they learn all of the various things they must learn from those helping them to become skating humans in order to realize the skating human image. Also, we will call students those who, under the supervision of those fostering the skating human, strive to learn that which they need to become skating humans.

Furthermore, study ability is ability that students possess to learn all the constructive knowledge required in order to become a skating human and realize the skating human image. Skill is a part of study ability and is the condition of the mastery of the necessary techniques required to become a skating human and realize the skating human image. Also, study process is the process by which, under the leadership of those fostering the skating human, those becoming skating humans learn all of the relevant knowledge.

Leadership. This is defined as the ability to lead those who will become skating humans on the part of those who will foster their becoming skating humans by giving them all the various knowledge they will need toward the goal of realizing the skating human image. Leadership ability is the ability of those fostering skating humans, with the goal of realizing the skating human image, to develop fully those becoming skating humans (students). The leadership process is the process by which those fostering skating humans, with the goal of realizing the skating human image, lead those becoming skating humans. Furthermore, evaluation is the process by which those fostering skating humans decide what level those becoming skating humans have reached and how far they have advanced in approaching the realization of the skating human image. Curriculum is the study route through which those fostering skating humans lead those becoming skating humans in order to realize the skating human image.

Educational Resources. A collective use of this term refers to all materials those fostering skating humans use to lead those becoming skating humans to realize the skating human image, along with all study materials used by those becoming skating humans, whose aim is to realize the skating human image. The educational resources play the role of the intermediary in the formation of the leadership and study of the skating human and are a necessary methodological element in the realization of the skating human image. The educational resources include natural educational resources and man-made educational resources. The former are sunshine, air, weather (clear, rainy, snowy, cloudy), air pressure (wind), water (water in a pool), earth (ice, ground), etc. The latter include gymnasiums or arenas (man-made ice ground), lighting, clothes, tools, shoes, stages, etc. Therefore, in the broad sense of the term, educational resources refers to the combination of natural educational resources and man-made educational resources, but when taken in the narrow sense of the term refers mostly to man-made educational resources.

The Construction Method of the Methodology of the Skating Human as National Theory in Every Nation in the World

It is imperative that we use the terminology of the structural elements of the methodology of the skating human, namely, *study* (*skill, study process*, etc.), *leadership* (*evaluation, curriculum, leadership process, leadership ability*, etc.), and *educational resources*, in order to realize the skating human image. However, it is also necessary to answer the question of how the content of these elements can be given substance. I will now present these kinds of problems related to the construction of the methodology of the skating human.

From the standpoint of those dealing with fundamental theory of physical education studies, it is possible to construct a methodology that answers these kinds of questions. The methodology of the skating human should use the original specialized vocabulary from each specialized area of physical education, and considering study, leadership, educational resources, etc., we can create a separate methodology from each field of physical education that serves to realize every partial image of the skating human in each era and each nation that emerges from that field. In regard to the methodology of the skating human from physical education physiology, for instance, while considering study, leadership, and educational resources we can construct an original methodology, using the specialized terms of physiology, such as *strength, physique, health, and flexibility*, that serve to realize the strength image, the physique image, the health image, and the flexibility image of the skating human.

Likewise, in regard to the methodology of the skating human from physical education psychology, while considering study, leadership, and educational resources we can construct an original methodology, using the specialized terms of psychology, such as *character; morale, mental health, flexibility*, etc., that serve to realize the character image, the morale image, the mental health image, the flexibility image, etc., of the skating human. In regard to the methodology of the skating human from physical education philosophy, while considering study, leadership, and educational resources we can construct an original methodology, using the specialized terms of philosophy, such as *mind, body, mind-body relationship, soul, flesh*, etc., that serves to realize the mind image, the body image, the mind-body relationship image, the soul image, the flesh image, etc., of the skating human. In regard to the methodology of the skating human from physical education science, while considering study, leadership, and educational resources we can construct an original methodology, using the specialized terms of educational science, such as *creativity, subjectivity, objectivity, cooperation, competition*, etc., that serve to realize the creativity image, the subjectivity image, the objectivity image, the cooperation image, the competition image, etc., of the skating human. In regard to the methodology of the skating human from physical education sociology, while considering study, leadership, and educational resources we can construct an original methodology as a national theory, using the specialized terms of sociology, such as *performer, amateur, professional, sports, physical education*, etc., that serve to realize the performer image, the amateur image, the professional image, the sports image, the physical education image, etc., of the skating human. In regard to the methodology of the skating human from physical education and sports biomechanics, while considering study, leadership, and educational resources we can construct an original methodology as a national theory using the specialized terms of biomechanics, such as *grasp, run, catch, walk, stand, hang, turn*, etc., that serve to realize the grasping image, the running image, the catching image, the walking image, the standing image, the hanging image, the turning image, etc., of the skating human.

Moreover, the construction of the original methodology of the skating human for each of these specialized fields of physical education must be living, changing entities, taking into account the realistic existence of variables such as nationality, race, age, sex, etc., to always be the best methodology for physical education researchers at the current time. Therefore, the research specialists in each field of physical education must, while referring to the knowledge in physical education history for advice, construct separate methodologies as national theories responsible for each specialized field.

In the above manner, it is possible to construct a methodology of the skating human for every country in the world. Thus we are able to form a national methodology of skating study in each country in the world and in each era by each national language.

Part IV

Theory of International Gymnastics Studies for the Achievement of Peace

1

A Word from the Author

The term *gymnastics human* is a symbolic term that works toward a national peace and a world peace. We, the world's physical education and sports scholars, must treat this word as dearly as our own lives. This is because, without the existence of the gymnastics human, none of the language concerning gymnastics and research concerning gymnastics could be formed. The existence builds and determines it all. The existence of gymnastics humans creates many national languages. However, the national languages are not able to create the human existence in all nations. They make American English, Japanese, German, French, Italian, Korean, British English, Spanish, Chinese, etc. The gymnastics humans in China speak Chinese. The gymnastics humans in Russia speak Russian. The gymnastics humans in the United States speak American English. The gymnastics humans also make other words like sound (noisy or nice), imitation sound, onomatopoeic words in the phenomenon of gymnastics. All national languages used in the phenomenon of gymnastics are a proof of the existence of gymnastics humans by nations. The term *gymnastics human* is the universal language of the world's physical education and sports scholars as long as the phenomenon of gymnastics continues actually in all the nations. It is a specialized term, even a holy term.

I present this book for the benefit of all the physical education and sports scholars of each of the world's nations alike.

2

Establishing the Hypothesis for Creating Gymnastics Studies

The following questions are the fundamental motives for attempting to create the theory of international gymnastics studies for the achievement of peace (principle of physical education and sports studies and research for all nations in the world):

1. Why, in the scholastic physical education programs of the education ministries of each country in the world, are teachers or professors using any types of gymnastics as the educational resources to lead students?

2. Why are the physical education and sports researchers of each country in the world conducting research concerning any types of gymnastics?

3. Why are physical educational teachers and physical education and sports researchers and professors of every country in the world conducting classes in schools, colleges, universities, and graduate schools concerning the theory of any types of gymnastics?

4. Why does the IOC adopt any types of gymnastics and include gymnastics in the Olympics?

5. Why does research concerning gymnastics belong to the physical education and sports studies?

6. Why is research concerning gymnastics worthy of a doctorate or master's degree in physical education and sports studies?

7. Why do we need physical education faculties in colleges, universities and graduate schools in the nation and the world?

8. Why do we physical education scholars need professors who offer lectures for their students in public and employ them?

We physical education and sports scholars, ask the questions above in order to restore social, national, and world trust in our profession. This means that we physical education scholars have social, national, and world problems. It also brings what education is in reality.

Currently there is no theory from the world's physical education and sports research that can answer these fundamental questions of gymnastics research. This is the most important problem that I have to take responsibility for as a physical education scholar in public. Therefore, I tried to think that I undertook the problem and tried to solve the problem and tried to build the theories by which I could answer all of the questions. The motives that I have to try the theory for studies of gymnastics are mentioned above.

Here, in order to ask myself and answer the question: "What are all types of gymnastics and, more generally, what is gymnastics?" I have formed the following hypothesis. 'When a human does gymnastics is when a human becomes a gymnastics human. (When a human does gymnastics is not not when a human becomes a human.)" As a reason for the formation of the hypothesis, I believe that to do gymnastics is to do gymnastics, and to do gymnastics is not not doing gymnastics. To do is to become.

I used this expression about apparatus in phenomenon of gymnastics as a reason. All the apparatus in gymnastics are connected to gymnastics human in fact. The apparatus themselves do not move at all but the apparatus are things that absorb entire energy of gymnastics human who tries to perform in gymnastics. Therefore I created this word "movement apparatus".

This new term (which will become a specialized term used among physical education and sports scholars) has been created in order to convert terms such as *gymnastics* and terms included in it (*parallel bars, uneven parallel bars, pommeled horse, rings, mat exercise, balance beam*, etc.) into moving, living worlds. Also, the world's physical education teachers take their responsibilities from the social reality of gymnastics being taught by sports leaders to sports students and followers.

Also, in this book I have used the term *movement human*. When we perceive the phenomenon of gymnastics, we see people moving. In order to express the existence of the moving human being (apart from the technique one may have in one's arms and legs) in one noun phrase, we say "movement human." This term refers to the entire existence of the human (individual) and some other (another person or something else) dynamically working together in both a passive and active relationship.

The term *gymnastics human* is used to represent collectively all of the various types of gymnastics, such as parallel bar human, uneven parallel bar human, pommeled horse human, ring human, balance beam human, etc. Each of these terms refers directly to the existence of the acting relationship between a human and apparatus in each type of gymnastics. It is this relationship, too, that gives life to and maintains the socially significant term *gymnastics*.

Next I would like to explain in detail what is directly indicated by the term *gymnastics human*. The object to which the words *gymnastics human* refers is the entirety of the acting relationship between a movement or non-movement apparatus and a movement human in the phenomenon of gymnastics or in the phenomenon in which an apparatus is dealt with. In the world of gymnastics, the movement human and movement apparatus together make up the gymnastics human. In this situation, the movement human is a movement human related to a movement apparatus and the movement apparatus is a movement apparatus related to movement human. Therefore, the two share a common point that connects them together. Specifically, this common point is the existential form in which the gymnastics human acts together in mutual independence and in certain aspects moves in a uniform motion. However, if we look objectively at them, we can divide the gymnastics human into a gymnastics human as a movement human and a gymnastics human as a movement apparatus.

Therefore, in presenting the theory, in order to refer directly to both the gymnastics human as a movement human and the gymnastics human as a movement apparatus, we will use the term *gymnastics human* for simplification. Only when we wish to make an explicit distinction between the two sides will we use the expressions *gymnastics human as a movement human* and *gymnastics human as a movement apparatus*. Therefore, the expression gymnastics human refers to both the movement apparatus and movement human sides of the gymnastics.

There are many reasons for the creation of the special term

gymnastics human, but the most important of these is the need to distinguish the general human existence from the existence experienced in the special world in which gymnastics is dealt with in physical education and sports studies and to make this special independence clear. In addition, it serves to help construct national theories (gymnastics studies) to explain the unique practice of gymnastics.

The next matter with which we must concern ourselves is the development of all types of gymnastics phenomena and phenomena that involve treatment of an apparatus in every country in the world. Specifically, in what form does this living phenomenon appear to our eyes? In other words, which actions in the living phenomenon of gymnastics are essential and which are nonessential? Understanding this distinction and synthesis will lead to a clear insight into this living phenomenon of gymnastics.

In order to answer these questions, I will examine the living phenomenon of gymnastics itself, relying on intuitive analysis and the integrated judgment method. As was stated in the hypothesis, the essence of the existence of the living phenomenon of gymnastics and the phenomenon in which an apparatus is dealt with and the nonessence of that existence (auxiliary actions to the existential essence) are manifested in the various aspects of the gymnastics human, such as the track-and-field human, the ball human, the flying human, the martial arts human, etc. Please see figure 28 for an explanation of this idea. There are, in other words, all the essential structural elements that form the living phenomenon of gymnastics.

If we analyze the primary factors that form the movement relying on our perceptions of the gymnastics phenomenon and then integrate these back together, we can come to understand the movement itself. For example, if we look at the action of the gymnastics human, we see that he acts on the ground, the air, the image, the ball, etc., in realities, to form the living phenomenon of gymnastics. The instant the gymnastics human acts in relation to ground he begins to exist as a track-and-field human. In that instant the gymnastics human acts in relation to another image, he begins to exist as a dance human. Furthermore, in the instant the gymnastics human acts to air, he begins to exist as a flying human. There are the auxiliary actions in the living

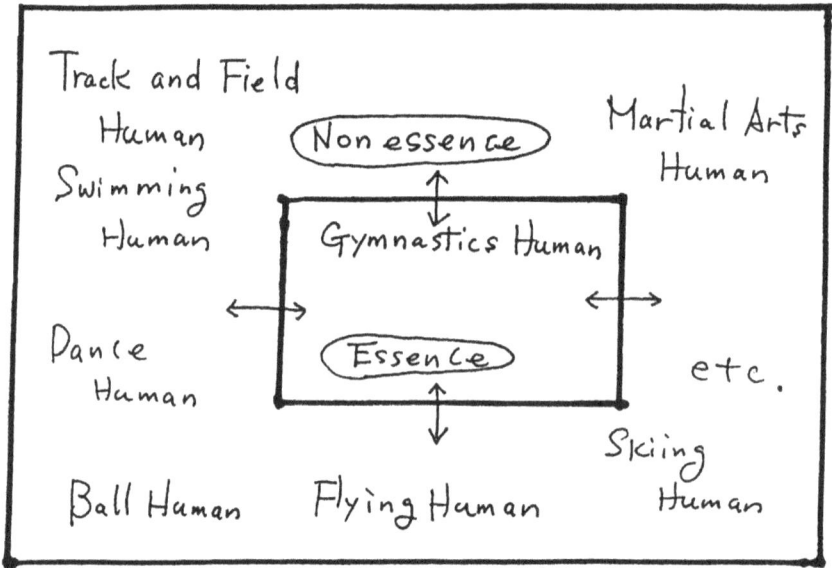

28. Formation elements of the living phenomenon of gymnastics in each nation in the world

phenomenon of gymnastics that create motion and that act indirectly on the movement of the gymnastics human.

In order to determine if figure 28 is true or false, let us try to return to the living phenomenon (fact) of each type of gymnastics. For instance, I explain the living phenomenon of the horizontal bar in gymnastics using this graph. We can say that in the actions of the bar human, the horizontal bar appears as the existential essence. At the same time, the phenomenon appears as a composition of transient aspects of the nonessential, such as the dance human (he may be doing horizontal movement with some image), the track-and-field human (he may perform horizontal bar movement with acting on the ground or the artificial ground, floorboards of gym), flying human (he may perform horizontal bar movement with acting in air), etc. The phenomenon of gymnastics human is, most importantly, the actions of the apparatus (including mat, horizontal bar, balance beam, etc.) on which there are made movements as a gymnastics human. I can explain concrete matters of actual gymnastics with figure 28. It means this figure 28 is true. So we need many kinds of special terms in order

130

to construct national gymnastics studies. If the horizontal bar movement is performed outdoors, the horizontal bar human may act on rain and water (like swimming human) or snow (like skiing human). The determining factor is the valuation of the gymnastics, but above all, it is determined by the action of the gymnastics human. Therefore, the gymnastics human in the phenomenon of gymnastics is essential existence. Why? I explain it in evidence of existence of gymnastics human, because existence of gymnastics human makes all things (national languages, special terms of gymnastics, actual sounds of gymnastics, etc.). The actions of gymnastic human mean movement apparatus for the sake of doing gymnastics and movement human for the sake of doing gymnastics.

Therefore, it is possible to say that all of the living phenomena of the various types of gymnastics can be found in every country in the world, being formed by a mixture of the characteristics of the living phenomena of gymnastics human, the track-and-field human, the flying human, the dance human, etc. Most important, all are formed from the existential essence of the gymnastics human, namely, the living actions of the gymnastics human that determine the process and result of the gymnastics. As evidence for this we can say that the points scored in a gymnastics event, which depend upon the actions of the gymnastics human in gymnastics, provide dynamic variation to the aspects of the phenomenon and the result of the gymnastics is determined by them. They also produce a lot of words in relation with the gymnastics in national languages and nonwords like sounds and imitation sounds in the phenomenon of gymnastics. Therefore, the action of the gymnastics human determine everything in the phenomenon of gymnastics.

I would like to put forth this idea in the form of a hypothesis: that the phenomenon of gymnastics is the mutual actions of apparatus and human, sometimes with music, talk, etc., namely, the gymnastics human. However, in order to do this I must provide some clear evidence that is able to confirm that this is the existential essence in the phenomenon of gymnastics. This would be the factual ground for the formation of these words. In order to speak scientifically about the phenomenon of gymnastics and phenomenon in which apparatus is dealt with, we must make this existential essence that will be the object of the analysis very clear. In other words, it is necessary to confirm whether or not the term *gymnastics human* is a term that possesses realistic qualities in the phenomenon of gymnastics.

Thus I began to think that I could incorporate this method into an ontology of the gymnastics human. In other words, using the term *gymnastics human*, I will explain in detail the reality of gymnastics. It should thus be possible to prove this hypothesis, the gymnastics human would be the existential essence in the phenomenon of gymnastics, and *gymnastics human* would become specialized terminology whose use would be required any time gymnastics research is being conducted. Furthermore, we would begin down the road toward the construction of a theory of gymnastics studies dealing with the entirety of practice and theory. It would be possible to advance the theory by means of a teleology and a methodology and, finally, to form gymnastics theory (a world united and different). A distinction would be made between the aspects of gymnastics studies that affect the daily lives of average humans and special areas of gymnastics studies. When names are given to these boundaries, gymnastics studies will be formed.

I have ascertained that the existence of the gymnastics human can be grasped as three aspects, and using them I hope to make this existence clear. Specifically, these are the movement-cultural existence of the gymnastics human, the educational existence of the gymnastics human, and the social existence of the gymnastics human. These all point to the fact that in every country in the world, the gymnastics human exists in many ways and forms a special world. I will now begin my undertaking to study the existence of this gymnastics human, who exists in every country in the world.

3

The Movement-Cultural Ontology of the Gymnastics Human

The gymnastics human lives in the movement culture, and the gymnastics human exists possessing movement-cultural aspects in all nations in the world. This comes from a connotative structure and a denotative structure. Together they maintain independent functions while living and existing as a whole.

The Connotative Structure

The gymnastics human as a movement human is organically composed with a head, a torso, hands, and feet. Internally, he is partially muscles, bones, organs, a brain, etc., which all rely on blood for their actions. However, the gymnastics human as movement human is actually made of many materials, such as a certain amount of air and various other objects, all of which will be acted upon by the existing life energy. These are based on factors of nature, which include gravity, temperature, climate, sunshine, rain, snow, etc., and artificial factors, which include gymnasiums, ground, lighting, etc., and they act on individual or group behavior and skill. However, these factors act together with factors dependent on the gymnastics human as a movement human himself, such as perception, thought, emotion, etc. Therefore, the gymnastics human as a movement human exists as a complex synthesis of the various factors that make up each specific human.

There are other aspects of the gymnastics human as an apparatus movement, including floor, vault, horizontal bar, parallel bars, rings, beams, pommelled horse, a symmetric bar, etc. Therefore, this term *gymnastics human* means specific human existence and apparatus existence in the phenomenon of gymnastics.

As individual actions, the two sides (the gymnastics human as a movement human and the gymnastics human as a movement apparatus) approach each other, come into contact, and separate from one another. These actions consist of various types, such as receiving, throwing, grasping, kicking, running, jumping, pushing, holding, etc.

As group actions, the two sides (the gymnastics human as a movement human and the gymnastics human as a movement apparatus) approach each other, come into contact, and separate from one another. These group actions consist of various types, such as yelling, using signals, watching, etc.

The actions of individual and group technical skills are based on the actions of eyes, ears, tongue, skin, etc., of the gymnastics human as a movement human and the actions of bones, bowels, and organs such as the heart, lungs, etc. Finally, the actions of thought, emotion, etc., also contribute. In other words, while the sensation/thought/emotion systems' parts have independent functions, they are organically and dynamically related and participate in the skilled actions of the gymnastics human as a movement human. In making value judgments about skilled actions, such as good/bad, achieved/not achieved, the gymnastics human as a movement human relies greatly on the actions of the sensation/thought/emotion system. The decisions and conflicts are: "my head hurts, but I have to keep performing hard," "I'm tired, time to quit soon," "I'll do horizontal bar movement and my horizontal bar movement is smooth; that horizontal bar is grasped cleanly," "I remember this so I'll do my best," "my hands hurt, but I have to try harder," "my teacher is watching the performances of my balance beam movement, so I'll to do my best," etc. Those sentences point to the dynamic actions of gymnastics human of sensation/thought/ emotion, sensation/emotion, sensation/thought, thought/sensation, emotion/sensation, emotion/thought/sensation, and so on (figure 29).

The Denotative Structure

The gymnastics human as a movement human appears in various movement-cultural aspects in all nations in the world. If we were to classify these movement-cultural aspects, we could classify them in the following four types.

The first type includes a kind of gymnastics event in which the

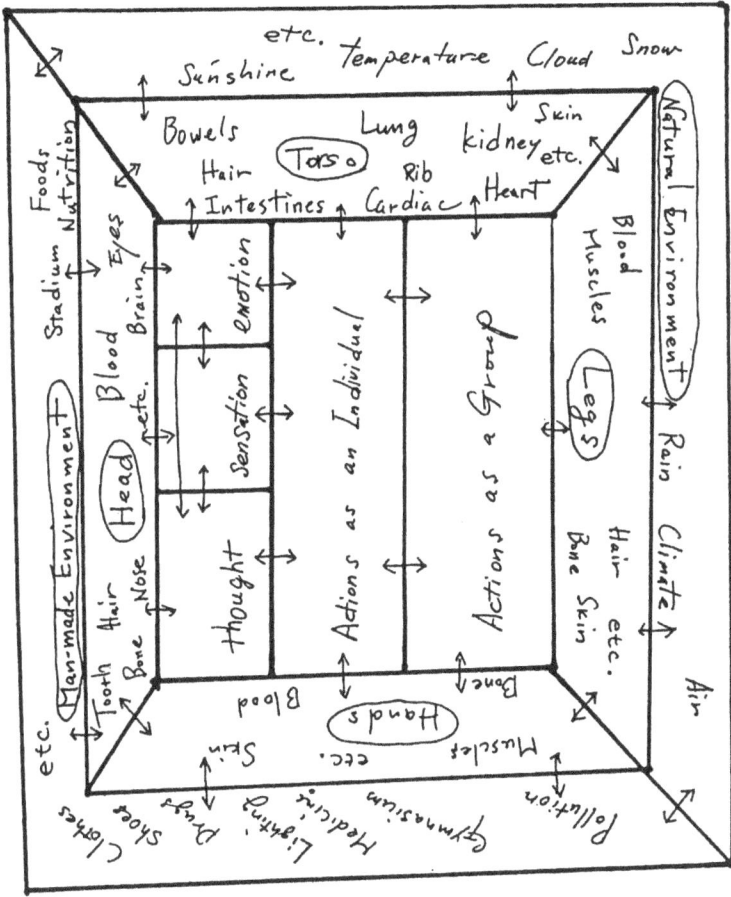

Figure 29. The many kinds of actions of the connotative structure of the gymnastics human in each nation in the world

movement apparatus (gymnastics human) either just separates from the human (gymnastics human) or just separates from itself. There are the vault human as movement human and boxer human as movement human in this type nowadays. However, the number of this kind of gymnastics event might be increased by some gymnastics specialists in the future.

The second type includes gymnastics events in which the action of the movement human (as the gymnastics human) and the movement apparatus (as the gymnastics human) are mutually disjunctive and conjunctive, such as rings human as movement human, floor human as movement human, beam human as movement human, horizontal bar human as movement human, etc.

While both type 1and 2 deal with individualistic movement-cultural properties, the following types 3 and 4 deal with movement-cultural properties that are oriented by the group, more than two people from the movement human (as gymnastics human).

The third type includes gymnastics events in which the actions of the group of gymnastics humans as movement humans attempt to approach the apparatus or separate from the apparatus. Today gymnastics of this type does not make an appearance in reality but have possibility like vault human as movement human in a competition among groups.

The fourth type of gymnastics human in the phenomenon of gymnastics is the gymnastics human as a movement human in the group and gymnastics human as movement apparatus in the group, who repeat actions of mutual approach, separation, and contact. The gymnastics human as a group event, for example horizontal bar human as movement human in a competition among more than two groups, belongs to this fourth type.

In this manner, it is possible to classify the movement-cultural existence of every gymnastics phenomenon based on the substance and type of actions of the gymnastics human. (Refer to figure 30). However, each gymnastics human as a movement human exists in a manner that presents unique aspects. The boxer human as movement human exists with unique aspects not found in horizontal bar human as movement human. (The boxer human as movement human is absolutely boxer human as movement human.) The floor human as movement human exists with unique aspects not found in horizontal bar human as movement human. (The floor human is absolutely floor human as movement human, in fact.) Therefore, each type of gymnastics human appears in his own unique movement-cultural aspects.

Vault-ness (the Vault Human as a Movement Human)

The gymnastics human as a movement human exists in aspects of vault movement. For example, there is either a direct or indirect relation to the apparatus of vault movement, the rules of vault movement, the facilities of vault movement, the terminology of vault movement, etc. The appearance of the vault human as a movement human forms the unique world of vault movement.

Beam-ness (the Beam Human as a Movement Human)

The gymnastics human as a movement human exists in aspects of beam movement. For example, there is either a direct or indirect relation to the apparatus of beam movement, the rules of beam movement, the facilities of beam movement, the terminology of beam movement, etc. the appearance of the beam human forma the unique world of beam movement.

Horizontal Bar-ness
(the Horizontal Bar Human as a Movement Human)

The gymnastics human as a movement human exists in aspects of horizontal bar movement. For example, there is either a direct or indirect relation to the apparatus of horizontal bar movement, the rules of horizontal bar movement, the facilities of horizontal bar movement, the terminology of horizontal bar movement, etc. The appearance of the horizontal bar human forms the unique world of horizontal bar movement.

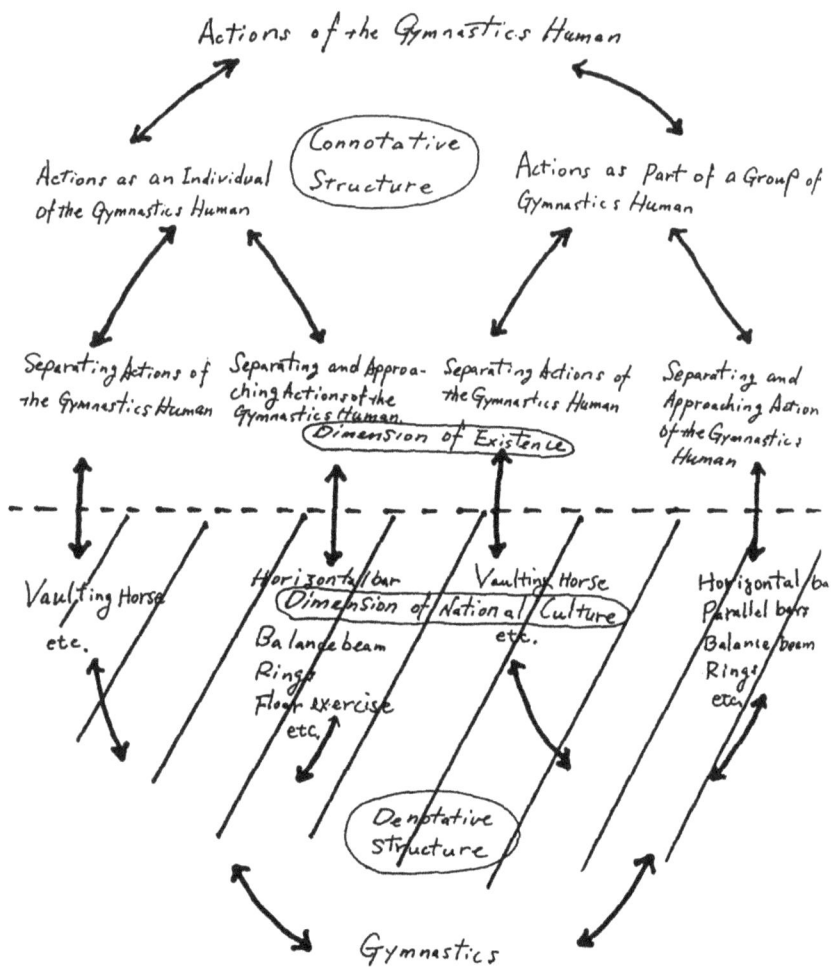

Actions of the Gymnastics Human

Connotative Structure

Actions as an Individual of the Gymnastics Human

Actions as Part of a Group of Gymnastics Human

Separating Actions of the Gymnastics Human

Separating and Approaching Actions of the Gymnastics Human.

Dimension of Existence

Separating Actions of the Gymnastics Human

Separating and Approaching Action of the Gymnastics Human

Vaulting Horse etc.

Horizontal bar

Dimension of National Culture

Balance beam
Rings
Floor exercise
etc.

Vaulting Horse
etc.

Horizontal bar
Parallel bars
Balance beam
Rings
etc.

Denotative Structure

Gymnastics

**Figure 30. The movement-cultural existence of the
gymnastics human in each nation in the world**

Floor Exercise-ness
(the Floor Exercise Human as Movement Human)

The gymnastics human as a movement human exists in aspects of floor exercise. For example, there is either a direct or indirect relation to the apparatus of floor exercise, the rules of floor exercise, the facilities of floor exercise, the terminology of floor exercise, etc. The appearance of the floor exercise human forms the unique world of floor exercise.

As there are several gymnastics events that have been introduced as mentioned above, the number of gymnastics events may increase in the future as new gymnastics events we have never seen emerge. In this way, the gymnastics human as a movement human exists in all the various movement-cultural aspects in every country in the world, in the United States as Americans, in Russia as Russians, in France as Frenchmen, in England as Englishmen, and in China as Chinese. The gymnastics human exists in these various movement-culture aspects.

4

The Educational Ontology
of the Gymnastics Human

In the special society of physical education in every country in the world, the gymnastics human as a movement human exists, possessing an aspect of physical education. Every type of gymnastics is evaluated educationally. Certainly, opinions are formed about whether a gymnastics builds a certain strength, develops character, fosters mental growth, fosters creativity, etc. The educational existence of the gymnastics human as a movement human comes from a connotative structure and a denotative structure. Each works based on an independent structure, and as a whole they exist educationally.

The Connotative Structure

In order to make clear the actions of the gymnastics human, we will analyze them and use integrated judgment, by looking both from the social actions of the gymnastics human toward the living energy and from the living energy toward the social actions of the gymnastics human. In this manner, we can grasp fully the entire substance of the actions of the gymnastics human. We have some factors that are expressed, such as body strength, flexibility, etc., while in contrast, some factors are expressive, such as the mind, soul, character, personality, condition of character, morale, flexibility, etc. These factors work in a living separate manner, and at the same time the actions of gymnastics human are in the integration of all of these living elements. By using these words to inquire about the nature of the actions of the gymnastics human, we can elucidate the concept of the gymnastics human. Therefore, these words refer to the various partial factors that make up the gymnastics human, and they are living words. The source of these words is based upon the supply and demand of living energy produced by the unification (actions of digestion, actions of oxidation) that takes place inside the individual of the mutually conflicting elements of air, food, and the gymnastics human. In other words, the source is the transformation of the various elements, such as body, body strength, flexibility of body, physique, physical condition, mind, soul, morale, flexibility of mind, personality, condition of character, etc, into a living entity. Therefore, the words *body, body strength, flexibility of body, physique, physical condition, mind, soul, morale, flexibility of mind, personality, condition of character*, etc., are all living words and are words that have come to refer to reality.

On the other hand, we have said that the action of the gymnastics human is formed from a synthesis of the various types of action of the gymnastics human expressed as mind, body, soul, physique, physical condition, body strength, flexibility of body, condition of character, morale, and flexibility of mind. It should be noted that in our analysis of the actions of the gymnastics human we said that there is both a movement apparatus and a movement human side to the gymnastics human, with mutually different objects. Since this is the case, it may not be appropriate to use the same type of language to explain both. However, based on the common point of view that both share as the gymnastics human, I will use the same language to explain them.

The analysis and synthesis of these two sides the gymnastics human as a movement human and the gymnastics human as a movement apparatus, are shown in figure 31 and figure 32.

Also making up the actions of the gymnastics human are skilled actions, which express technique. However, if we analyze these skilled actions, we can see that they are made up of actions of the conduct of the gymnastics human and the substance of the kind of technique being expressed. In other words, the actions of the conduct of the gymnastics human, together with the substance of the technique, make up the reality of the skilled action of the gymnastics human and exist united in reality. These exist in a relationship that is mutually life giving and enlivened, creating the phenomenon of the skilled existence of the gymnastics human.

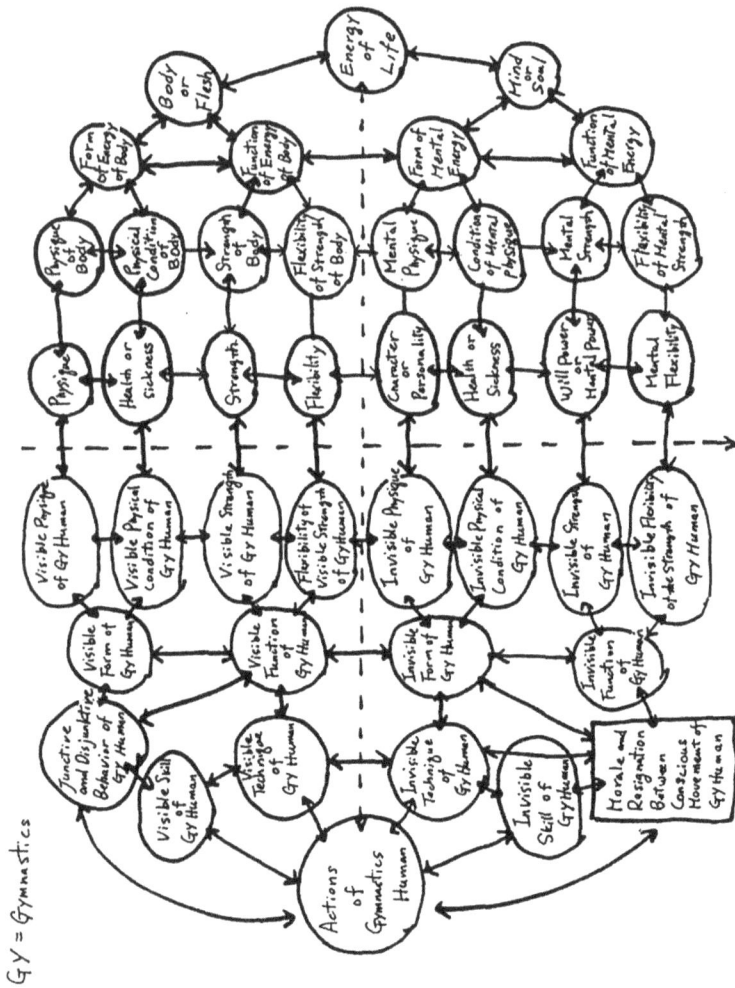

Figure 31. Action types of the gymnastics human in each nation in the world

GY = Gymnastics

I   The Visible Physique of the Gymnastics Human
    Movement Apparatus : Shape, Color, Material, Weight, Size etc.
    Movement Human   : Height, Arm Extension, Weight, Color of Skin etc

II The Condition of the Visible Physique of the Gymnastics Human
    Movement Apparatus : Quality of Firmness of the Movement Apparatus
    Movement Human   : Quality of the Visible Physique of Movement Human

III The Function of the Visible Physique   Gymnastics Human
    Movement Apparatus : Function of Movement Apparatus etc.
    Movement Human   : Endurance, Speed, Sphere of Movement, etc.

IV The Condition of Visible Function of the Gymnastics
    Movement Apparatus : Condition of Visible Function of Movement Apparatus
    Movement Human   : Condition of Visible Function of Movement Human
                         Effective Physical Ability and Flexibility of Movement
                                                                    Human etc

- -

V   The Invisible Physique of the Gymnastics   Human
    Movement Apparatus : Invisible Shape
    Movement Human   : Invisible Physique

VI The Condition of the Invisible Physique of the Gymnastics Human
    Movement Apparatus : Condition of Invisible Shape
    Movement Human   : Condition of Invisible Physique

VII The Function of the Invisible Physique of the Gymnastics Human
    Movement Apparatus : Function of Invisible Shape
    Movement Human   : Function of Invisible Physique

VIII The Condition of the Invisible Physical Function of the Gymnastics Human
    Movement Apparatus : Condition of Invisible Function.
    Movement Human   : Condition of Invisible physical Function.

Figure 32. The types and contacts of the actions of the gymnastics human in each nation in the world

The Denotative Structure

In regard to the denotative structure of the educational existence of the gymnastics human, I have attempted some analytical speculation that will explain it, as shown in figure 33.

Here I will explain each of the educational elements of the gymnastics human dealt with in the second analysis of the educational phenomenon of the gymnastics human.

Society

The gymnastics human functions in the special society of gymnastics. However, in order to create this special society, he must work by accepting and approving all of the factors. Specifically, the gymnastics human as a movement human that takes on the special social role of player acts both socially and morally. The gymnastics human as a movement human acts in participation with the humans that take on the social roles of judges, teachers, leaders, etc., and even with things that are set up for the purpose of becoming a gymnastics human as a movement human, such as unique facilities, equipment, rules, etc. In this manner, the phenomenon of gymnastics is when as the gymnastics human as a , movement human is enlarged from some person to some thing and from some thing to some person, he acts both socially and a morally. However, while the society of the gymnastics human as a movement human provides the nature of a special society, in order that gymnastics occurs in general society, it exists in the twofold relationship with general society and the special society of gymnastics.

Discovery-ness

The gymnastics human as a movement human acts creatively. At the same time, a gymnastics human as a movement apparatus also acts creatively. In the action of the gymnastics human, there are situations in which new technical content or form, no similar example to which existed in the past, are added. There new techniques are conceptualized and given special names. This itself points to the discovery-ness

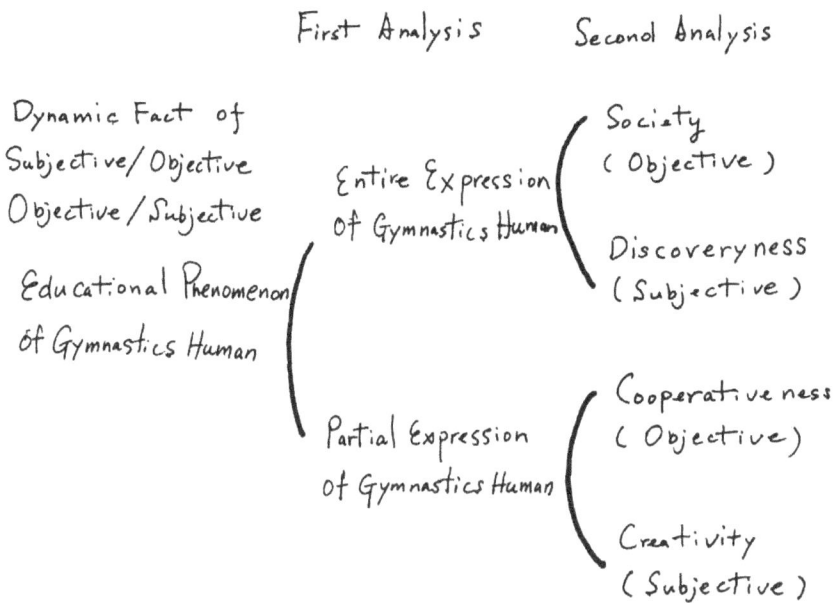

Figure 33. The educational existence of the gymnastics human in each nation in the world

of the gymnastics human. For example, names in the events of gymnastics itself point to the discovery-ness of the gymnastics human. For example, we are able to find so many things from gymnastics in the Olympics. The original words for gymnastics that the Olympics created were proof of the discovery-ness of gymnastics human. There is a certain manner in which the Olympics brought about the birth of the new gymnastics. In this way, there are situations in which a new gymnastics human is given existence and movement-cultural history is formed. The discovery-ness of the gymnastics human consists of both the creative and historical expansion aspects of these actions.

Cooperativeness

In the phenomenon of gymnastics, there are many cases in which the gymnastics human acts in a group. In these cases, cooperative intentions are demanded of the gymnastics human. This cooperativeness depends on the mutual relationship between acting gymnastics humans that have taken on the social role of the player (athlete) and therefore this is a social action. There is cooperativeness from a unified standpoint and cooperativeness from a different standpoint. For example, the general factors associated with the individual gymnastics human such as the school region, age, sex, etc., may be identical or different. Also, the various factors from the special standpoint of gymnastics such as skill level of the gymnastics human, the player role, companions, etc., may be identical or different.

In this way, the actions of the cooperativeness of the gymnastics human exist as the nature of the identities and differences between general things and the special things limited only to gymnastics. So if we try to limit it to only the cooperativeness in the special society of gymnastics, the cooperativeness of identity recognition of the gymnastics human is based on the recognition of the technical standpoint and the cooperativeness of difference recognition is based on the recognition of the existential standpoint.

Creativity

The gymnastics human, in the living, always-changing space of gymnastics, acts while at every moment faced with the problem: "In what way should I best handle the apparatus?" The gymnastics human as apparatus movement, who has been acted on by the gymnastics human as a movement human, is a concrete expression of the skill of the gymnastics human as a movement human himself. This is something that indicates the level of skill. Therefore, the gymnastics human as movement apparatus demands skill from the gymnastics human as a movement human, and conversely, the gymnastics human as a movement human, exists while demanding skill from the gymnastics human as a movement apparatus. Through the skill demands of these two sides, the gymnastics human creates. For example, the gymnastics human as a movement apparatus is thrown by the gymnastics human as a movement human, who has taken the social role of a gymnastics movement as a performer and a skill. Then the gymnastics human as a movement human tries to face this movement apparatus and, through the apparatus as a movement apparatus as an extension of the individual's body, tries to respond to the skilled action of the movement apparatus as apparatus. As a result, the excellent performance as a gymnastics human, apparatus, special terms of gymnastics, and so forth, will be created.

The creativity of the gymnastics human can be seen in the creativity of the partial cause/effect actions of playing, of going inside, doing well, and failing. Through this partial cause/effect process, the action of winning, the action of losing, and the action of a draw are created. Creativity can be seen in the partial cause/effect actions in the entire process of gymnastics, from the start to finish. Furthermore, the creativity generates the subjective emotions of happiness, vexation, anger, and sorrow at every instant in the gymnastics human as a movement human and the gymnastics human as a movement apparatus. In the special living space of gymnastics, the unknown space of gymnastics, and the regulated space of the gymnastics, are acting creatively in an original way. These actions bring about a reformation of the self-consciousness of the possibilities of ability in the gymnastics human who has taken on the special role of performer. In this special society, it gives meaning to life.

In this way, the gymnastics human exists educationally. At the same time, he exists as the educational being in scholastic physical education in every country in the world and is an expression of every country in the world (each national language) by his existence.

5

The Social Ontology
of the Gymnastics Human

The gymnastics human exists within general society. There he exists in each nation while possessing an aspect of social existence in which he lives trying to create original plans. For example, from the factual phenomenon of gymnastics all kinds of words have been derived, such as *physical education, recreation*, etc. On the other hand, in the social actions of the gymnastics human there are various kinds of sociological terms that have been created, such as *fair, unfair, cooperative*, etc. This can be said to be implicit proof that the gymnastics human exists socially. Concerning the social existence of the gymnastics human, in order to grasp his factual living state as a living state, I will divide this into a connotative structure and a denotative structure and explain each. Therefore, the social existence of the gymnastics human is the entirety of the independent actions of connotative structure and denotative structure.

The Connotative Structure

Let us consider the basic aspects of the actions of the gymnastics human. In the case of the individual, it is the actions of mutual separation-contact within the gymnastics human. In the case of the group, it is the actions of mutual separation-contact between many gymnastics humans. In other words, the basic principle is the entirety of the motion that occurs when the gymnastics human as a movement apparatus and the gymnastics human as a movement human mutually separate, approach, and have contact.

If we apply this fact to each kind of the entire phenomenon of gymnastics, it will be understood easily. This is shown in figure 34.

In other words, in order to grasp this dynamic separation/contact relationship within the gymnastics human, one must begin by looking

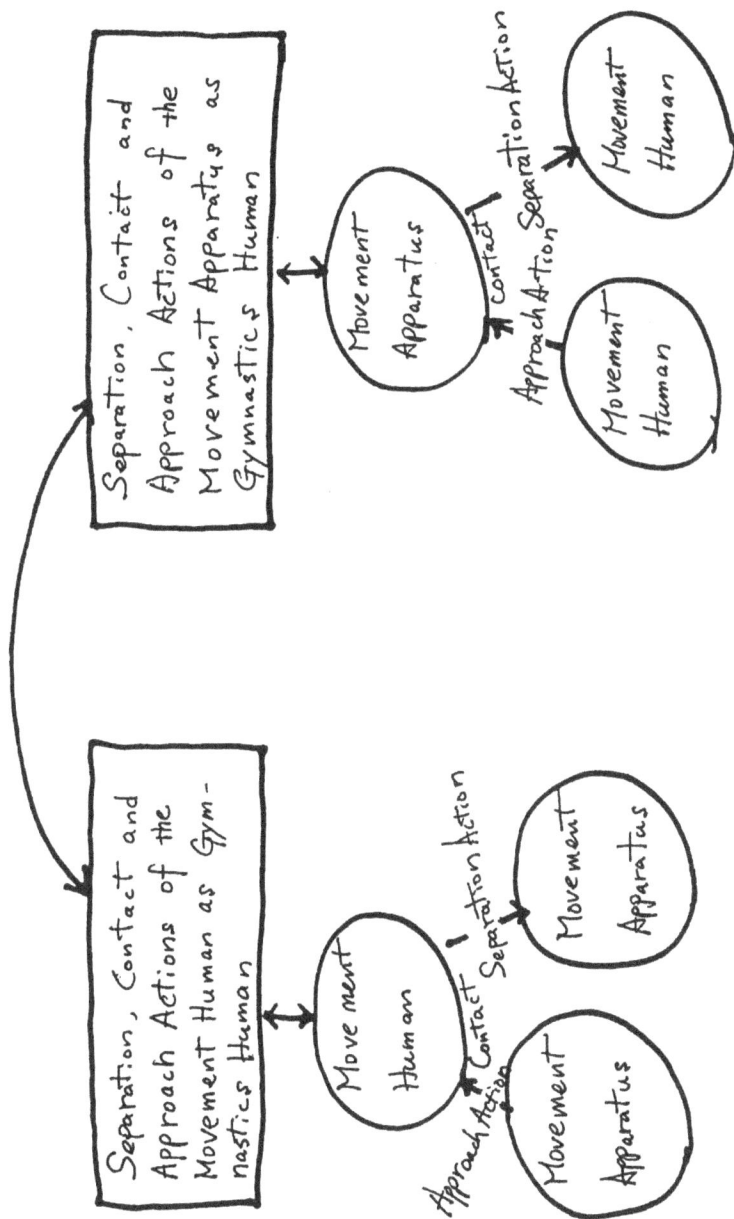

Figure 34. Separation, contact and approach actions of the gymnastics human in each nation in the world

objectively from the actions of the body of the gymnastics human. Meanwhile, there are also the actions of the mind of the gymnastics human, namely, the separation/contact movement of consciousness. Those actions come from the fact that when dealing with the apparatus, the gymnastics human as a movement human recognizes the apparatus by the action of unconscious-conscious. The strength, or perhaps weakness, of the actions of the consciousness of the gymnastics human as a movement human is located in the polarized structure of the morale and resignation of the consciousness. The strength or weakness depends throughout on the manner in which the consciousness moves between those polarizations (figure 35).

As the gymnastics human as a movement human lives, breathes, and goes to the gymnastics human as a movement apparatus, and as the gymnastics human as a movement apparatus lives, breathes, and goes to the gymnastics human as a movement human, the morale strengthens the consciousness. In other words, the morale strengthens the unified perception of both sides of the gymnastics human, the gymnastics human as a movement human and the gymnastics human as a movement apparatus. It also promotes the manifestation of living as a gymnastics human. For example, in a hotly contested gymnastics competition, the performer himself and each act that the performer does come to be perceived as a unified dimension.

Because the morale is a living thing, it promotes flattering aspects, but since it is caused through the consciousness's condition of resignation, it moves to the resignation, which is a different kind of element. Primarily, the morale of the gymnastics human is in the dimension of time, which has a passive nature and has some bad points, but in the dimension of space the morale has an active nature. The morale possesses these kinds of properties.

However, the resignation of the gymnastics human is the condition of the consciousness of the preparatory steps for displaying the consciousness of morale. Therefore, the resignation of the gymnastics human, in relation to the morale, is an element of denial, but on the other hand, it provides a kind of quality that serves to support morale as well. In the realm of space the resignation of the gymnastics human is weak and passive, but in the realm of time it is strong and active.

The connotative structure of the social existence of the gymnastics

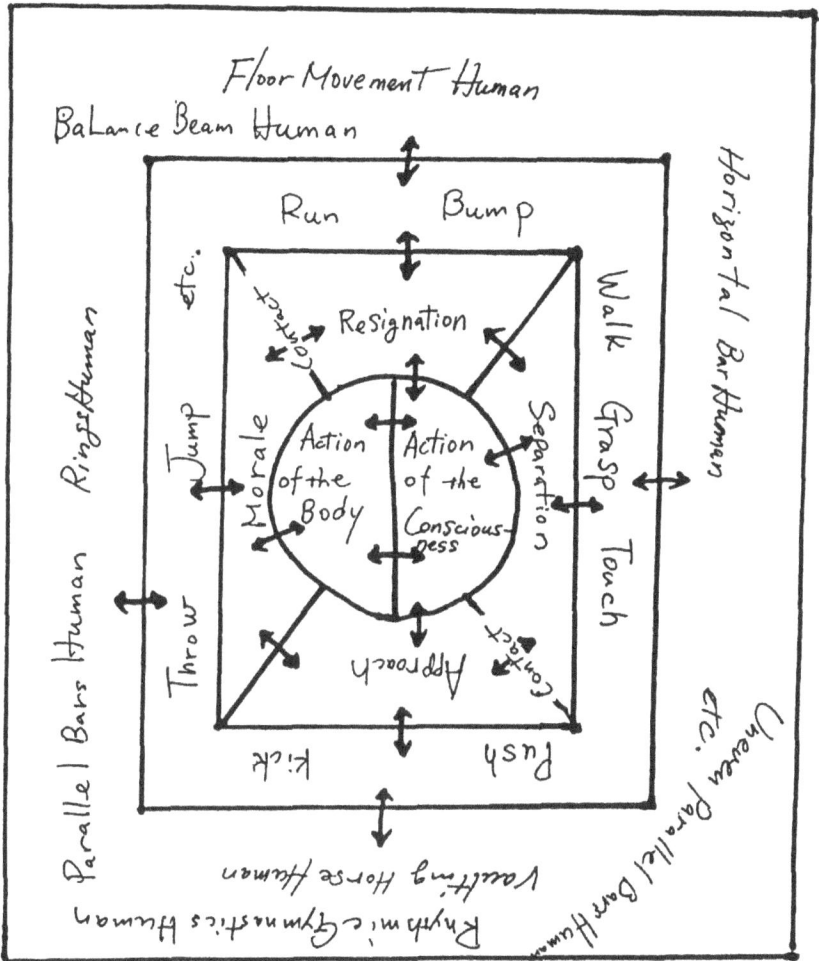

Figure 35. Relations between existence of the gymnastics human and the words or language connecting phenomena of gymnastics in each nation in the world

human presents the mutual actions of separation-contact within the gymnastics human. Objectively, the body acts by the separation-contact actions, and at the same time, subjectively, the mind acts by the separation-contact actions. Together they act as a whole. Within these actions, the changes in consciousness are acting, namely, by presenting the aspects of morale and resignation.

Concerning the actions of the gymnastics human, we use many different expressions to indicate them. These different expressions all rely on the aspects of the actions of the gymnastics human. Refer to figure 36.

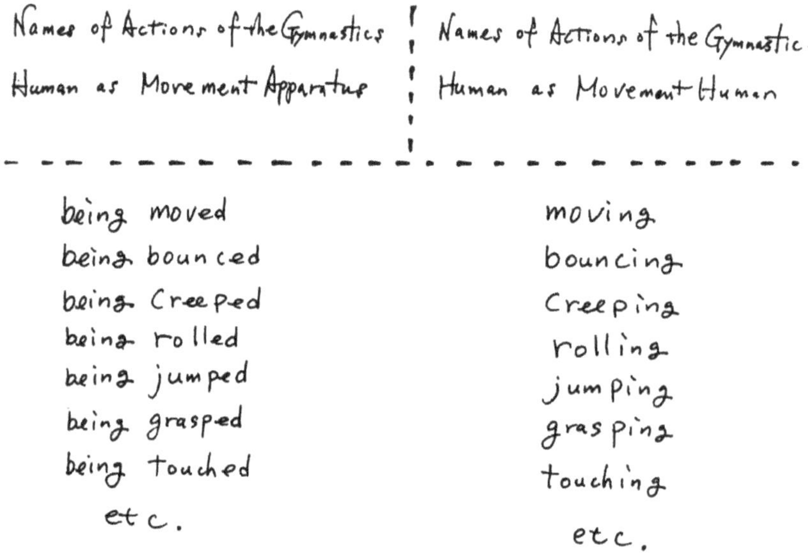

Names of Actions of the Gymnastics Human as Movement Apparatus	Names of Actions of the Gymnastics Human as Movement Human
being moved	moving
being bounced	bouncing
being creeped	creeping
being rolled	rolling
being jumped	jumping
being grasped	grasping
being touched	touching
etc.	etc.

Figure 36. Natural expressions related to the actions of the gymnastics human in each nation in the world

For example, in order to create sentences for classifications within the types of gymnastics human, such as the action of the gymnastics, one would proceed in the following way.

The horizontal bar human as a movement human grasps at the same time the horizontal bar human as a movement apparatus is grasped (the action of the horizontal bar human). The beam human as movement human jumps at the same time the beam human as a movement beam is jumped (the action of the beam human).

In the preceding manner, the actions of the connotative structure of the gymnastics human themselves act in an original way. At the same time, they also act with aspects of the denotative structure.

The Denotative Structure

In the following way, I have analyzed and gained insight into the denotative elements of the social existence of the gymnastics human and I have attempted to extract the denotative elements themselves. (See figure 37.)

Using figure 37, I will explain each of the social factors of the gymnastics human listed in the second analysis.

Recreation-ness/Competitiveness

First there is recreation-ness, in which the gymnastics human amuses himself with entertaining gymnastics, such as when a group of coworkers or a family enjoys gymnastics. There is also competitive-ness, which includes tension of seriousness, such as when competitive leagues are sponsored by all kinds of competitive groups. The recreation-ness of gymnastics humans fosters a place for the meeting of the hearts of the gymnastics human as a movement human comrade and the gymnastics human as a movement human and the gymnastics human as a movement apparatus comrade. It is a softening aspect that encourages mutual understanding. Then there is competitiveness, which is the aspect of the gymnastics human where, within the rules of competition, a gymnastics human as a movement human comrade or perhaps a gymnastics human as a movement human and a gymnastics human as a movement image comrade, facing one another, act with bravery and valorous determination. The greater the scale of the competitive league, the more the spirit intensifies, and the competitiveness of the gymnastics human appears more conspicuous. For instance, this is the case in all the types of gymnastics in international leagues, etc.

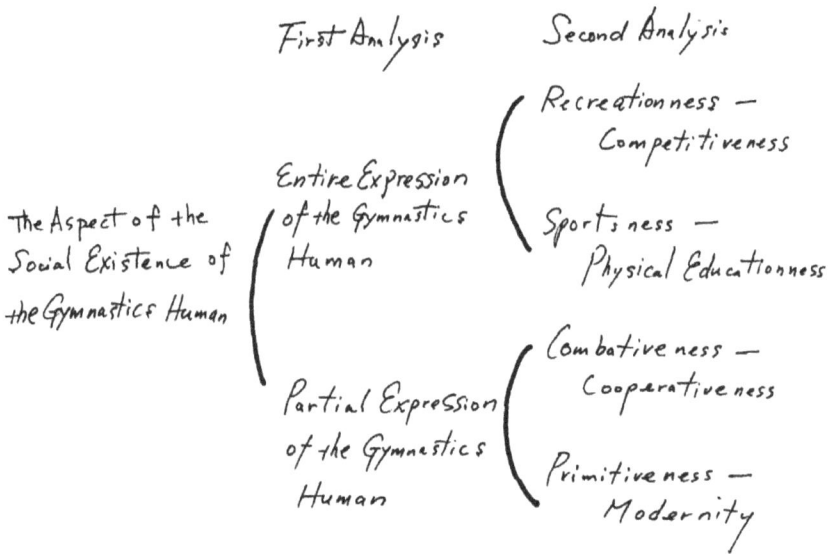

First Analysis   Second Analysis

The Aspect of the Social Existence of the Gymnastics Human

Entire Expression of the Gymnastics Human
- Recreationness — Competitiveness
- Sportsness — Physical Educationness

Partial Expression of the Gymnastics Human
- Combativeness — Cooperativeness
- Primitiveness — Modernity

Figure 37. The social existence of the gymnastics human in each nation in the world

In the phenomenon of gymnastics, based on the fundamental structure of the teacher and pupil, the educational environment and content are given in the school's gym or a corresponding place. This is the physical education-ness of the gymnastics human performing in each gymnastic event. The physical education-ness of the gymnastics human is an educational phenomenon that depends on the sum total of the teacher and pupil. This is an aspect of the special society called school and an aspect of the actions of the gymnastics human that comes from a regionally narrow scope. The student who is recognized by the school side, perhaps specially selected, from nursery school through elementary, junior high, and high school, will be acting the role of the physical education-ness of gymnastics human. On the other hand, the phenomenon of gymnastics in general society is an expression of the sports-ness of the gymnastics human. We can see the sports-ness of the gymnastics human because the sphere of gymnastics belongs to sports. It is of course possible for gymnastics to belong in the realm of sports. If that is the case, the sports-ness of gymnastics human would be the aspect of the gymnastics human in which, in the social phenomenon that relies on the sum total of leaders and followers, a wide range of many kinds of gymnastics would be developed with no relevance to sex, age, or occupation. Furthermore, there are the phenomena of vault movement, floor movement, rings movement, beam movement etc., expressions of the sports-ness of gymnastics human.

Combativeness/Cooperativeness

In the actions of the gymnastics human, there are the elements of the contrasting actions of combativeness and cooperativeness. The action of a behavior (or performance) of an individual gymnastics human as a movement human on a team of gymnastics humans is an expression of cooperativeness. This action of the behavior between companion gymnastics humans creates a oneness of the team/individual and builds many conscious states. It conspicuously expresses the cooperativeness of the gymnastics humans. This aspect can also be seen in the phenomenon where a group performs gymnastics, whereas actions of the gymnastics human, the skilled actions of the gymnastics human, as an individual, are sublimated to the skilled actions of the gymnastics humans, as a group. Namely, when there is a lack in the skilled actions of one gymnastics human as a movement human, it is compensated for by the skilled actions of some other individual gymnastics human as a movement human. In addition, there is also the aspect in which in order for one gymnastics human as a movement human as an individual to do skilled actions, some different gymnastics human as a movement human as an individual tries to give assistance. In these forms, this aspect appears.

In contrast to this, there are also times when, with a severe attitude toward other gymnastics humans (competitors), the gymnastics human as an individual feels other gymnastics humans are rivals or opponents. This is an expression of the combativeness of the gymnastics human. It is most conspicuous in the setting of vehement competition between gymnastics humans. Combativeness can be seen in every phenomenon of gymnastics and every phenomenon in which apparatus is dealt with. It is the moment when the skilled actions of the gymnastics human as an individual are steeply opposed to the skilled actions of some other gymnastics human as an individual and they feel each other to be rivals. It also can be the movement of rivals that appears between the skilled actions of gymnastics humans of a group.

Primitiveness/Modernity

In gymnastics, there is the primitiveness of the gymnastics human, in which the gymnastics human engages in direct apparatus (or body of apparatus) contact. In gymnastics such as parallel bar movement, beam movement, etc. (barefoot, uncovered palms of the hands, etc.) there is direct contact with the apparatus in the actions toward the gymnastics human as a movement human that has taken on the role of performer, such as the situations of handstanding, touching, turning, etc. Therefore, the primitiveness of the gymnastics human involves giving a direct impact to body of apparatus of gymnastics human, but the opportunities to handle the apparatus are relatively frequent.

On the other hand, there is an aspect of modernity of the gymnastics human in which in the relation between gymnastics human(human side) the gymnastics human (apparatus side) acts by using equipment, gloves, towel, powder to stop slipping, shoes, music, etc., horizontal bar movement, rings movement, etc, by getting supporter, powder, bandage, etc. There are gymnastics events that conspicuously express the modernity of the gymnastics human. In the modernity of the gymnastics human, the impact of the apparatus received by the body of the gymnastics human as a movement human is small. The handling of the image is relatively rare, and the freedom of the gymnastics movement is limited.

Moreover, to say that here in the denotative structure we have come up with a comprehensive list of all of the words that refer to the social existence of gymnastics human would be added. I have aimed only for a coordinated understanding of the social existence of the gymnastics human and an understanding of it as a living existence. Furthermore, if we look at all the various elements of the social existence of the gymnastics human, such as the amateurness or professionalness of gymnastics human, the fair play-ness of the gymnastics human and the playfulness of the gymnastics human, we can see that these elements are vital elements that act to stir up the social aspects of gymnastics human. In this manner, in every country in the world, the gymnastics human expresses the originality of each country and carries on a social existence. In the stream of time of past-present-future, this existence lives in the present as realistic beings and this existence is variable and alive.

6

Generalizations from the Ontology
of the Gymnastics Human

Up to this point, the three existences of the gymnastics human, namely, the movement-cultural, educational, and social existences have been explained clearly. The *gymnastics human*, when taken as in the hypothesis, is language that refers to the existential essence of the phenomenon of gymnastics and the phenomena in which an apparatus is dealt with. In other words, we have confirmed the fad that the words *gymnastics human* are alive and exist, forming the special expanding world of gymnastics and dealing with the image of gymnastics in every country in the world. We have also confirmed the fad that these words refer directly to a special kind of human. The gymnastics human exists as the expression of each country in the world, in the United States as an American, in Russia as a Russian, in China as a Chinese, in Japan as a Japanese, in Sweden as a Swede, etc. They speak American English, Chinese, Korean, German, British English, Italian, French, Spanish, etc., in phenomena of gymnastics. In the present of the ever-flowing stream of past-present-future, with living and variable aspects, it exists and lives.

Now, as a result of the clear evidence of the existential essence of gymnastics and the clear evidence of the existence of the gymnastics human in the phenomenon of gymnastics, the following kinds of questions can now be answered:

Question 1: What is the phenomenon of gymnastics?
Answer: This is the phenomenon in which a human and apparatus become gymnastics human through doing the gymnastics. It is a special world in which the gymnastics human performs (or acts).

Question 2: What does it mean to do gymnastics?
Answer: This is when some humans become gymnastics humans, who

can be divided into, on the one hand, a movement human and, on the other hand, a movement apparatus for doing gymnastics.

For example (more concreteness):

Question 1: What is horizontal bar movement?
Answer: This is when a human and horizontal bar become a horizontal bar human.

Question 2: What does it mean to do beam movement?
Answer: This means becoming a beam human, who can be divided into a movement human as a beam human and a movement apparatus as a beam human.

Question 3: What does it mean in physical education to do gymnastics?
Answer: This is the conduct by which the human and apparatus become gymnastics human (as movement human and movement apparatus) and both of these are physical education-ized and try to become physical education-ized.

Question 4: What does it mean in sports to do gymnastics?
Answer: This is the conduct in which the human and apparatus become gymnastics human in both sides, and both of these are sports-ized and try to become sports-ized.

Any other questions concerning the phenomenon of the gymnastics itself can be answered from the educational, social, and movement-cultural ontologies previously presented.

Furthermore, this gymnastics human encompasses every type of gymnastics human. Namely, it is the existence of the rings human, the existence of the vault human, the existence of the horizontal bar human, the existence of the beam human, etc. also, depending on the differences in sex, age, race, school, occupation, etc., the above exist as different expressions.

In the above manner, through the movement of speculation, the establishment of the ontology of the gymnastics human, from both an abstract standpoint and a concrete standpoint, from the existence to being and from being to existence, became possible. Here we can generalize this system as the ontology of the gymnastics human.

Finally, while I have referred to the existence of the gymnastics human as a special existence of the human in gymnastics, I must now go on to present the existence of a purpose in the existence of the gymnastics human. Namely, the existence of the gymnastics human I have presented up until now is an existence that acts in order to realize the gymnastics human image. It is that purpose for which the existence is acting. Therefore, I must now go on to develop a presentation concerning the gymnastics human image-the teleology of the gymnastics human. I would like to affirm the gymnastics human image that comes from the existence of the gymnastics human, who exists with special aspects in gymnastics.

7

The Teleology of the
Gymnastics Human

Up to this point, I have contemplated the existential essence in the phenomena of all types of gymnastics. I have shown clearly and confirmed that in every country in the world, every type of gymnastics human exists in the world of each type of gymnastics. However, at the same time, this existence includes the purpose of the gymnastics human, namely, the gymnastics human image. It is not simply the existence of the gymnastics human, but also an existence that tries to realize the ideal image that the gymnastics human must attain. Above all, the practice of all types of gymnastics that is being conducted in scholastic physical education in every country in the world is for the sake of realization of all types of the gymnastics human image by all types of the gymnastics human. Also, there is the necessity for physical education and sports studies research concerning all types of gymnastics in every country in the world (such as physical education and sports studies philosophy, physical education and sports studies psychology, physical education and sports studies physiology, physical education and sports studies sociology, physical education and sports studies history, etc.) in order to plan the realization of the gymnastics human image, in the practice of gymnastics or the practice where an apparatus is dealt with, in physical education.

At this point I will go on to speculate about what kind of special ideal image is meant by the purpose of the gymnastics human or, more specifically, the gymnastics human image.

The gymnastics human image is, of course, the purpose of the practice of gymnastics, but it is necessary to explain clearly what in reality it is to which this word directly refers. It refers to the ideal image in which the actions of the gymnastics human as a movement human and the actions of the gymnastics human as an apparatus movement in the practice of gymnastics are existing together, doing superior actions. The gymnastics human image is the ideal image that is living and exists ideally from one era to the next era in every country in the world. This is determined by the research of the physical education and sports theory specialists (such as physical education and sports studies philosophers, physical education and sports studies psychologists, physical education and sports studies physiologists, physical education and sports studies sociologists, physical education and sports studies historians, etc.) that are living in each era in every country in the world. The term *gymnastics human image* refers directly to the ideal existence that adds weight, depth, size, and breadth to that acting existence.

In the nature of the substance of the gymnastics human there are really two different kinds of nature. Also, these two natures dynamically act together and form the firm gymnastics human image. The first is the part of the purpose that has a universal nature that is common, no matter what the time, no matter what the place, no matter what the country. For example, all of the superior actions of the movement human and the movement apparatus (in other words, the attempt to realize the gymnastics human image) even though there are differences between the histories, cultures, ideas, races, etc., of the countries in the world, share a common universal nature.

The second is the concrete purpose of the gymnastics human, which is variable depending on the time, the society, the nation, age, sex, and other variables from country to country. In every country there is originality in history, ideas, culture, and natural language. The gymnastics human image of a certain era in each country of the world has the aspects of that era. Furthermore, from the point of view of age, the various types of gymnastics human image for children are different from the various types of gymnastics human image for old people. From the point of view of sex, the gymnastics human images for males and females are different. The images of the gymnastics human are not identical, due to the various differences. Therefore, as opposed to the purpose of the universal substance of the gymnastic human, this points to the variable, concrete purpose of the gymnastics human.

The constitution of the teleology of the gymnastics human relies on the support/being-supported relationship between these two sides, which is a relationship that acts dynamically and mutually to support each side. The gymnastics human image of the former is the purpose of the gymnastics human, while the gymnastics human image of the latter is the goal of the gymnastics human. The difference between these words clearly points to the difference between the universal purpose and the variable purpose. Therefore, the gymnastics human image consists of the purpose substance as its core, and that which surrounds the purpose substance is the goal substance. The dynamic relationship between them assumes the character of abstract/concrete-concrete/abstract. Because of this, the gymnastics human image possesses unifying qualities that transcend the realities of nationality, age, sex, etc. (time and space), but at the same time this teleology is also one that sees those realities as realities. This can be summarized in figure 38.

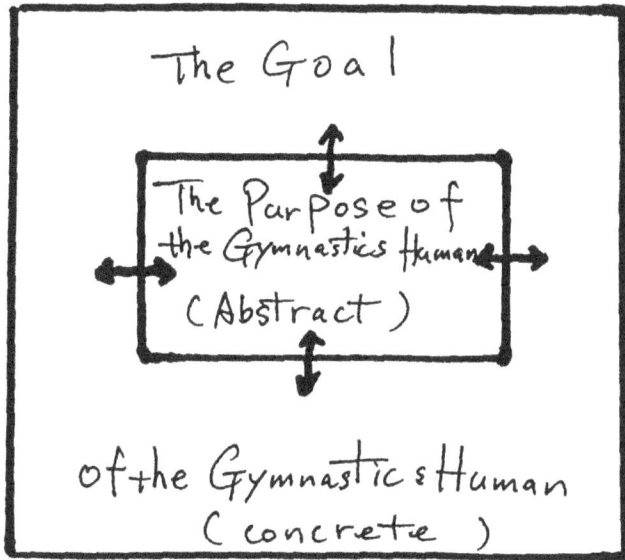

The Goal

The Purpose of the Gymnastics Human
(Abstract)

of the Gymnastics Human
(concrete)

**Figure 38. Constitution of the
gymnastics human image in each nation in the world**

Next I would like to go on to explain the purpose of the gymnastics human. Specifically, of what substance is the gymnastics human image itself constructed? I will explain this point.

The structure of the gymnastics human image is made up of two types: a connotative structure and a denotative structure. These form the living, unified whole. There are the actions of all of the many element images, and as a whole they act ideally. If we broadly divide these various idealistic elements, they come from the connotative structure and the denotative structure. (Refer to figure 39).

In physical education and sports, the gymnastics human forms the special society of gymnastics. He works ideally in a unique way. At the same time, he is regulated in a unique way and exists ideally.

The Image of Connotative Structure

In the actions of the gymnastics human image, there is the image of connotative structure. This acts as the foundation for the generation of the image of denotative structure and thus is a vitally important area. The image of connotative structure itself is formed from the various element images that become the many different ideals. It is formed from the ideal of the image of life energy that comes from physical education and sports nutrition studies and physical education and sports hygiene, the ideal of the image of the body and the image of the mind (mind-body image) that comes from physical education and sports philosophy, the ideal of the image of body strength, the image of flexibility, the image of physique, and the image of physical condition (the image of health) that come from physical education and sports physiology, etc. The physical education and sports studies researchers of every country in the world will go on to prove the realistic existence of the gymnastics human. Relying on the leadership of this proof, the previous images of the connotative structure of the gymnastics human will be concretely alive and acting ideal images. Then, in order that the physical education and sports studies researchers of every country in the world expand on the substance of the words of these various elements, and in order to promote understanding of these words as living things, the research of purpose will proceed. As a result, to the question: "Why are the educational ministries of every country in the world conducting and practicing all kinds of gymnastics in scholastic physical education?" one will be able to provide a direct answer from the various fields of physical education and sports studies, namely, physical education and sports philosophy, physical education and sports psychology, physical

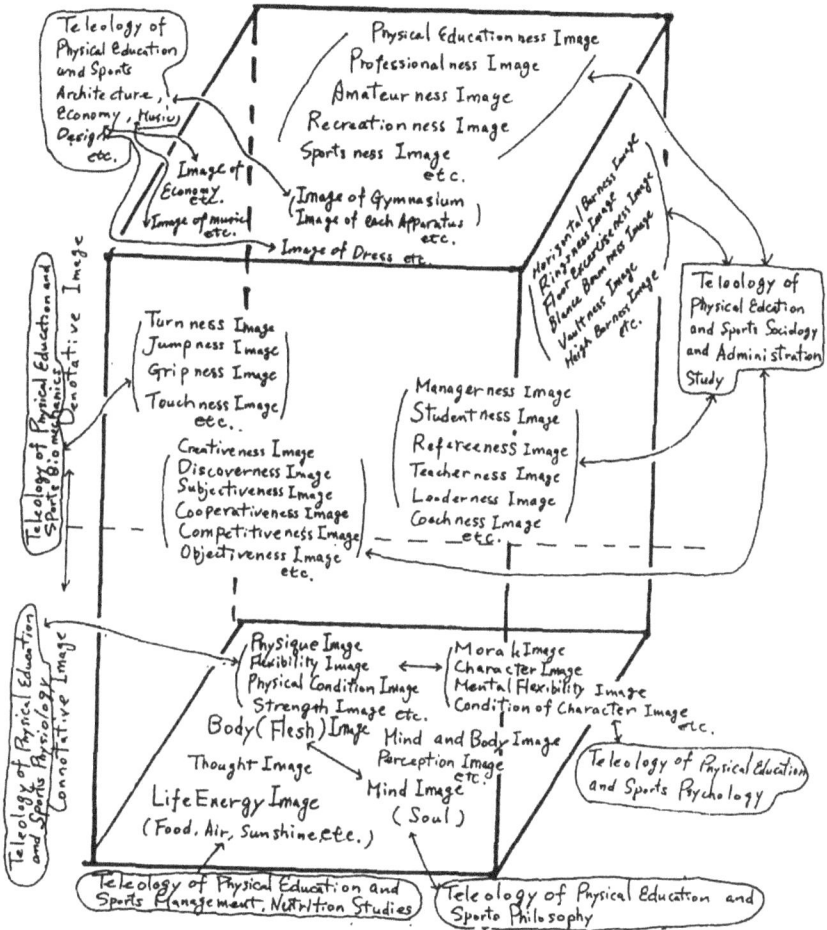

Figure 39. The gymnastics human image in each nation in the world

education and sports physiology, physical education and sports sociology, physical education and sports history, etc. For example, from physical education and sports philosophy, all types of gymnastics are practiced in scholastic physical education in order to realize the image of the mind and body of all types of the gymnastics human image. The content of the image of the mind and body can be explained relying on the research of physical education and sports philosophers. Of course, the contents of the partial element images presented there are ideal contents drawn from the proof of all of the specialist researchers in physical education and sports studies, and at the same time, in the space of the various elements in the image of connotative structure, they are doing superior actions.

Also, there are the various elements that do superior actions in the image of the denotative structure as well. For ample, the image of body strength is formed by the superior inner actions of body strength itself, acting in superior actions in relation to the various elements, such as morale, flexibility, cooperativeness, competitiveness, physical condition, creativeness, etc.

shown above, the image of connotative structure in the gymnastic human image is the entirety of the various elements of the connotative structure that have been amassed by the physical education and sports studies researchers in every country in the world and the physical education and sports studies research of every era. However, this image of connotative structure not only acts in the image of connotative structure but works in the image of denotative structure. So what kind of substance of ideal images makes up the image of the denotative Structure of the gymnastics human? I will go on to deal with this question.

The Image of Denotative Structure

In the action of the gymnastics human image as a g human image, there is an image of denotative structure. In the ideal image that is generated from the image of connotative structure, the origin of the formation of the image of denotative structure is included. Inside the denotative structure itself, which acts as the denotative structure, are the actions of the various element images.

Looking from the specialized point of view of the physical education and sports sociologists and scholastic physical education and considering the existential direction of the gymnastics human, if an inquiry is made to determine the ideal images of that existence, then in the following way the idealistic elements of the denotative structure become visible. The image of sports-ness, the image of physical education-ness, the image of amateurness, the image of professionalness, the image of recreation-ness, the image of teacher-ness, the image of student-ness, the image of leader-ness, the image of manager-ness, the image of coach-ness, the image of director-ness, the image of follower-ness, the image of vault movement-ness, the image of horizontal bar movement-ness, the image of pommeled horse movement-ness, the image of rings movement-ness, the image of beam movement-ness, the image of creativeness, the image of cooperative-ness, the image of competitiveness, the image of objectiveness, the image of discovery-ness, the image of subjective-ness, etc. From the above kinds of images of elements, the image of the denotative structure in the gymnastics human image is formed. The various images of elements above are the various aspects of the gymnastics human image, and they are things that have been culled from researchers in physical education and sports sociology and scholastic physical education. Then the images of the various elements in the denotative structure act in a way that promotes the idealistic condition of the connotative structure, while at the same time they are the superior denotative elements that act in a way that promotes the idealistic condition of the elements in the image of the denotative structure. Therefore, each of the elements in the denotative structure itself is an element that is superior and acts ideally.

In the above manner, the gymnastics human image itself is the purpose of the existence of the gymnastics human in every country in the world. Therefore, this is limited by the existence of the gymnastics human and, in reality, there is a purpose in straining to derive the gymnastics human image from this existence. For example, in order to explain this gymnastics human image as a gymnastics human image in reality, we can divide the gymnastics human image into its various different types, such as the horizontal bar movement image, the pommeled horse movement image, the rings movement image, the floor movement image, and so on. We can concretely express the goal of the gymnastics human if we look, for instance, at the box horse human from various points of view. From the point of view of school level, there are box horse human images in the elementary school and the high school. From the point of view of sex, there are the male rings human image and the female beam human image. From the point of view of age, there are the ten-year-old horizontal bar human image and the forty-year-old horizontal bar human image. From the point of view of nationality, there are the rings human image as an American, the rings human image as a Japanese, the rings human image as a Russian, the rings human image as a Swede, the rings human image as an Australian, the rings human image as a Frenchman, the rings human image as a German, the rings human image as an Italian, and so on. In other words, because the existence of all types of the gymnastics human in every country of the world is different, the purpose of the gymnastics human can be materialized as different goals by the different nationalities, national languages, backgrounds of national histories, and other national differences. On the other hand, while the gymnastics human image can make as its purpose the various unique gymnastics human images of each country in the world, from a global, humanistic, common point of view, it can also present a purpose that is the gymnastics human image as a world citizen. Provided that the existence of all types of the gymnastics human practicing all kinds of gymnastics in all places around the world can be confirmed, this purpose can be erected as a common purpose of all types of the world citizen (or perhaps mankind) gymnastics human image.

Above I have presented the purpose of the gymnastics human or, more specifically, the substance of the gymnastics human image (limited to only the important substance necessary in gymnastics theory). As a result, we have reached a point at which the following kinds of questions can be answered:

Question 1: Why are the educational ministries of every country in the world practicing all types of gymnastics in scholastic physical education?
Answer: All types of gymnastics are being practiced in scholastic physical education in every country in the world in order to realize all

types of the gymnastics human image as the specific humans of every country in the world.

Question 2: Why are the educational ministries of every country in the world offering classes on the theory concerning all types of gymnastics in scholastic physical education?
Answer: This is so that in the scholastic physical education of every country in the world physical education teachers will show the peaceful practice of all types of gymnastics to the students and explain the practice of all types of gymnastics to the students and the students will understand them.

Question 3: Why are the physical education and sports researchers of every country in the world conducting research in fields such as physical education and sports psychology, physical education and sports philosophy, physical education and sports physiology, physical education and sports history, physical education and sports sociology, etc.? Furthermore, is it necessary in human society, the human nation, and the human world?
Answer: It is absolutely necessary for national formation of physical education and sports studies (including gymnastics study). This is so that the place of gymnastics in every country in the world will be realized. This research is the guarantee of the sound practice of gymnastics in every country. Also, through this research we, all physical education and sports scholars, can build the national theory of gymnastics in every country in the world that supports human nations and the human world.

Question 4: Why must a World Physical Education and Sports Academy be established?
Answer: Relying on the development of this type of research, the gymnastics human image in every country in the world and the gymnastics human image of each era of mankind will be constructed, thus developing the guarantee of peace in every country and world peace. Also, the academy will nurture physical education and sports researchers who will contribute to peace in every country and to world peace or will work as responsible professors in the future at colleges,

universities, and graduate schools who support the nation and world as a human society through their true theory or knowledge.

Question 5: Why must a Physical Education and Sports Academy be established in every country in the world?

Answer: Physical education and sports researchers (from all the fields) are necessary to conduct the national gymnastics theory in every country and to guarantee that the practice of gymnastics in every country in the world is a peaceful practice. And through these efforts, we are able to promise prosperity of nation and prosperity of mankind. (Ministries of education in every nation have to answer all questions concerning gymnastics in public because of letting pupils practice some kinds of gymnastics, from elementary school to graduate school. Instead of the ministries of education in all nations, we scholars of physical education and sports in all nations take responsibility for answering the questions concerning gymnastics in public.)

Other questions we can pose in order to recover our professional trust in all nations is: Why do we need doctors for physical education and sports studies? Why do we have to plan the doctoral programs in graduate schools in all nations? What does this word professor mean for physical education and sports studies? More sharply, why do we need professors for our studies, physical education and sports studies? Does *professor* mean a player of talk without responsibilities for actual physical education and sports practices? Why do we need faculties of physical education in colleges, universities, and graduate schools for the human nation, mankind, etc.?

In addition, any questions concerning the purpose of formation related to all types of gymnastics in every country in the world can be answered from the teleology of the gymnastics human. Also, from this purpose it is necessary to go on to develop support for peace in every country and world peace.

Furthermore, from the presentation of the ontology and teleology of gymnastics human in every country in the world, we must now go on to develop the methodology of the gymnastics human in every country in the world by which the existence of the gymnastics human in every country in the world realizes the gymnastics human image of every country in the world. This will deal with the method by which the existence of the gymnastics human in every country in the world realizes the gymnastics human image. The methodology will be organically connected to the ontology and the teleology and will have the unique quality of working together with them. This kind of undertaking will work through the realization of the establishment of universal gymnastics theory, which unites all countries in the world and accept differences between all countries in the world.

8

The Methodology of the
Gymnastics Human

The methodology of the gymnastics human is an original theoretical area that deals with both the movement human and the movement apparatus sides of the phenomenon of all types of gymnastics. These two sides, which are referred to directly by the term *gymnastics human*, can be said, depending on how they work together, to emphasize the movement apparatus as a gymnastics human, only the ability required for the movement apparatus is required of the movement human as a gymnastics human. On the other hand, if we emphasize the movement human, only the ability required for the movement human is required of the movement apparatus. This means that skillful movement is needed. Therefore, achieving the required ability that is possible when both sides accept each other's demands is imperative. This type of method is the only advanced method by which the gymnastics human image can be realized in each nation in the world. Toward that end, there are notably two methodologies: one in relation to the time (era, etc.) and one in relation to space (nation, etc.). The former considers the experience of becoming a gymnastics human in terms of time, while the latter considers the experience of becoming a gymnastics human in terms of space. Therefore, the method that realizes the gymnastics human image must give the appropriate weight to experience in time and experience in space.

The Theoretical Foundation and Ground for the
Formation of the Gymnastics Human Methodology

Before presenting the methodology of the gymnastics human, it is necessary to first make clear the reasons why it is possible to present such a methodology. In order to do this, we must look at the theoretical foundation and the ground for the methodology. The theoretical foundation for the formation of the methodology of the gymnastics human relies on the educational, social, and movement-cultural ontologies of the gymnastics human and the teleology of the gymnastics human already presented. The ground for the formation of this methodology is the fact that in scholastic physical education in every country around the world gymnastics is being practiced. The former is based on the development of the theory, while the latter comes from the practice of gymnastics.

The Characteristics of the Methodology of the Gymnastics Human

There are two characteristics associated with the content of the methodology of the gymnastic human. First, it is an unchangeable, universal, abstract methodology, applicable to any country at any time. Second, as countries (space) and eras (time) change, it is a concrete, realistic methodology that changes accordingly. The methodology of the gymnastics human is constructed with the former at the core, while the latter surrounds it, both working together to preserve the relationship. More specifically, the former is the area of the methodology based on the common qualities of all countries and constructed by the physical education and sports researchers of every country in the world so that the practice of gymnastics in scholastic physical education in every country in the world serves to realize the gymnastics human image. Meanwhile, the latter is the area of the methodology that has the quality of grasping the differences in the realistic aspects of the gymnastics human, i.e., the country, era, age, sex, school, etc., as differences in realistic aspects.

Elements of the Formation of the Contents of the Methodology of the Gymnastics Human

In regard to the formation of the methodology of the gymnastics human, both the theoretical foundation and the practical ground have been presented already. However, I believe that the latter, the practical ground, gives an extraordinarily important reason for the formation of the methodology of the gymnastics human. Namely, because of the existence of the practice of gymnastics in physical education programs: the existence of the practice of gymnastics in society, and the existence of physical education teachers, mentors, and students who play a function in society, the need for the methodology of the gymnastics human becomes apparent.

In that case, physical education teachers and mentors are those who lead students to become gymnastics humans and realize the gymnastics human image, while students and followers who receive all forms of gymnastics education are those who look toward becoming all forms of gymnastics humans and realizing all forms of the gymnastics human image. Therefore, the human relationship between the teachers and mentors and students and followers in the phenomenon of gymnastics will all become the gymnastics human and realize the gymnastics human image. It is a mutual relationship that exists to realize the gymnastics human image.

Those fostering the gymnastics human have had experience in the past of fully (deeply and widely) becoming a gymnastics human in order to realize the gymnastics human image. They are those who possess the leadership qualifications to be able to realize the gymnastics human image. On the other hand, those becoming gymnastics humans must receive leadership in order to realize the gymnastics human image. They are those of whom study skills are demanded.

With the relationship between physical education teachers who try to realize the gymnastics human image and foster gymnastics humans as students who study while looking toward becoming gymnastics human and realizing the gymnastics human image as the ground, the various structural elements of the methodology of the various kinds of gymnastics humans are formed. Specifically, these elements include study, leadership, evaluation, curriculum, educational resources, study ability, study processes, leadership ability, skill, etc. Classifying these elements into large groups, we may divide them into study, leadership, and educational resources. The terms *skill, study, ability, study process*, etc., are technical terms connected with the student or follower becoming a gymnastics human and trying to realize the gymnastics human image and therefore are study terms. The terms *leadership ability, evaluation, curriculum*, etc., are all terns connected with the teachers and mentors trying to realize the gymnastics human image and turn their students into gymnastics humans and are therefore leadership terms. Finally, that which brings the leadership and study together at the place of the gymnastics is the educational resources. The structural elements of the methodology of the gymnastics human are systematized in the manner described in figure 40.

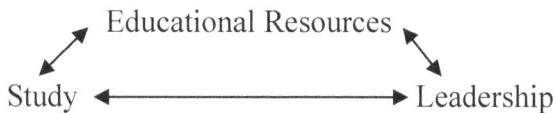

Figure 40. The structural elements of the methodology of the gymnastics human in each nation in the world

Study. This is the state of those becoming gymnastics humans in which they learn all of the various things they must learn from those helping them to become gymnastics humans in order to realize the gymnastics human image.

Also, we will call students those who, under the supervision of those fostering the gymnastics human, strive to learn that which they need to become gymnastics humans. Furthermore, study ability is ability that students possess to learn all the constructive knowledge required in order to become a gymnastics human and realize the gymnastics human image. Skill is a part of study ability and is a condition of the mastery of the necessary techniques required to become a gymnastics human and realize the gymnastics human image. Also, study process is the process by which, under the leadership of those fostering the gymnastics humans, those becoming gymnastics humans learn all of the relevant knowledge.

Leadership. This is defined as the ability to lead those who will become gymnastics humans on the part of those who will foster their becoming gymnastics humans by giving them all the various knowledge they will need toward the goal of realizing the gymnastics human image. Leadership ability is the ability of those fostering gymnastics humans, with the goal of realizing the gymnastics human image, to fully develop those becoming gymnastics humans. The leadership process is the process by which those fostering gymnastics human, with the goal of realizing the gymnastics human image, lead those becoming gymnastics humans. Furthermore, evaluation is the process by which those fostering gymnastics humans decide what level those becoming gymnastics humans have reached and how far they have advanced in approaching the realization of the gymnastics human image. Curriculum is the study route through which those fostering gymnastics humans lead those becoming gymnastics humans in order to realize the gymnastics human image.

Educational Resources. We collectively use this term to refer to all materials those fostering gymnastics humans use to lead those becoming gymnastics humans to realize the gymnastics human image, along with all study materials used by those becoming gymnastics humans aiming to realize the gymnastics human image. The educational resources play the role of intermediaries in the formation of the leadership and study of the gymnastics human and are necessary methodological elements in the realization of the gymnastics human image. The educational resources include natural educational resources and man-made educational resources. The former are sunshine, air, weather (clear, rainy, snowy, cloudy), air pressure (wind), water (water in a pool), earth (ground), etc. The latter include gymnasiums, lighting, clothes, tools, shoes, stages, etc. Therefore, in the broad sense of the term, *educational resources* refers to the combination of natural educational resources and man-made educational resources, but when taken in the narrow sense of the word refers mostly to man-made educational resources.

The Constructive Method of the Methodology of the Gymnastics Human as National Theory in Every Nation in the World

It is imperative that we use the terminology of the structural elements of the methodology of the gymnastics human, namely, *study* (*skill, study process*, etc.) *leadership* (*evaluation, curriculum, leadership process, leadership ability*, etc.), and *educational resources*, in order to realize the gymnastics human image. However, it is also necessary to answer the question of how the content of these elements can be given substance. I will now present these kinds of problems related to the construction of the methodology of the gymnastics human.

From the standpoint of those dealing with the fundamental theory of physical education studies, it is possible to construct a methodology that answers these kinds of questions. The methodology of the gymnastics human should use the original specialized vocabulary from each specialized area of physical education and considering study, leadership, educational resources, etc., we can create a separate methodology from each field of physical education that serves to realize every partial image of the gymnastics human in each era and each nation that emerges from that field. In regard to the methodology of the gymnastics human from physical education physiology, for instance, while considering study, leadership, and educational resources, we can construct an original methodology, using the specialized terms of physiology, such as *strength, physique, health, and flexibility*, that serve to realize the strength image, the physique image, the health image, and the flexibility image of the gymnastics human.

Likewise, in regard to the methodology of the gymnastics human from physical education psychology, while considering study, leadership, and educational resources we can construct an original methodology, using the specialized terms of psychology, such as *character, morale, mental health, mental flexibility*, etc., that serve to realize the character image, the morale image, the mental health image, and the mental flexibility image of the gymnastics human. In regard to the methodology of the gymnastics human from physical education philosophy, while considering study, leadership, and educational resources we can construct an original methodology, using the specialized terms of philosophy, such as *mind, body, mind-body relationship, soul, flesh*, etc., that serve to realize the mind image, the body image, the mind-body relationship image, the sad image, and the flesh image of the gymnastics human. In regard to the methodology of the gymnastics human from physical education educational science, while considering study, leadership, and educational resources we can construct an original methodology, using the specialized terms of educational science, such as *creativity, subjectivity, objectivity, cooperation, competition*, etc., that serve to realize the creativity image, the subjectivity image, the objectivity image, the cooperation image, and the competition image of the gymnastic human. In regard to the methodology of the gymnastics human from physical education sociology, while considering studs leadership, and educational resources we can construct an original methodology as a national theory, using the specialized terms of sociology, such as *performer, amateur, professional, sports, physical education*, etc., that serve to realize the performer image, the amateur image, the professional image, the sports image, the physical education image, etc., of the gymnastics human. In regard to the methodology of the gymnastics human from biomechanics, while considering study, leadership, and educational resources we can construct an original methodology as a national theory, using the specialized terms of biomechanics, such as *grasp, run, catch, walk, stand, hang, turn*, etc., that serve to realize the running image, the grasping image, the catching image, the walking image, the standing image, etc., of gymnastics human. Moreover, the construction of the original methodology of the gymnastics human for each of these specialized fields of physical education must be living, changing entities, taking into account the realistic existence of things such as nationality, race, age, sex, etc., to always be the best methodology for physical education researchers at the current time. Therefore, the research specialists in each field of physical education must, while referring to the knowledge of physical education history for advice, construct separate methodologies as national theories responsible for each specialized field.

In the above manner, it is possible to construct a methodology of the gymnastics human for every country in the world. Thus we are able to form a national methodology of gymnastics study in each country in the world in each national language.

Part V

Theory of International Skiing Studies for the Achievement of Peace

1

A Word from the Author

The term *skiing human* (or *snow human*) is a symbolic term that works toward a national peace and a world peace. We, the world's physical education and sports scholars, must treat this word as dearly as our own lives. This is because without the existence of the skiing human, none of the language concerning skiing and research concerning skiing could be formed. The existence builds and determines it all. The existence of skiing humans creates many national languages. However, the national languages are not able to create the human existence in all nations. They make American English, Japanese, German, French, Italian, Korean, British English, Spanish, Chinese, etc. The skiing human in China speaks Chinese. The skiing human in Russia speaks Russian. The skiing human in the United States speak American English. The skiing humans also make other words like sound (noisy or nice), imitation sound, onomatopoeic words in the phenomenon of skiing. All national languages making the phenomenon of skiing are proof of the existence of skiing human in each nation. The term *skiing human* is the universal language of the world's physical education and sports scholars as long as the phenomenon of skiing continues in all the nations. It is a specialized term, even a holy term.

I present this book for the benefit of all the physical education and sports scholars of each of the world's nations alike.

2

Establishing the Hypothesis for Creating Skiing Studies

The following questions are the fundamental motives for attempting to create the theory of international skiing studies for the achievement of peace (principle of physical education and sports studies for all nations in the world):

1. Why, in the scholastic physical education programs of the education ministries of each country in the world, are teachers or professors using any types of skiing as educational resources to lead students?
2. Why are the physical education and sports researchers of each country in the world conducting research concerning any types of skiing?
3. Why are physical education teachers and physical education and sports researchers and professors of every country in the world conducting classes in schools, colleges, universities, and graduate schools concerning the theory of any types of skiing?
4. Why does the IOC adopt any types of skiing and do skiing in the Olympics?
5. Why does the research concerning skiing belong to the physical education and sports studies?
6. Why is the research concerning skiing worthy of doctorate degrees or master's degrees in physical education and sports studies?
7. Why do we need physical education faculties in colleges, universities, and graduate schools in the nation and the world?
8. Why do we physical education scholars need professors who offer lectures for their studies in public and employ them?

We physical education scholars created the above-mentioned

questions in order to get social, national, and world trust for our profession in public. It means that we physical education scholars have social, national, and world problems. It also considers what education is in reality.

Currently there is no theory in the world's physical education and sports research that can answer these fundamental questions of skiing research. This is the most important problem that I have to take responsibility for as a physical education scholar in public. Therefore, I undertook the problem and tried to solve it and to build the theories so that I could answer all of the questions. The motive that I have to try the theory for studies of skiing is mentioned above.

Here, in order to ask and answer the question: "What are all types of skiing and, more generally, what is skiing?" I have formed the following hypothesis. "When a human does skiing is when a human becomes a skiing human. (When a human does skiing is not when a human becomes a human.)" As a reason for the formation of the hypothesis, I believe that to do skiing is to do skiing, and to do skiing is not not doing skiing. To do is to become.

This new term (which will become a specialized term used among physical education and sports scholars) has been created in order to convert terms such as skiing and terms included in it (*jump skiing, downhill skiing*, etc.) into moving, living worlds. Also, the world's physical education teachers take their responsibilities from the social reality of skiing being taught by sports leaders to sports students and followers.

Also in this book I have used the term *movement human*. When we perceive the phenomenon of skiing, we see people moving on snow. In order to express the existence of the moving human being (apart from the technique one may have in one's arms and legs) in one noun phrase, we say "movement human." This term refers to the entire existence of the human (individual) and some other (another person or something else) dynamically working together in both a passive and active relationship.

The term *skiing human* is used to represent collectively all of the various types of skiing, such as ski-jumping human, etc. Each of these terms refers directly to the existence of the acting relationship between human and snow in each type of skiing. It is this relationship, too, that gives life to and maintains the socially significant term *skiing*.

Next I would like to explain in detail what it is directly indicated the term *skiing human* refers to. The object to which the words *skiing human* refers is the entirety of the acting relationship between a movement human and a movement snow in the phenomenon of skiing or in the phenomenon in which skiing is dealt with. In the world of skiing, the movement human as skiing human and movement snow, as skiing human together make up the skiing human. In this situation, the movement human is a movement human related to a movement human as skiing human and the movement snow as skiing human is a movement human as skiing human related to movement snow as skiing human. Therefore, the two share a common point that connects them together.

Specifically, this common point is the existential form in which the skiing humans act together in mutual independence and in certain aspects move in a uniform motion. However, if we look objectively at them, we can divide the skiing human into a skiing human as a movement human and a skiing human as a movement snow.

Therefore, in presenting the theory, in order to refer directly to both the skiing human as a movement human and the skiing human as a movement snow sides, we will use the term *skiing human* for simplification. Only when we wish to make an explicit distinction between the two sides we will use the expression *skiing human as a movement human and skiing human as a movement snow*. Therefore, the expression skiing human refers to both the movement human as skiing human and movement snow as skiing human sides of the skiing.

There were many reasons for the creation of the special term *skiing human*, but the most important of these was the need to distinguish the general human existence from the existence experienced in the special world in which skiing is dealt with in physical education and sports studies and to make this special independence clear. In addition, it serves to help construct national theories (skiing studies) to explain the unique practice of skiing.

The next matter with which we must concern ourselves is the development of all types of skiing phenomena and phenomena that involve the applied exercises of skiing in every country in the world. Specifically, in what form does this living phenomenon appear to our eyes? In other words, which actions in the living phenomenon of skiing are essential and which are nonessential? Understanding this distinction and synthesis will lead to a clear insight into this living phenomenon of skiing.

In order to answer these questions, I will examine the living phenomenon of skiing itself, relying on intuitive analysis and the integrated judgment method. As I stated in the hypothesis, the essence of the existence of the living phenomenon of skiing and the phenomenon in which the applied exercises of skiing are dealt with and the nonessence of that existence (auxiliary actions to the existential essence) are manifested in the various aspects of the skiing human, such as the track-and-field human, the ball human, the flying human, the dance human, etc. Please see figure 41 for an explanation of this idea. There are, in other words, all the essential structural elements that form the living phenomenon of skiing.

If we analyze the primary factors that form the movement relying on our perceptions of the skiing phenomenon and then integrate these back together, we can come to understand the movement itself. For example, if we look at the action of the skiing human, we see that he acts on the ground, the air, the image, the ball, the human, etc., in reality, to form the living phenomenon of skiing. The instant the skiing human acts in relation to ground without snow he begins to exist as a track-and-field human. The instant the skiing human acts momentarily in relation to another image, he begins to exist as a dance human.

Furthermore, in the instant the skiing human acts momentarily in air, he begins to exist as a flying human. There are the auxiliary actions in the living phenomenon of the skiing that create motion and that act indirectly on the movement of the skiing human.

In order to determine if figure 41 is true or false, let us try to return to the living phenomenon (fact) of each type of skiing. For instance, I explain the living phenomenon of ski-jumping human in the skiing using this graph. We can say that in the actions of the skiing human, ski-jumping human appears as the existential essence. At the same time, the phenomenon appears as a composition of transient aspects of the nonessential, such as the dance human (he may be ski-jumping momentarily with some image), the track-and-field human (he may perform ski-jumping on the ground or the artificial ground), the flying

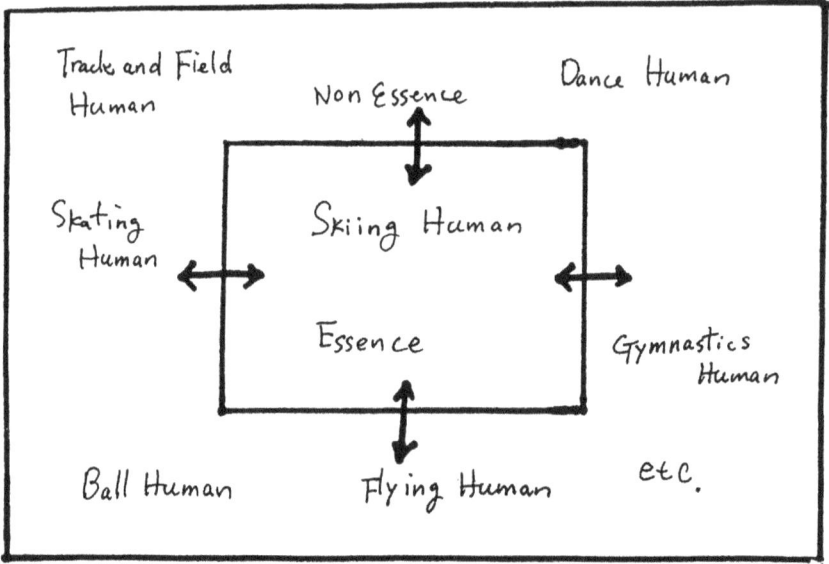

**Figure 41. Formation elements of the living phenomenon
of skiing in each nation in the world**

human (he may perform ski-jumping with acting in air), etc. The
phenomenon of skiing; human is, most important, the actions of the
skiing human as movement snow when there is created movement
human as a skiing human. I can explain concrete matters of actual
skiing with this figure 41. That means this figure 41 is true.

So we need many kinds of special terms in order to construct
national skiing studies. If the ski jumping is performed outdoors, the
ski-jumping human may act momentarily in rain and water (like
swimming human). The determining factor is the valuation of the
skiing, but above all, it is determined by the action of the skiing
human. Therefore, the skiing human in the phenomenon of skiing is
essential existence. Why? I explain it in evidence of existence of
skiing human, because existence of skiing human makes all of things
(national languages, special terms of skiing, actual sounds of
phenomenon of skiing, etc.). The actions of skiing human mean
movement human as skiing snow for the sake of doing skiing and
movement human as skiing human for the sake of doing skiing.

Therefore, it is possible to say that all of the living phenomena of the various types of skiing can be found in every country in the world, being formed by a mixture of the characteristics of the living phenomena of the martial arts human, the track-and-field human, the flying human, the dance human, etc. Most important, all are formed from the existential essence of the skiing human, namely, the living actions of the skiing human that determine the process and result of the skiing. As evidence for them, we can say that the points scored in a skiing competition, which depend upon the actions of the skiing human in skiing, provide dynamic variation to the aspects of the phenomenon and the result of skiing is determined by them. They also produce a lot of words (specific terms) in relation to the skiing in national languages and nonwords like sounds and imitation sounds in the phenomenon of skiing. Therefore, the action of skiing human determines everything in the phenomenon of skiing.

I would like to put this idea (that the phenomenon of skiing is the mutual actions of specific humans, that is, skiing human as a movement human and skiing human as a movement snow, namely, the skiing human) in the form of a hypothesis. However, in order to do this I must provide some clear evidence that is able to confirm that this is the existential essence in the phenomenon of skiing. This would be the factual ground for the formation of these words. In order to speak scientifically about the phenomenon of the movement human as skiing human and phenomenon in which movement snow as skiing human is dealt with, we must make this existential essence that will be the object of the analysis very clear. In other words, it is necessary to confirm whether or not the term *skiing human* is a term that possesses realistic qualities in the phenomenon of skiing.

Thus I began to think that I could incorporate this method into an ontology of the skiing human. In other words, using the term *skiing human*, I will explain in detail the reality of skiing. Thus, should it be possible to prove this hypothesis, the skiing human would be the existential essence in the phenomenon of skiing and *skiing human* would become specialized terminology whose use would be required any time skiing research is being conducted. Furthermore, we would begin down the road toward the construction of a theory of skiing studies dealing with the entirety of practice and theory. It would be possible to advance the theory by means of a teleology and a methodology and, finally, form skiing theory (a world united and different). A distinction would be made between the aspects of skiing studies that affect the daily lives of actual humans and special areas that the skiing human lives in the skiing studies and practices. When names are given to these boundaries, skiing studies will be formed.

I have ascertained that the existence of the skiing human can be grasped as three aspects, and in this way I hope to make this existence clear. Specifically, these are the movement-cultural existence of the skiing human, the educational existence of the skiing human, and the social existence of the skiing human. These all point to the fact that in every country in the world the skiing human exists in many ways and forms a special world. I will begin my undertaking from my understanding of this skiing human–the skiing human that exists in every country in the world.

3

The Movement-Cultural Ontology of the Skiing Human (or Snow Human)

The skiing human lives in the movement culture and the skiing human exists possessing movement-cultural aspects in all nations in the world. This comes from a connotative structure and a denotative structure. Together they maintain independent functions while living and existing as a whole.

The Connotative Structure

The skiing human as a movement human is organically composed with a head, a torso, hands, and feet. Internally, he is partially muscles, bones, organs, a brain, etc., which all rely on blood for their actions. However, the skiing human as movement human is actually made of many materials, such as a certain amount of air, and various other objects, all of which will be acted upon by the existing life energy. These are based on factors of nature, which include gravity, temperature, climate (sunshine, rain, snow), etc., and dual factors which include mi-, ground, lighting, etc., and they act on individual or group behavior and skill. However, these factors act together with factors dependent on the skiing human as a movement human himself, such as perception, thought, emotion, etc. Therefore, the skiing human as a movement human exists as a complex synthesis of the various factors that makeup each specific human.

There are other aspects of the skiing human as an object movement, including alpine-skiing human, freestyle-skiing human, cross-country-skiing human, ninety-meter ski-jumping human, biathlon-skiing human, slalom-skiing human, etc. Therefore, this term, *skiing human*, means specific human existence and snow existence for skiing in the phenomenon of skiing.

As individual actions, the two sides (the skiing human as a

movement human and the skiing human as a movement snow) approach each other, come into contact, and separate from one another. These actions consist of various types, such as pushing, touching, grasping, kicking, punching, jumping, striking, holding, thrusting, etc.

As group actions, the two sides (the skiing human as a movement human and the skiing human as a movement snow) approach each other, come into contact, and separate from one another. These group actions consist of various types, such as yelling, using signals, watching, etc.

The actions of individual and group technical skills are based on the actions of eyes, ears, tongue, skin, etc., of the skiing human as a movement human and the actions of bones, bowels, and organs such as the heart, lungs, etc. Finally, the actions of thought, emotion, etc., also contribute. In other words, while the sensation/thought/emotion system's parts have independent functions, they are organically and dynamically related and participate in the skilled actions of the skiing human as a movement human. In making value judgments about skilled actions, such as good/bad, achieved/not achieved, the skiing human as a movement human relies greatly on the actions of the sensation/thought/emotion system. The decisions and conflicts are that "my head hurts, but I have to keep performing hard," "I'm tired, so I'll quit soon," "I challenge the snow as an alpine-skiing human, so I'll do my best," "my hands hurt, but I have to try harder," "my teacher is seeing my slalom performances so I'll try to do my best," etc. Those phrases point to the dynamic actions of skiing human of sensation/thought/emotion, sensation/emotion, sensation/thought, thought/sensation, emotion/sensation, emotion/thought/sensation, and so on (figure 42).

The Denotative Structure

The skiing human as a movement human exists in various movement-cultural aspects in all nations in the world. If we were to classify these movement-cultural aspects, we could classify them in the following four types, because basic forms of all movement humans are composed by approaching actions to someone and some substances

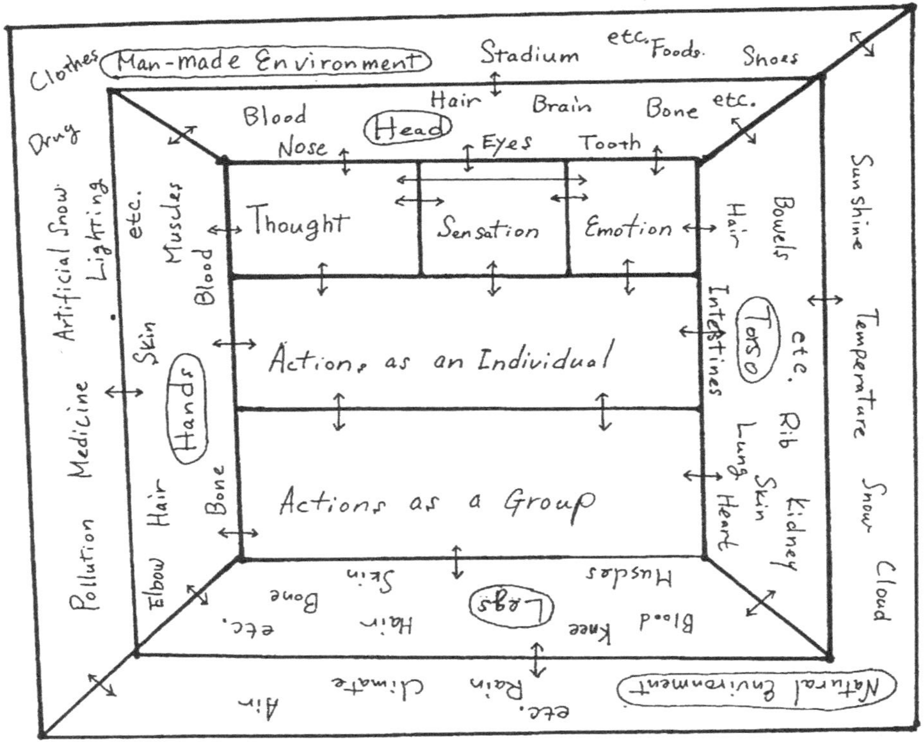

Figure 42. The many kinds of actions of the connotative structure of the skiing human in each nation in the world

(including water, image, air, ball, etc.), touching actions to someone, and some substances, and separating actions to someone and some substances, in fact. When we watch all actions of movement human we can confirm three kinds of characterized actions through existence of movement human in physical education and sports practices.

The first type includes a kind of skiing event in which either the movement human as skiing human just approaches the movement snow as skiing human or the movement snow as skiing human just approaches the movement human as skiing human. There is ski-jumping human as movement human as an example of this type nowadays. However, the number of this kind of skiing event might be increased by some skiing specialists in the future.

The second type includes skiing events in which the action of the movement human (as the skiing human) and the movement snow (as the skiing human) are mutually disjunctive and conjunctive, such as alpine-skiing human as movement human, slalom- skiing human as movement human, biathlon-skiing human as movement human, cross-country-skiing human as movement human, etc.

While both type 1 and type 2 deal with individualistic movement/cultural properties, both the following type 3 and type 4 deal with movement/cultural properties that are oriented by the group of more than two people from the movement human (as skiing human).

The third type includes skiing events in which the actions of the group skiing human as a movement human attempt to approach the other group skiing human as snow movement or separate from the other group skiing human as snow movement. Today skiing of this type appears as combined skiing jumps but has possibilities like 70-meter skiing jump human as movement human and 100-meter skiing jump human as movement human in a competition among groups.

The fourth type of skiing human in the phenomenon of skiing is the skiing human in whom the skiing human as a movement human in the group and the skiing human as a movement human in the group repeat actions of mutual approach, separation, and contact. The skiing human works as a group event, for example. There are possible relay cross-country skiing humans as movement human in the group and relay slalom skiing humans as movement human in the group in a competition among more than two groups that belong to this fourth type.

In this manner, it is possible to classify the movement-cultural existence of every skiing phenomenon based on the substance and type of actions of the skiing human. (Refer to figure 43.) However, each skiing human as a movement human exists in a manner that presents unique aspects. The alpine skiing human as movement human exists with unique aspects not found in slalom skiing human as movement human. (The alpine skiing human as movement human is absolutely alpine skiing human as movement human.) The slalom skiing human as movement human exists with unique aspects not found in cross-country skiing human as movement human. (The slalom skiing human is absolutely slalom skiing human as movement human, in fact.) Therefore, each type of skiing human appears in his own unique movement-cultural aspects.

Ski Jump-ness
(the Ski-Jumping Human as a Movement Human)

The ski-jumping human as a movement human exists in aspects of ski jumping. For example, there is either a direct or indirect relation to the apparatus of ski jumping, the rules of ski jumping, the facilities of ski jumping, the terminology of ski jumping, etc. The appearance of the ski-jumping human as a movement human forms the unique world of ski jumping.

Alpine Skiing-ness
(the Alpine-Skiing Human as a Movement Human)

The alpine-skiing human as a movement human exists in aspects of alpine skiing. For example, there is either a direct or indirect contact with the apparatus of alpine skiing, the rules of alpine skiing, the facilities of alpine skiing, the terminology of alpine skiing, etc. The appearance of the alpine skiing forms the unique world of alpine skiing.

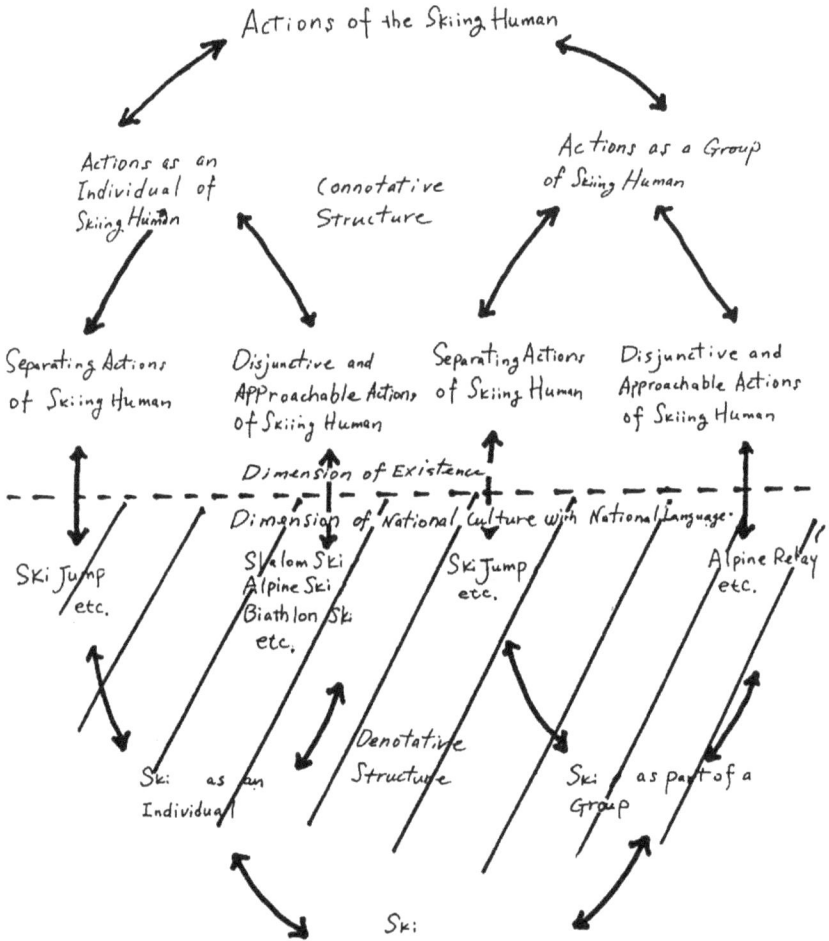

Actions of the Skiing Human

Actions as an Individual of Skiing Human

Connotative Structure

Actions as a Group of Skiing Human

Separating Actions of Skiing Human

Disjunctive and Approachable Actions of Skiing Human

Separating Actions of Skiing Human

Disjunctive and Approachable Actions of Skiing Human

Dimension of Existence

Dimension of National Culture with National Language

Ski Jump etc.

Slalom Ski Alpine Ski Biathlon Ski etc.

Ski Jump etc.

Alpine Relay etc.

Denotative Structure

Ski as an Individual

Ski as part of a Group

Ski

Figure 43. The movement-cultural existence of the skiing human in each nation in the world

194

Slalom Skiing-ness
(the Slalom-Skiing Human as a Movement Human)

The slalom-skiing human as a movement human exists in aspects of slalom skiing. For example, there is either a direct or indirect relation to the apparatus of slalom skiing, the rules of slalom skiing, the terminology of slalom skiing, the facilities of slalom skiing, etc. The appearance of the slalom-skiing human as a movement human forms the unique world of slalom skiing.

Biathlon Skiing-ness
(the Biathlon-Skiing Human as a Movement Human)

The biathlon-skiing human as a movement human exists in aspects of biathlon. For example, there is either a direct or indirect contact with the apparatus of biathlon, the rules of biathlon, the facilities of biathlon, the terminology of biathlon, etc. The appearance of the biathlon-skiing human forms the unique world of biathlon.

As there are several skiing events that have been introduced in the above-mentioned, the number of new skiing events may increase in the future as new skiing events we have never seen emerge. In this way, the skiing human as a movement human exists in all the various movement-cultural aspects in every country in the world, in the United States, as Americans, in Russia as Russians, in France as Frenchmen, in England as Englishmen, and in China as Chinese. And skiing human also exists in fact as student, as teacher, as professor, as instructor, as boy student, as girl student, as graduate student, as leader, as observer, as onlooker, etc., in any place in all nations in the world. The ski human exists in these various movement-cultural aspects.

4

The Educational Ontology of the Skiing Human (or Snow Human)

In the special society of physical education in every country in the world, the skiing human as a movement human exists possessing an aspect of physical education. Every type of skiing is evaluated educationally. Certainly, opinions are formed about whether a skiing human builds a certain strength, develops character, fosters mental growth, fosters creativity, etc. The educational existence of the skiing human as a movement human comes from a connotative structure and denotative structure. Each works based on an independent structure, and as a whole they exist educationally.

The Connotative Structure

In order to make clear the actions of the skiing human, we will analyze them and use integrated judgment, by looking both from the social actions of the skiing human toward the living energy and from the living energy toward the social actions of the skiing human. In this manner, we can grasp fully the entire substance of the actions of the skiing human. We have some factors that are expressed, such as body strength, flexibility, etc., while in contrast, some factors are expressive, such as the mind, soul, character, personality, condition of character, morale, flexibility, etc. These factors work in a living, separate manner, and at the same time the actions of skiing human are in the integration of all these living elements. By using these words to inquire about the nature of the actions of the skiing human, we can elucidate the concept of the skiing human. Therefore, these words refer to the various partial factors that make up the skiing human, and they are living words. The source of these words is based upon the supply and demand of living energy produced by the unification (actions of digestion, actions of oxidation) that takes place inside the individual of the mutually conflicting elements of air and food and the skiing human. In other words, the source is the transformation of the various elements, such as body strength, flexibility of body, physique, physical condition, mind, soul, morale, flexibility of mind, personality, condition of character, etc., into a living entity. Therefore, the words *body strength, flexibility of body, physique, physical condition, mind, soul, morale, flexibility of mind, personality, and condition of character* are all living words and are words that have come to refer to reality.

On the other hand, we have said that the action of the skiing human is formed from a synthesis of the various types of action of the skiing human expressed as mind, body, soul, physique, physical condition, body strength, flexibility of body, condition of character, morale, and flexibility of mind. It should be noted that in our analysis of the actions of the skiing human we said that there is both a movement human and movement snow side of the skiing human, with mutually different objects. Since this is the case, it may not be appropriate to use the same type of language to explain both. However, based on the common point of view that both share as the skiing human, we will use the same language to explain them.

The analysis and synthesis of these two sides, the skiing human as a movement human and the skiing human as a movement snow, are shown in figure 44 and figure 45.

Also making up the actions of the skiing human are skilled actions, which express technique. However, if we analyze these skilled actions, we can see that they are made up of actions of the conduct of the skiing human and the substance of the kind of technique being expressed. In other words, the actions of the conduct of the skiing human, together with the substance of the technique, make up the reality of the skilled actions of the skiing human and exist united in reality. These exist in a relationship that is mutually life giving and enlivened, creating the phenomenon of the skilled existence of the skiing human.

The Denotative Structure

In regard to the denotative structure of the educational existence of

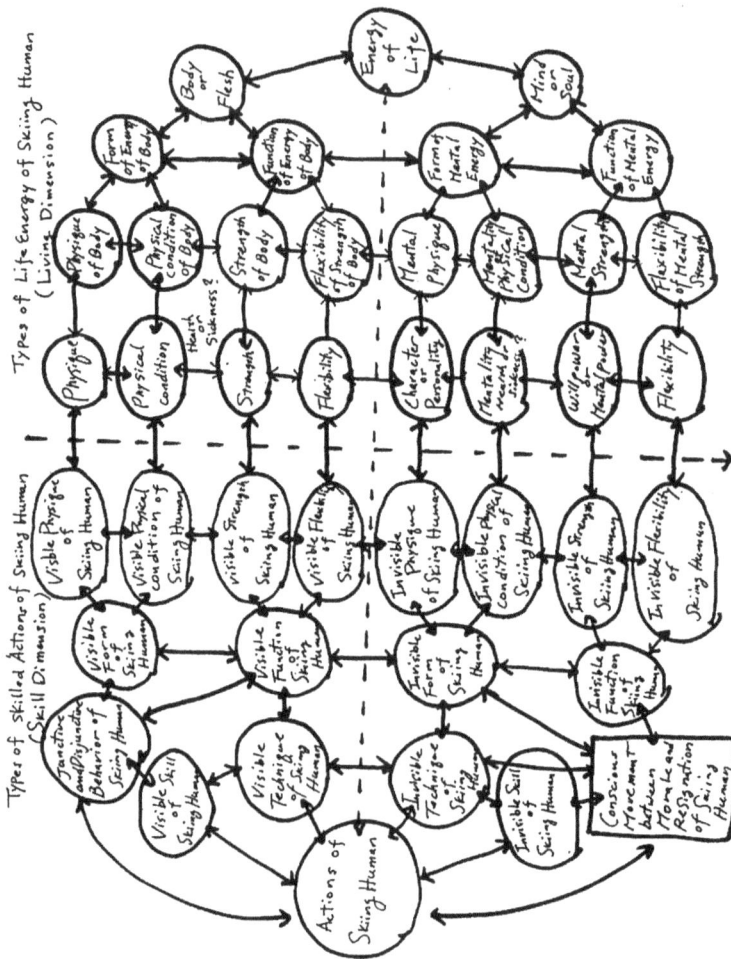

Figure 44. Types of action of the skiing human in each nation in the world

the skiing human. I have attempted some analytical speculation that will explain it, as shown in figure 46.

Here I will explain each of the educational elements of the skiing human dealt with in the second analysis of the educational phenomenon of the skiing human.

Society

The skiing human functions in the special society of skiing. However, in order to create this special society, he must work by accepting and approving all of the factors. Specifically, the skiing human as a movement human that takes on the special social role of player acts both socially and morally. The skiing human as a movement human acts in participation with the special humans that take on the social roles of judges, teachers, leaders, etc., and even with things that are set up for the purpose of becoming a skiing human as a movement human, such as unique facilities, equipment, rules, etc. In this manner, the phenomenon of skiing is when, as the skiing human as a movement human is enlarged from some person to some thing and from some thing to some person, he acts both socially and morally. However, while the society of the skiing human as a movement human provides the nature of a special society, in order that skiing occurs in general society, it exists in the twofold relationship with general society and the special society of the skiing.

Discovery-ness

The skiing human as a movement human acts creatively. At the same time, skiing human as a snow movement also acts creatively. In the action of the skiing human, there are situations in which new technical content or form, no similar example to which existed in the past, is added. There new techniques are conceptualized and given special names. This itself points to the discovery-ness of the skiing human. Names in the events of skiing itself point to the discovery-ness of the skiing human. For example, we are able to find so many things from skiing in the Olympics. The original words for skiing that the

I   The Visible Physique of the Skiing Human
     Movement Human : Size. Weight. color of Skin. stature. etc.
     Movement Snow : Size. Depth. Color. Weight etc.

II   The Condition of the Visible Physique of the Skiing Human
     Movement Human : Quality of the visible Physique of the Skiing Human
     (Effector not)
     Movement Snow : Quality of the Visible Shape of the Skiing Human

III   The Function of the Visible Physique of Skiing Human
     Movement Human : Endurance, Speed, Power etc
     Movement Snow : Support of Endurance, Support of Speed, Support of Power etc

IV   The Condition of the Visible Function of Skiing Human
     Movement Human : Effective physical Ability and Flexibility of the Skiing Hu
     Movement Snow : Support of Effective physical Ability and Flexibility of the S
     Human

- -

V   The Invisible Physique of the Skiing Human
     Movement Human : Invisible Physique of the Skiing Human
     Movement Snow : Invisible Shape of the Skiing Human.

VI   The Condition of the invisible Physique of the Skiing Human
     Movement Human : Condition of the invisible Physique of the Skiing Hu
     (Mental Effort or not)
     Movement Snow : Condition of the invisible shape of the Skiing Hum

VII   The Function of the invisible Physique of the Skiing Human
     Movement Human : Mental Endurance, Mental Speed, Mental power etc
     Movement Snow : Support of Mental Endurance, Support Mental speed
     Support of Mental power etc.

VIII   The Condition of the invisible Function of the Skiing Human
     Movement Human : Flexibility of Mental Endurance, Effective Ment
     Ability. etc
     Movement Snow : Support of Flexibility of Mental Endurance, Supp
     of Effective Mental Ability etc.

Figure 45. The types and contents of the actions of the
skiing human in each nation in the world

First Analysis Second Analysis

Subjective / Objective
Objective / Subjective
Dynamic Fact

Educational
Phenomenon of
the Skiing Human

Entire Expression of
Skiing Human

Society
(Objective)

Discovery ness
(Subjective)

Partial Expression
of Skiing Human

Cooperative ness
(Objective)

Creativity
(subjective)

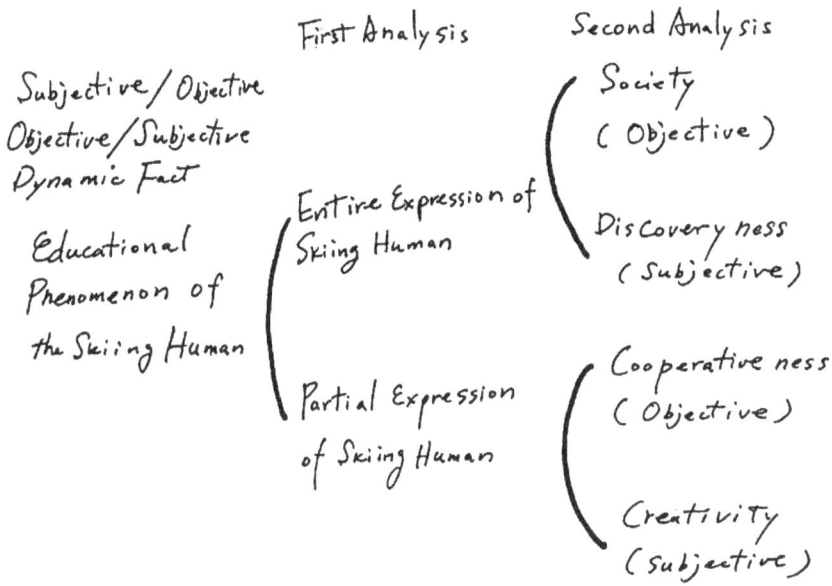

Figure 46. The educational existence of the
skiing human in each nation in the world

Olympics created were proof of the discovery-ness of skiing human. There is a certain matter in which the Olympics brought about the birth of the new skiing. In this way, there are situations in which a new skiing human given movement-cultural existence in history is formed. The discovery-ness of the skiing human consists of both the creative and historical expansion aspects of these actions.

Cooperativeness

In the phenomenon of skiing, there are many cases in which the skiing human acts in a group. In these cases, cooperation intentions are demanded of the skiing human. This cooperativeness depends on the mutual relationship between acting skiing humans that have taken on the social role of the player (athletes), and therefore this is a social action. There is cooperativeness from a unified standpoint and cooperativeness from a different standpoint. For example, the general factors of the school associated with the individual skiing human, religion, age, sex, etc., may be identical or different. Also, the various factors of the special standpoint of the skiing such as skill level of the skiing human, the player (athlete) role, companions, etc., may be identical or different.

In this way, the actions of the cooperativeness of the skiing human exist as the nature of the identities and differences of the special things limited only to the skiing. So if we try to limit it to only the cooperativeness in the special society of skiing, the cooperativeness of identity recognition of the skiing human is based on the recognition of technical standpoint and the cooperativeness of difference recognition is based on the recognition of existential standpoint.

Creativity

The skiing human, in the living, always-changing space of skiing, acts while at every moment being faced with the problem: "In what way should I best handle skiing human as the snow movement I have?" The skiing human as movement human, who has been acted on by a skiing human as snow movement, is a concrete expression of the skill of the skiing human as a movement human himself. It is something that indicates the level of skill. Therefore, the skiing human as a movement human demands skill from the skiing human as a movement snow, and conversely, the skiing human as a movement human exists while demanding skill from a skiing human as a snow movement. Through the skill demands of these two sides, the skiing human creates. For example, a skiing human as a snow movement is thrown by the skiing human as a movement human, who has taken the social role of skiing human as an athlete and a skill. Then the skiing human as a movement human tries to face this snow movement and, through the skiing human of snow movement as an extension of the individual's body, tries to respond to the skilled action of the skiing human as a snow movement. As a result, the excellent performance of a skiing human, tools, special terms of skiing, and so forth, will be created.

The creativity of the skiing human can be seen in the creativity of the partial cause/effect action of playing and the action of going inside and the action of doing well and the action of failure. Through this partial cause/effect process, the action of winning, the action of losing, and the action of a draw are created. Creativity can be seen in the partial cause/effect actions in the entire process of the skiing, from start to finish. Furthermore, the creativity generates the subjective emotions of happiness, vexation, anger, and sorrow at every instant in skiing human as a movement human, and skiing human as snow movement, in the special living space of the skiing, the unknown space of the skiing, and regulated space of the skiing, is acting creatively in an original way. These actions being about a reformation of the self-consciousness of the possibilities of ability in the skiing human who has taken the special role of performer. In this special society, it gives meaning to life.

In this way, the skiing human exists educationally. At the same time, he exists as the educational being in scholastic physical education in every country in the world and is an expression of every country in the world (each national language) by his existence.

5

The Social Ontology of the
Skiing Human (or Snow Human)

The skiing human exists within general society. There he exists in each nation while possessing an aspect of social existence in which he lives trying to plan original plans. For example, from the factual phenomenon of the skiing all kinds of words have been derived, such as *physical education, recreation*, etc. On the other hand, in social actions of skiing human there are various kinds of sociological terms that have been created, such as *fair, unfair, cooperative*, etc. This can be said to be implicit proof that the skiing human exists socially concerning the social existence of the skiing human. In order to grasp his factual living state as a living state, I will divide this into a connotative structure and a denotative structure and explain each. Therefore, the social existence of the skiing human is the entirety of the independent actions of connotative structure and denotative structure.

The Connotative Structure

Let us consider the basic aspects of the actions of the skiing human. In the case of the individual, it is the actions of mutual separation/contact within the skiing human. In the case of the group, it is the actions of mutual separation/contact among many skiing humans. In other words, the basic principle is the entirety of the motion that occurs when the skiing human as a snow movement and the skiing human as a movement human mutually separate, approach, and have contact.

If we apply this fact to each kind of the entire phenomenon of skiing, it will be understood easily. This is described by figure 47.

In other words, in order to grasp this dynamic separation/contact relationship between the skiing humans, one must begin by looking objectively from the actions of the skiing human. Meanwhile, there are also the actions of the mind of the skiing human, namely, the separation/contact movement of consciousness. Those actions come from the fact that when dealing with the apparatus, the skiing human as a movement human recognizes a skiing human as movement snow by the action of unconscious-conscious. The strength, or perhaps weakness, of the actions of the consciousness of the skiing human as a movement human is located in the polarized structure of the morale and resignation of the consciousness. The strength or weakness depends throughout on the manner in which the consciousness moves between those polarizations (figure 48).

As the skiing human as a movement human lives, breathes, and goes to the skiing human as a movement snow, and as a skiing human as a movement snow lives, breathes, and goes to the skiing human as a movement human, the morale strengthens the consciousness. In other words, the morale strengthens the unified perception of both sides of the skiing human, the skiing human as a movement human and the skiing human as a movement snow. It also promotes the manifestation of living as a skiing human. For example, in a hotly contested skiing event, the performer himself and each action that the performer does come to be perceived as a unified dimension.

Because the morale is a living thing, it promotes flattering aspects, but since it is caused through the consciousness's condition of resignation, it moves to the resignation, which is a different kind of element. Primarily, the morale of the skiing human is not in the dimension of time, which has a passive nature and has some bad points, but in the dimension of space it has an active nature. The morale possesses these kinds of properties.

However, the resignation of the skiing human is the condition of the consciousness of the preparatory steps for displaying the consciousness of morale. Therefore, the resignation of the skiing human, in relation to the morale, is an element of denial, but on the other hand, it provides a kind of quality that serves to support morale as well. In the realm of space the resignation of the skiing human is weak and passive, but in the realm of time it is strong and active.

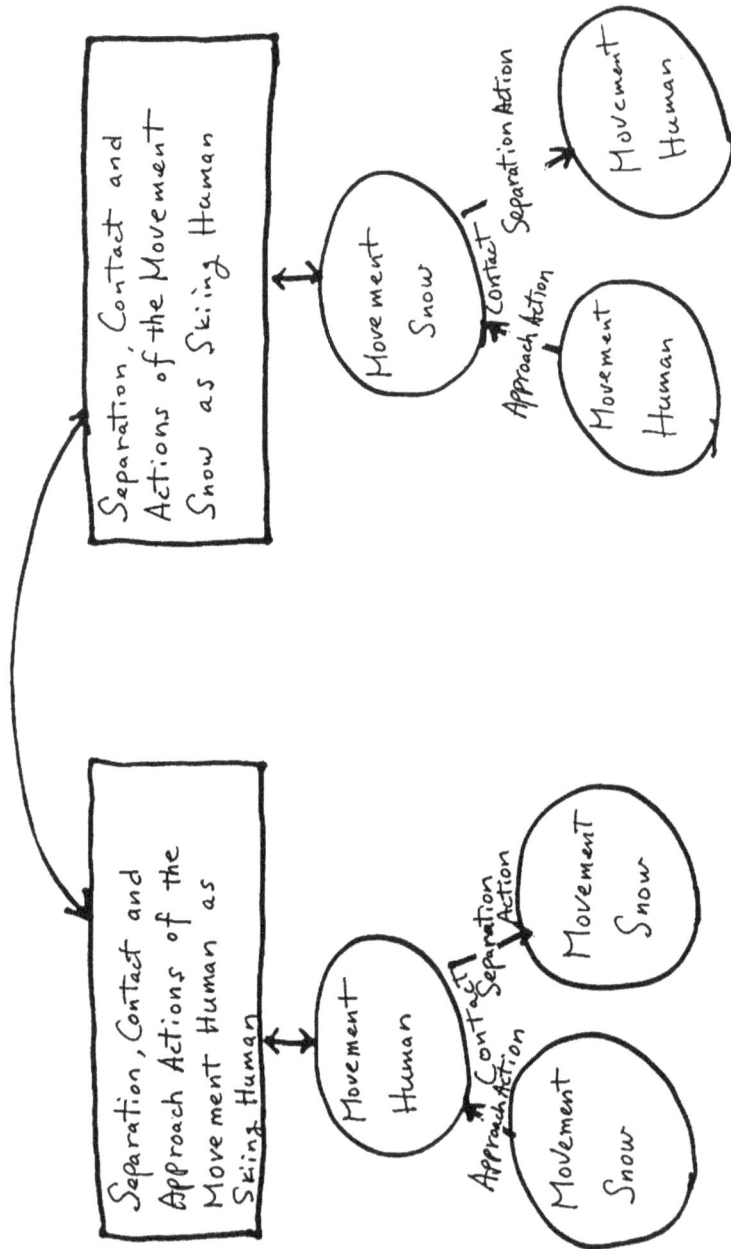

Figure 47. Separation, contact and approach actions of skiing human in each nation in the world

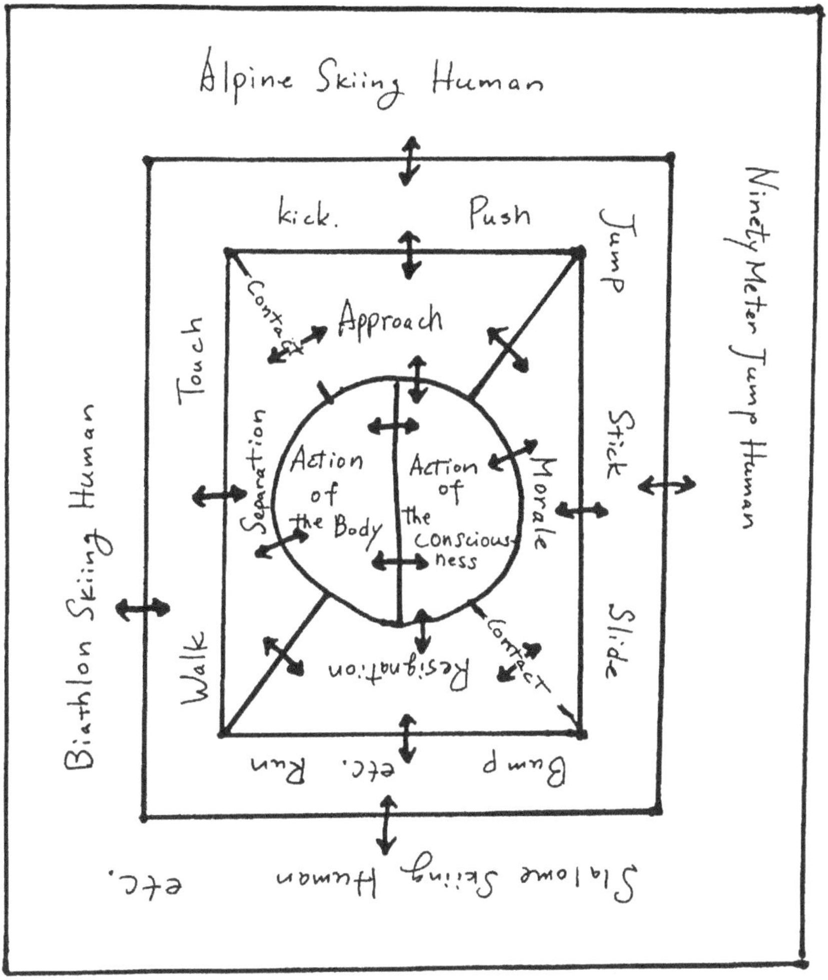

Figure 48. Relations between existence of the skiing human and the words or language connecting phenomena of the skiing human in each nation in the world

The connotative structure of the social existence of the skiing human presents the mutual actions of separation/contact between the skiing humans. Objectively, the body acts by the separation/contact actions, and at the same time, subjectively, the mind acts by the separation/contact actions. Together they act as a whole. Within these actions, the changes in consciousness are acting, namely, by presenting the aspects of morale and resignation.

Concerning the actions of the skiing human, we use many different expressions to indicate them. These different expressions all rely on the aspects of the actions of the skiing human. (Refer to figure 49).

For example, in order to create sentences for classification within the types of skiing human, such as the action of the skiing human, one would proceed in the following way. The alpine-skiing human as a movement human jumps (action of skier) at the same time the skiing human as a movement snow is jumped (action of snow for skiing). The slalom-skiing human as movement human pushes, at the same time the slalom-skiing human as a movement snow is pushed.

In the above manner, the actions of the connotative structure of the skiing human themselves act in an original way. At the same time, they also act with aspects of denotative structure.

The Denotative Structure

In the following way, I have analyzed and gained insight into the denotative elements of the social existence of the skiing human, and I have attempted to extract the denotative elements themselves. (See figure 50).

In the chart, I show each of the social factors of the skiing human listed in the second analysis.

Recreation-ness/Competitiveness

First there is recreation-ness, in which the skiing human amuses himself with entertaining skiing, such as when a group of coworkers or a family enjoys skiing. There is also competitiveness, which includes tension of the kind of seriousness such as when competitive leagues

Names of Actions of the Skiing Human as Movement Snow	Names of Actions of the Skiing Human as Movement Human
being pushed	Pushing
being moved	Moving
being slid	Sliding
being rolled	Rolling
being Stuck	Sticking
being touched	Touching
being Skied	Skiing
being jumped	Jumping
etc.	etc.

Figure 49. Natural expressions related to the actions of skiing human in each nation in the world

are commissioned through the sponsorship of all kinds of competitive groups. The recreation-ness of the skiing human fosters a place for the meeting of the hearts of the skiing human as a snow movement and the skiing human as a movement human. It is a softening aspect that pursues mutual understanding. On the other hand there is the competitiveness, which is the aspect of the skiing human where, within the rules of competition, a skiing human as a snow movement or perhaps a skiing human as a movement human and a skiing human as a snow movement act with bravery and valorous determination. The greater the scale of the competitive league, the more the spirit intensifies, and the competitiveness of the skiing human appears more conspicuous. For instance, this is the case in all the types of skiing in international leagues, etc.

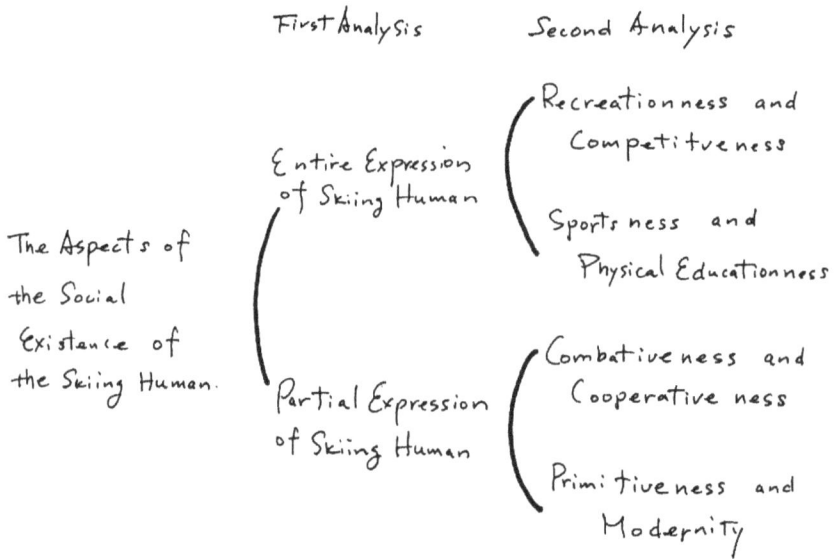

First Analysis   Second Analysis

Recreationness and
Competitveness

Entire Expression
of Skiing Human

Sportsness and
Physical Educationness

The Aspects of
the Social
Existance of
the Skiing Human.

Partial Expression
of Skiing Human

Combativeness and
Cooperative ness

Primitiveness and
Modernity

Figure 50. The social existence of the skiing human in each nation in the world

Sports-ness/Physical Education-ness

In the phenomenon of skiing, based on the fundamental structure of the teacher and pupil, the educational environment and content are given in the school's gym or a corresponding place. This is the physical education-ness of the skiing human performing in each skiing event. The physical education-ness of the skiing human is an educational phenomenon that depends on the sum total of the teacher and pupil. This is an aspect of the special society called school and an aspect of the actions of skiing humans as teacher (or professor) and students (as they are driven by sociological terms) that comes from a regionally narrow scope. The student, who is recognized by the school side, perhaps specially selected, from nursery school through elementary, junior high, and high school, will be acting the role of the physical education-ness of skiing human. On the other hand, the phenomenon of the skiing in general society is an expression of the sports-ness of the skiing human. We can see the sports-ness of the skiing human because a sphere of skiing belongs to sports. It would be possible for skiing to belong in the realm of sports. If it were so, the sports-ness of skiing human would be the aspect of the skiing human in which, in the social phenomenon that relies on the sum total of leaders and followers, a wide range of many kinds of skiing would be developed with no relevance to sex, age, or occupation. Furthermore, there are the phenomena of slalom skiing, ski jumping, alpine skiing, etc. All of these are expressions of the sports-ness of skiing human.

Combativeness/Cooperativeness

In the actions of the skiing human, there are the elements of the contrasting actions of combativeness and cooperativeness. The action of an individual skiing human as a movement human on a team of skiing humans is an expression of cooperativeness. This action of the play between companion skiing humans creates a oneness of the team/individual and builds many conscious states. It conspicuously expresses the cooperativeness of skiing human. This aspect can also be seen in the phenomenon where a group does skiing, whereas actions of the skiing human, the skilled actions of the skiing human as an individual, are sublimated to the skilled actions of the skiing human as a group. Namely, when there is a lacking in the skilled actions of one skiing human as a movement human, it is compensated for by the skilled actions of some other skiing human as a movement human as an individual. In addition, them is also the aspect in which in order for one skiing human as a movement human as an individual to do skilled actions, some different skiing human as a movement human as an individual tries to give assistance. In these forms, this aspect appears.

In contrast to this, there are also times when, with a severe attitude toward other skiing humans, the skiing human as an individual feels other skiing humans are rivals or opponents. This is an expression of the combativeness of the skiing human. It is most conspicuous in the setting of vehement competition between skiing humans. Combativeness can be seen in every phenomenon of skiing and every phenomenon in which the skiing human as movement on snow-covered ground is dealt with. It is the moment when the skilled actions of the skiing human as an individual are steeply opposed to the actions of another skiing human as snow movement, and he feels it as a rival. It also can be the movement of rivals that appears between the skilled actions of skiing humans of a group.

Primitiveness/Modernity

In skiing, there is the primitiveness of the skiing human, in which the skiing human engages in direct skiing human as snow movement contact. In skiing such as playing with snowballs by children, building of snowmen by children, etc. (barefoot, uncovered palms of the hands, etc.) there is momentary direct contact with the snow movement as skiing human in the actions toward the skiing human as a movement human that has taken on the role of performer, such as the situations of hand grabbing, touching, kicking, etc. Therefore, the primitiveness of the skiing human involves giving a direct impact to the body of skiing human, but the opportunities to handle the skiing human as movement snow are relatively frequent.

On the other hand, there is an aspect of modernity of the skiing human in which in the relation between skiing human (human side) the skiing human (snow side) acts by using equipment, uniform, shoes, music, etc. Alpine skiing, slalom, biathlon, ski jumping, etc., by getting specific uniforms, skiwear, ski poles, ski boots, ski gloves, etc., are skiing events that conspicuously express the modernity of the skiing human. In the modernity of the skiing human, the impact of the snow received by the body of the skiing human as a movement human is small. The handling of the snow is relatively rare, and the freedom of the skiing movement is limited.

Moreover, to say that here in the denotative structure we have come up with a comprehensive list of all of the words that refer to the social existence of skiing human would be addled. I have aimed only for a coordinated understanding of the social existence of the skiing human and an understanding of it as a living existence. Furthermore, if we look at all the various elements of the social existence of the skiing human, such as the amateurness or professionalness (there is not at present) of the skiing human, the fair play-ness of the skiing human, and the playfulness of the skiing human, we can see that these elements are vital ones that act to stir up the social aspects of skiing human. In this manner, in every country in the world, the skiing human expresses the originality of each country and carries on a social existence. In the stream of time of past-present-future, this existence lives in the present as realistic beings and is variable and alive.

6

Generalizations from the Ontology of the Skiing Human (or Snow Human)

Up to this point, the three existences of the skiing human, namely, the movement-cultural, educational, and social existence, have been explained clearly. *Skiing human*, when taken as in the hypothesis, is language that refers to the existential essence of the phenomenon of skiing and the phenomenon in which snow is dealt with. In other words, we have confirmed the fact that the words *skiing human* are alive and exist, forming the special expanding world of skiing and dealing with an image for skiing in every country in the world. We have also confirmed the fact that these words refer directly to a special kind of human. The skiing human exists as the expression of each country (national language) in the world, in the United States as Americans, in Russia as Russians, in China as Chinese, in Japan as Japanese, in Sweden as Swedes, etc. The skiing human speaks American English, Chinese, Korean, German, British English, Italian, French, Spanish, etc. in the phenomena of skiing. In the present of the ever-flowing stream of past-present-future, with living and variable aspects, it exists and lives.

Now, as a result of the clear evidence of the existential essence of the skiing and the clear evidence of the existence of the skiing human in the phenomenon of skiing, the following kinds of questions can now be answered:

Question 1: What is the phenomenon of skiing?
Answer: The phenomenon of skiing is the phenomenon in which a human and snow become skiing human through doing the skiing. It is a special world in which the skiing human performs (or acts).

Question 2: What does it mean to ski?
Answer: This is an action by which some humans become skiing

humans, who can be divided into, on the one hand, movement human and, on the other hand, a snow movement for doing skiing!

For example (more concreteness):

Question 1: What is the alpine skiing?
Answer: Alpine skiing is a practice by which human and snow become an alpine skiing human.

Question 2: What does it mean to do alpine skiing?
Answer: This means becoming an alpine-skiing human, who can be divided into a movement human as a skiing human and a movement snow as a skiing human.

Question 3: What does it mean in physical education to ski?
Answer: This is the conduct in which the human and snow become skiing human (as movement human and movement snow) and both of these are physical education-ized and try to become physical education-ized.

Question 4: What does it mean in sports to ski?
Answer: This is the conduct in which the human and snow become skiing human in both sides, and both of these are sports-ized and try to become sports-ized.

For any other questions concerning the phenomenon of skiing itself, they can be answered from the movement-cultural, educational, and social ontologies presented previously.

Furthermore, this skiing human encompasses every type of skiing human. Namely, it is the existence of the slalom-skiing human, the existence of the free-style-skiing human, the existence of the biathlon-skiing human, the existence of the ski-jumping human, etc. Also, depending on the differences in sex, age, race, school, occupation, etc., the above specific humans in phenomena of skiing exist as different expressions.

In the above manner, through the movement of speculation, the establishment of the ontology of the skiing human, from both an abstract standpoint and a concrete standpoint, from the existence to being and from being to existence, became possible. Here we can generalize this system as the ontology of the skiing human.

Finally, while I have referred to the existence of the skiing human as a special existence of the human in skiing, I must now go on to present the existence of a purpose in the existence of the skiing human. Namely, the existence of the skiing human that I have presented until now is an existence that acts in order to realize the skiing human image. It is that purpose for which the existence is acting. Therefore, I must now go on to develop a presentation concerning the skiing human image-the teleology of the skiing human in each nation and each era. I would like to affirm the skiing human image that comes from the existence of the skiing human, who exists with special aspects in the skiing.

7

The Teleology of the Skiing Human
(or Snow Human)

Until this point, I have contemplated the existential essence in the phenomenon of all types of skiing. I have clearly shown and confirmed that in every country in the world every type of skiing human of each type of skiing exists. However, at the same time, this existence includes the purpose of the skiing human, namely, the skiing human image. It is not simply the existence of the skiing human, but also an existence that tries to realize the ideal image that the skiing human must attain. Above all, the practice of all types of skiing that is being conducted in scholastic physical education and sports in every country in the world is being practiced for the sake of the realization of all types of skiing human image by all types of the skiing human. Also, there is the necessity for physical education and sports studies research concerning all types of skiing in every country in the world (such as physical education and sports studies philosophy, physical education and sports studies psychology, physical education and sports studies physiology, physical education and sports studies sociology, physical education and sports studies history, etc.) in order to plan the realization of the skiing human image, in the practice of the skiing of the applied practice where skiing is dealt with, in physical education.

At this point I will go on to speculate about what kind of special ideal image is meant by the purpose of the skiing human in the world or, more specifically, by the skiing in all nations in the world.

The skiing human image in all nations in the world is of course, the purpose of the practice of the skiing, but it is necessary to explain clearly what in reality it is that this word directly refers to. It refers to the ideal image in which the actions of the skiing human as a movement human and the actions of the skiing human as a movement snow in the practice of skiing are existing together doing superior actions. The skiing human image is the ideal image that is living and existing ideally from one era to the next era in every country in the world. This is determined by the research of the physical education and sports theory specialists (such as physical education and sports studies philosophers, physical education and sports studies psychologists, physical education and sports studies physiologists, physical education and sports studies sociologists, physical education and sports studies historians, etc.) that are living in each era in every country in the world. The words *skiing human image* refer directly to the ideal existence that adds weight, depth, size, and breadth to that acting existence.

In the nature of the substance of the skiing human there are really two different kinds of nature. Also, these two natures dynamically act together and form the firm skiing human image. The first is the part of the purpose that has a universal nature that is common, no matter what the time, no matter what the place, no matter what the country. For example, all of the superior actions of the movement human as skiing human and the movement human as skiing snow–in other words, the attempt to realize the skiing human image–even though there are differences between the histories, cultures, ideas, races, and languages of the countries in the world, share a common universal nature.

The second is the concrete purpose of the skiing human, which is variable depending on the time, the society, the nation, age, sex, and other variables from country to country. In every country, there is originality in history, ideas, culture, and national language. The skiing human image of a certain era in each country of the world has the aspects of that era. Furthermore, from the point of view of age, the various types of the skiing human image for children are different from the various types of the skiing human image for old people (figure 51). From the point of view of sex, the skiing human images for males and females are different. The images of the skiing human are not identical, due to the various differences among people. Therefore, as opposed to the purpose of the universal substance of the skiing human, this points to the variable, concrete purpose of the skiing human. The constitution of the teleology of the skiing human relies on the support/being-supported relationship between these two sides, which is a relationship that acts dynamically and mutually to support each side. The skiing human image of the former is the

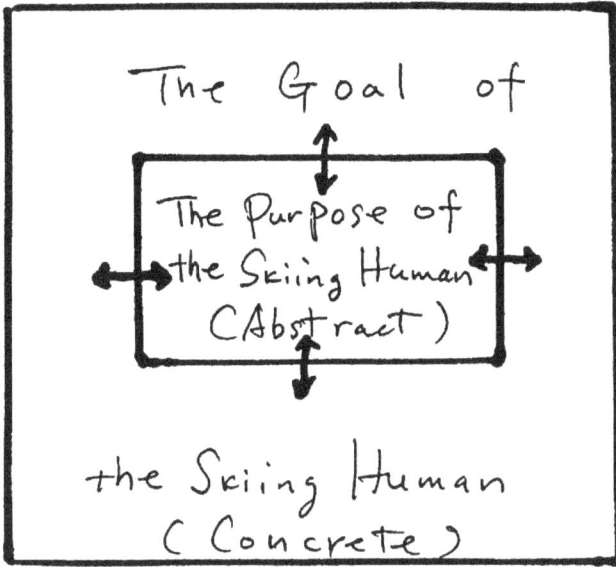

Figure 51. Constitution of the skiing human image in each nation in the world

purpose of the skiing human, while the skiing human image of the latter is the goal of the skiing human. The difference between these clearly points to the difference between the universal purpose and the variable purpose. Therefore, the skiing human image consists of the purpose substance as its core, and that which surrounds the purpose substance is the goal substance. The dynamic relationship between them assumes the character of abstract/concrete-concrete/abstract. Because of this, the skiing human image possesses unifying qualities that transcend the realities of nationality, age, sex, etc. (time and space), but the same time, this teleology is also one that sees those realities as realities. This is summarized in figure 51.

Next I would like to go on to explain the purpose of the skiing human. Specifically, of what substance is the skiing human image itself constructed? I will now explain this point.

The structure of the skiing human image is made up of two types: a connotative structure and a denotative structure. These form the living, unified whole. There are the actions of all of the many element images, and as a whole they act ideally. If we broadly divide these various idealistic elements, they come from the connotative structure and the denotative structure. (Refer to figure 52.)

In physical education and sports, the skiing human forms the special society of skiing in general society. He works ideally in a unique way. At the same time, he is regulated in a unique way and exists ideally in general society.

The Image of Connotative Structure

In the actions of the skiing human image, there is the image of connotative structure. This acts as the foundation for the generation of the image of denotative structure, and so this is a vitally important area. The image of connotative structure itself is formed from the various element images that become the many different ideals. It is formed from the ideal of the image of life energy that comes from physical education and sports nutrition studies and physical education and sports hygiene, the ideal of the image of the body and the image of the mind (mind-body image) that come from physical education and sports philosophy, the ideal of the image of body strength, the image of flexibility, the image of physique, and the image of physical condition (the image of health) that come from physical education and sports physiology, etc. The physical education and sports studies researchers of every country in the world will go on to prove the realistic existence of the skiing human. Relying on the leadership for this proof, the previous images of the connotative structure of the skiing human will be concretely alive and acting as an ideal image. Then, in order that the physical education and sports studies researchers of every country in the world expand on the substance of the words of these various elements, and in order to promote understanding of these words as living things, the research into purpose will proceed. As a result, to the question: "Why are the educational ministries of every country in the world conducting and practicing all kinds of skiing in scholastic physical education?" one will be able to provide a direct answer from the various fields of physical education and sports studies, namely, physical education and sports philosophy, physical education and sports psychology, physical education and sports physiology, physical education and sports sociology, physical education and sports history, etc. For example,

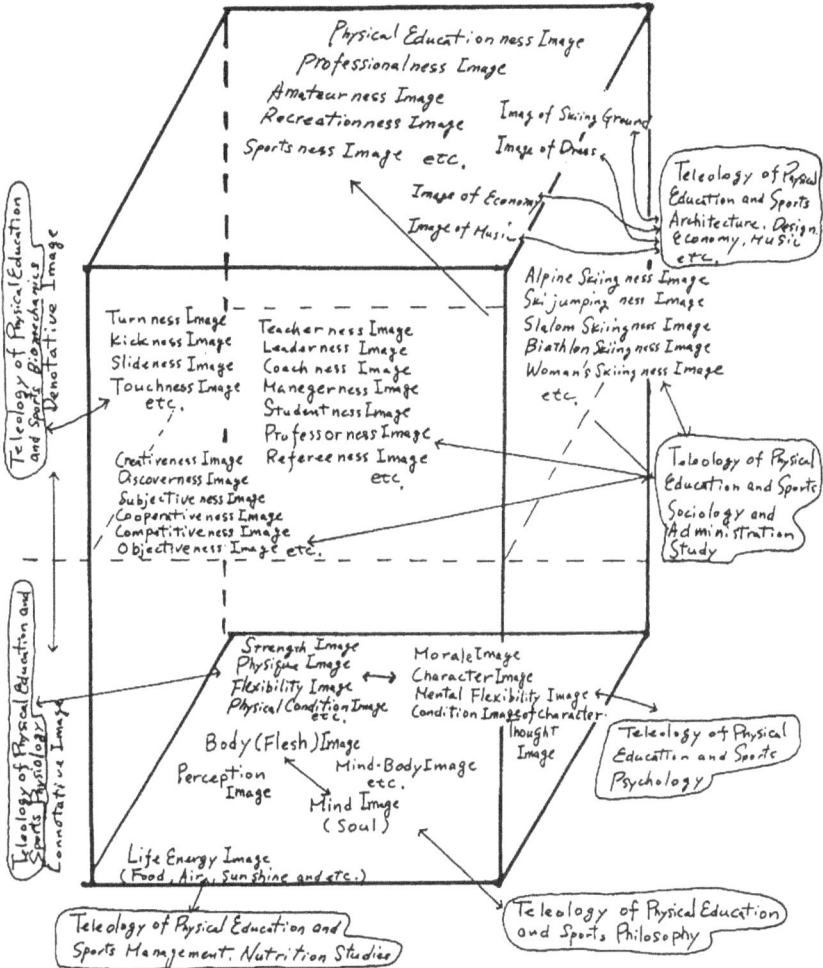

Physical Education ness Image
Professional ness Image
Amateur ness Image
Recreation ness Image
Sports ness Image etc.

Image of Skiing Ground
Image of Dress

Image of Economy
Image of Music

Teleology of Physical Education and Sports Architecture, Design, Economy, Music etc.

Teleology of Physical Education and Sports Biomechanics. Denotative Image

Turn ness Image
Kick ness Image
Slide ness Image
Touch ness Image
etc.

Teacher ness Image
Leader ness Image
Coach ness Image
Manager ness Image
Student ness Image
Professor ness Image
Referee ness Image
etc.

Alpine Skiing ness Image
Ski jumping ness Image
Slalom Skiing ness Image
Biathlon Skiing ness Image
Woman's Skiing ness Image
etc.

Creativeness Image
Discoverness Image
Subjective ness Image
Cooperative ness Image
Competitive ness Image
Objective ness Image etc.

Teleology of Physical Education and Sports Sociology and Administration Study

Teleology of Physical Education and Sports Physiology. Connotative Image

Strength Image
Physique Image
Flexibility Image
Physical Condition Image
etc.

Morale Image
Character Image
Mental Flexibility Image
Condition Image of character
Thought Image

Teleology of Physical Education and Sports Psychology

Body (Flesh) Image
Perception Image
Mind·Body Image etc.
Mind Image (Soul)

Life Energy Image (Food, Air, Sunshine and etc.)

Teleology of Physical Education and Sports Management. Nutrition Studies

Teleology of Physical Education and Sports Philosophy

Figure 52. The skiing human image in each nation in the world

according to physical education and sports philosophy, all types of skiing are practiced in scholastic physical education and sports in order to realize the image of the mind and body of all types of the skiing human. The content of the image of the mind and body can be explained relying on the research of physical education and sports philosophers. Of course, the content of the partial element images presented there all is ideal content that is drawn from the proof of all of the specialist researchers in physical education and sports studies, and at the same time, in the space of the various elements in the image of connotative structure, they are things that are doing superior actions.

Also, there are the various elements that do superior actions in the image of the denotative structure as well. For example, the image of body strength is the result of superior inner actions of body strength itself, acting in superior actions in relation to the various elements, such as morale, flexibility, cooperativeness, competitiveness, physical condition, creativeness, etc.

As is shown above, the image of the connotative structure in the skiing human image is the entirety of the various elements of the connotative structure that have been amassed by the physical education and sports studies researchers in every country in the world and the physical education and sports studies research of each era. However, this image of connotative structure not only acts in the image of connotative structure but works in the image of denotative structure. So what kind of substance of ideal images makes up the image of the denotative structure of skiing human? I will now go on to deal with this question.

The Image of Denotative Structure

In the actions of the skiing human image, there is an image of denotative structure. In the ideal image that is generated from the image of connotative structure, the origin of the formation of the image of the denotative structure is included. Inside the denotative structure itself, which acts as the denotative structure, are the actions of the various element images.

Looking from the specialized point of view of the physical

education and sports sociologists and scholastic physical education and considering the existential direction of the skiing human, if an inquiry is made to determine the ideal images of that existence, then in the following way, the idealistic elements of the denotative structure become visible. The image of sports-ness, the image of professional-ness, the image of recreation-ness, the image of teacher-ness, the image of student-ness, the image of leader-ness, the image of manager-ness, the image of coach-ness, the image of director-ness, the image of follower-ness, the image of slalom-ness, the image of freestyle-ness, the image of ninety- meter ski jumping-ness, the image of alpine skiing-ness, the image of biathlon-ness, the image of cross-country skiing-ness, the image of creativeness, the image of cooperativeness, the image of competitiveness, the image of objectiveness, the image of discovery-ness, the image of subjectiveness, etc. From the above kinds of images of elements, the image of the denotative structure in the skiing human image is formed. The above various images of elements are the various aspects of the skiing human image, and they are things that have been culled from researchers in physical education and sports sociology and scholastic physical education. Then the images of the various elements in the denotative structure act in a way that promotes the idealistic condition of the connotative structure, while at the same time they are the superior denotative elements that act in a way that promotes the idealistic condition of the elements in the image of the denotative structure. Therefore, each of the elements in the denotative structure themselves is an element that is superior and acts ideally.

In the above manner, the skiing human image itself is the purpose of the existence of the skiing human in every country in the world. Therefore, this is limited by the existence of the skiing human, and in reality there is a purpose in straining to derive the skiing human image from this existence. For example, in order to explain this skiing human image as a skiing human image in reality, we can divide the skiing human image into its various different types, such as the biathlon-ness image, the cross-country-ness image, the alpine skiing-ness image, the freestyle skiing-ness image, the slalom-ness image, and so on. We can express concretely the goal of the skiing human if we look, for instance, at the slalom from various points of view. From the point of view of school level, there are slalom human images in the elementary school and the high school. From the point of view of sex, there are the male slalom human image and the female slalom human image. From the point of view of age, there are the ten-year-old slalom human image and the forty-year-old slalom human image. From the point of view of nationality, there are the slalom human image as an American, the slalom human image as a Japanese, the slalom human image as a Russian, the slalom human image as a Swede, the slalom human image as an Australian, the slalom human image as a Frenchman, the slalom human image as a German, the slalom human image as an Italian, and so on. In other words, because the existence of all types of the slalom human in every country of the world is different, the purpose of the slalom human can be materialized as different goals by the nationalities, national languages, backgrounds of national histories, and other national differences. On the other hand, while the skiing human image can make as its purpose the various unique human images of each country in the world, from a global, humanistic, common point of view, it can also present a purpose that is the skiing human image as a world citizen, provided that the existence of all types of the skiing human practicing all kinds of skiing in all places around the world can be confirmed, this purpose can be erected as a common purpose of all types of the world citizen, or perhaps mankind, skiing human image.

Above, I have presented the purpose of the skiing human or, more specifically, the substance of the skiing human image (limited to only the important substance necessary in skiing theory). As a result, we have reached a point at which the following kinds of questions can be answered:

Question 1: Why are the educational ministries of every country in the world practicing all types of skiing in scholastic physical education?
Answer: All types of skiing are being practiced in scholastic physical education in every country in the world in order to realize all types of the skiing human image as the specific humans of every country in the world.

Question 2: Why are the educational ministries of every country in the world offering classes on the theory concerning all 'types of skiing in scholastic physical education?

Answer: This is so that in the scholastic physical education of every country in the world, physical education teachers will show the peaceful practice of all types of skiing to the students, and so that they will explain the practice of all types of skiing to the students and the students will understand them.

Question 3: Why are the physical education and sports researchers of every country in the world needed for conducting research in fields such as physical education and sports psychology, physical education and sports philosophy, physical education and sports physiology, physical education and sports history, physical education and sports sociology, etc.? Furthermore, is it necessary in human society, the human nation, and the human world?

Answer: It is absolutely necessary for national formation of physical education and sports studies (including skiing study). This is so that the place of skiing in every country in the world will be realized. This research is the guarantee of the sound practice of skiing every country. Also, through this research we, all physical education and sports scholars, can build the national theory of the skiing in every country in the world that supports the human nations and human world.

Question 4: Why must a World Physical Education and Sports Academy be established, in fact?

Answer: Relying on the development of this type of research, the skiing human image in every country in the world and the skiing human image of each era of mankind will be constructed, thus developing the guarantee of peace in every country and world peace. Also, the academy will nurture physical education and sports researchers who will contribute to peace in every country and to world peace or will work as responsible professors in the future at colleges, universities, and graduate schools who support the nation and world as a human society through their true theory or knowledge?

Question 5: Why must a Physical Education and Sports Academy be established in every country in the world?

Answer: Physical education and sports researchers (from all the fields) are necessary to conduct the national skiing theory in every country and guarantee that the practice of skiing in every country in the world is a peaceful practice. And through these efforts, we are able to promise prosperity of the nation and prosperity of mankind. (The ministry of education in every nation currently has to answer all of the questions concerning skiing in public because of letting pupils and students practice some kinds of skiing, performing from elementary school to graduate school. Instead of the ministry of educations in all nations, we scholars of physical education and sports in all nations take responsibility to answer the questions concerning skiing in public.)

Another question we can pose in order to recover our professional trust in all nations is: Why do we need doctors of physical education and sports studies? Why do we have to plan the doctoral programs in graduate schools in all nations? What does this term *professor of physical education and sports studies* mean? More sharply, why do we need a professor for our studies, physical education and sports studies? Does professor mean a player of talk without responsibilities for actual physical education and sports practices? Why do we need faculties of physical education in colleges, universities, and graduate schools for the human nation and mankind, etc.?

In addition, any questions concerning the purpose of formation related to all types of skiing in every country in the world can be answered from the teleology of the skiing human. Also, from this purpose it is necessary to go on to develop support for peace in every country and world peace.

Furthermore, from the presentation of the ontology and teleology of skiing human in every country in the world we must now go on to develop the methodology of the skiing human in every country in the world by which the existence of the skiing human in every country in the world realizes the skiing human image of every country in the world. This will deal with the method by which the existence of the skiing human in every country in the world realizes the skiing human image. The methodology will be organically connected to the ontology and the teleology and will have the unique quality of working together with them. This kind of undertaking will work through the realization of the establishment of universal skiing theory, which unites all countries in the world and accepts differences among all countries in the world.

8

The Methodology of the Skiing Human
(or Snow Human)

The methodology of the skiing human is an original theoretical area that deals with both the movement human and the snow movement sides of the phenomenon of all types of skiing. These two sides, which are referred to directly by the term *skiing human*, can be said to work together to emphasize the movement snow as a skiing human. Only the ability required for the movement snow as a skiing human is required of the movement human as a skiing human. (It means qualified snow for skiers in sociological expression.) On the other hand, if we emphasize the movement human as skiing human, only the ability required for the movement human as skiing human is required of the movement human as skiing human. (It means that skillful movement of skier is needed.) Therefore, achieving the required ability that is possible when both sides accept each other's demands is imperative. This type of method is the only advanced method by which the skiing human image can be realized in each nation in the world. Toward that end, there are notably two methodologies, one in relation to time (era, etc.) and one in relation to space (nation, etc.). The former considers the experience of becoming a skiing human in terms of time, while the latter considers the experience of becoming a skiing human in terms of space. Therefore, the method that realizes the skiing human image must give the appropriate weight to experience in time and experience in space.

Theoretical Foundation and Ground for the
Formation of the Skiing Human Methodology

Before presenting the methodology of the skiing human, it is necessary to first make clear the reasons why it is possible to present such a methodology. In order to do this, we must look at the theoretical foundation and the ground for the methodology. The theoretical foundation for the formation of the methodology of the skiing human relies on the educational, social, and movement-cultural ontologies of the skiing human and the teleology of the skiing human already presented. The ground for the formation of this methodology is the fact that in scholastic physical education in every country around the world skiing is being practiced. The former is based on the development of the theory, while the latter comes from the practice of skiing.

The Characteristics of the Methodology of the Skiing Human

There are two characteristics associated with the content of the methodology of the skiing human. First, it is an unchangeable, universal, abstract methodology, applicable to any country at any time. Second, as countries (space) and eras (time) change, it is a concrete, realistic methodology that changes accordingly. The methodology of the skiing human is constructed with the former at the core, while the latter surrounds it, both working together to preserve the relationship. More specifically, the former is the area of the methodology based on the common qualities of all countries and constructed by the physical education and sports researchers of every country in the world so that the practice of skiing in scholastic physical education in every country in the world serves to realize the skiing human image in each era. Meanwhile, the latter is the area of the methodology that has the quality of grasping the differences between the realistic aspects of the skiing human by country, era, age, sex, school, etc., as differences in realistic aspects.

Elements of the Formation of the Contents of the Methodology of the Skiing Human

In regard to the formation of the methodology of the skiing human, both the theoretical foundation and the practical ground have been presented already. However, I believe that the latter, the practical ground, gives an extraordinarily important reason for the formation of the methodology of the skiing human. Namely, because of the existence of the practice of skiing in physical education programs, the existence of the practice of skiing in society, and the existence of physical education teachers, mentors, and students who play a function in society, the need for the methodology of the skiing human becomes apparent.

In that case, physical education teachers and mentors are those who lead students to become skiing humans and realize the skiing human image, while students and followers who receive all forms of skiing education are those who look toward becoming all forms of skiing humans and realizing all forms of the skiing human image. Therefore, the human relationship of the teachers and mentors and students and followers in the phenomenon of the skiing will all become the skiing human and realize the skiing human image. It is a mutual relationship that exists to realize the skiing human image.

Those fostering the skiing human have experience in the past of fully (deeply and widely) becoming skiing humans in order to realize the skiing human image. They are those who possess the leadership qualifications to be able to realize the skiing human image. On the other hand, those becoming skiing humans must receive leadership in order to realize the skiing human image. They are those of whom study ability is demanded.

With the relationship between physical education teachers who try to realize the skiing human image and foster students as skiing humans, who study while looking toward becoming skiing humans and realizing the skiing human image, as the ground, the various structural elements of the methodology of the various kinds of skiing human are formed. Specifically, these elements include study, leadership, evaluation, curriculum, educational resources, study ability, study processes, leadership ability, skill, etc. Classifying these elements into large groups, we may divide them into study, leadership, and educational resources. All the terms of study skill, ability, study process, etc., are technical terms connected with the student or following becoming a skiing human and trying to realize the skiing human image, and they therefore belong to the terms of the study. The terms *leadership ability, evaluation, curriculum*, etc., are all terms connected with the teachers and mentors trying to realize the skiing human image and turn their students into skiing humans and are therefore leadership terms. Finally, that which brings the leadership and study together at the place of the skiing is the educational resources. The structural elements of the methodology of the skiing human are systematized in the manner described in the figure below.

Study. This is the state of those becoming skiing humans in which they learn all of the various things they must learn from those helping them to become skiing humans in order to realize the skiing human image.

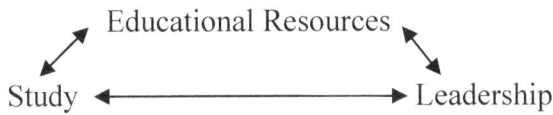

Figure 53. The structural element of the methodology of the skiing human in each nation in the world

Also, we will call students those who, under the supervision of those fostering the skiing human, strive to learn that which they need to become skiing humans. Furthermore, study ability is ability that students possess to learn all the constructive knowledge required in order to become a skiing human and realize the skiing human image. Skill of study is a part of study ability and is the condition of the mastery of the necessary techniques required to become a skiing human and realize the skiing human image. Also, study process is the process by which, under the leadership of those fostering the skiing human, those becoming skiing humans learn all of the relevant knowledge.

Leadership. This is defined as the ability to lead those who will become skiing human by those who will foster their becoming skiing humans by giving them all the various knowledge they will need toward the goal of realizing the skiing human image. Leadership ability is the ability of those fostering skiing humans, with the goal of realizing the skiing human image, to fully develop those becoming skiing humans (students). The leadership process is the process by which those fostering skiing humans, with the goal of realizing the skiing human image, lead those becoming skiing humans. Furthermore, evaluation is the process by which those fostering skiing humans decide what level those becoming skiing humans have reached and how far they have advanced in approaching the realization of the skiing human image. Curriculum is the study route through which those fostering skiing humans lead those becoming skiing humans in order to realize the skiing human image.

Educational Resources. We collectively use this term to refer to all materials those fostering skiing humans use to lead those becoming skiing humans to realize the skiing human image, along with all study materials used by those becoming skiing humans aiming to realize the skiing human image. Therefore, the educational resources play the role of intermediary in the formation of the leadership and study of the skiing human and are a necessary methodological element in the realization of the skiing human image. The educational resources include natural educational resources and man-made educational resources. The former are sunshine, air, weather (clear, rainy, snowy, cloudy), air pressure (wind), water (water in a pond or lake), earth (ski ground), etc. The latter include gymnasium (man-made ski ground), lighting, clothes, tools, shoes, stages, etc. Therefore, in the broad sense of the term, *educational resources* refers to the combination of natural educational resources and man-made educational resources, but when taken in the narrow sense of the word refers mostly to man-made educational resources.

The Construction Method of the Methodology of the Skiing Human as National Theory in Every Nation in the World

It is imperative that we use the terminology of the structural elements of the methodology of the skiing human, namely, *study* (*skill, study process, learning*, etc.) *leadership* (*evaluation, curriculum, leadership process, leadership ability*, etc.), and *educational resources*, in order to realize the skiing human image. However, it is also necessary to answer the question of how the content of these elements can be given substance. I will now present these kinds of problems related to the construction of the methodology of the skiing human.

From the standpoint of those dealing with fundamental theory of physical education studies, it is possible to construct a methodology that answers these kinds of questions. The methodology of the skiing human should use the original specialized vocabulary from each specialized area of physical education, and considering study, leadership, educational resources, etc., we can create a separate methodology from each field of physical education that serves to realize every partial image of the skiing human in each era and each nation that emerges from that field. In regard to the methodology of the skiing human from physical education physiology, for instance, while considering study, leadership, and educational resources we can construct an original methodology, using the specialized terms of physiology, such as *strength, physique, health*, and *flexibility*, that serve to realize the strength image, the physique image, the health image, and the flexibility image of the skiing human.

Likewise, in regard to the methodology of the skiing human from physical education psychology, while considering study, leadership, and educational resources we can construct an original methodology, using the specialized terms of psychology, such as *character, morale, mental health, flexibility*, etc., that serve to realize the character image, the morale image, the mental health image, the flexibility image, etc., of the skiing human. In regard to the methodology of the skiing human from the physical education philosophy, while considering study, leadership, and educational resources we can construct an original methodology, using the specialized terms of philosophy, such as *mind, body, mind-body relationship, soul, flesh*, etc., that serves to realize the mind image, the body image, the mind-body relationship image, the soul image, the flesh image, etc., of the skiing human. In regard to the methodology of the skiing human from physical education educational science, while considering study, leadership, and educational resources we can construct an original methodology, using the specialized terms of educational science, such as *creativity, subjectivity, objectivity, cooperation, competition*, etc., that serve to realize the creativity image, the subjectivity image, the objectivity image, the cooperation image, the competition image, etc., of the skiing human. In regard to the methodology of the skiing human from physical education sociology, while considering study, leadership, and educational resources we can construct an original methodology as a national theory, using the specialized terms of sociology, such as performer, amateur, professional, sports, physical education, etc., that serve to realize the performer image, the amateur image, the professional image, the sports image, the physical education image, etc., of the skiing human. In regard to the methodology of the skiing human from physical education and sports biomechanics, while considering study, leadership, and educational resources we can construct an original methodology as a national theory, using the specialized terms of biomechanics, such as *jump, land, run, walk, stand, hang, turn*, etc., that serve to realize the jumping image, the landing image, the running image, the walking image, the standing image, etc., of the skiing human. Moreover, the construction of the original methodology of the skiing human for each of these specialized fields of physical education must be living, changing entities, taking into account the realistic existence of things such as nationality, race, age, sex, etc., to always be the best methodology for physical education researchers at the current time. Therefore, the research specialists in each field of physical education must, while referring to the knowledge of physical education history for advice, construct separate methodologies as national theories responsible for each specialized field.

In the above manner, it is possible to construct a methodology of the skiing human for every country in the world. Thus we are able to form a national methodology of skiing study in each country in the world and in each era by each national language.

Part VI

Theory of International Dance Studies for the Achievement of Peace

1

A Word from the Author

The term dance human is a symbolic term that works toward national peace and world peace. We, the world's physical education and sports scholars, must treat this term as dearly as our own lives. This is because without the existence of the dance human, none of the language concerning dance and research concerning dance could be formed. The existence builds and determines it all. The dance humans use American English, Japanese, German, French, Italian, Korean, British English, Spanish, etc., in the phenomenon of dance. For example, the dance humans in China speak Chinese in the phenomenon of dance, the dance humans in Russia speak Russian in the phenomenon of dance, and the dance humans in the United States speak American English in the phenomenon of dance. The dance humans also use other words like sound (noisy or nice), imitation sound, and onomatopoeic words in the phenomenon of dance. All the national language making in the phenomenon of dance is proof of the existence of dance human. The term dance human will be the universal language of the world's physical education and sports scholars as long as the phenomenon of dance continues actually in all the nations. It is a specialized term, even a holy term. Dance human is dance human. The dance human is not human, because dance human indicates people dancing in the phenomenon of dance.

I present this chapter for the benefit of all the physical education and sports scholars of each of the world's nations.

2

Establishing the Hypothesis for Creating Dance Studies

The following questions are the fundamental motives for attempting to create the theory of international dance studies for the achievement of peace (principle of physical education and sports studies and research for all nations in the world):

1. Why, in the scholastic physical education programs of the education ministries of each country in the world, are teachers or professors using any types of dances as the educational resource to lead students?
2. Why are the physical education and sports researchers of each country in the world conducting research concerning any types of dances?
3. Why are physical education teachers and physical education and sports researchers and professors of every country in the world conducting classes in schools, colleges, universities, and graduate schools concerning the theory of any types of dances?
4. Why does the research concerning the dances belong to the physical education and sports studies?
5. Why is the research concerning the dances worthy of doctorates or master's degrees in physical education and sports studies?

Currently there is no theory in the world's physical education and sports research that can answer these fundamental questions of dance research. I have been speculating about such a fundamental question as a theory or principle of physical education and sports studies. And I believe that this is a very important question or problem to which a solution must be found. Therefore, I have undertaken this task. By pointedly asking myself these questions and trying to answer them, and from the reality of dance and dialogue of the dances, I have endeavored to construct this theory. These problems, which are the motives for this research and contemplation I have undertaken, are vitally important and are the fundamental driving force behind this research and contemplation.

Here, in order to answer the question: "What are all types of dance and, more generally, what is dance?" I have formed the following hypothesis: "When a human does a dance is when a human becomes a dance human. (When a human does a dance is not not when a human becomes a human.)" As a reason for the formation of the hypothesis, I believe that to do a dance is to do a dance, and to do a dance is not not doing a dance. To do is to become.

This new term, which will become a specialized term used among physical education and sports scholars, has been created in order to connect terms such as *dance* and terms included in it (*ballet, social dance, folk dance, creative dance*, etc). This new term is also a word that specialists in physical education and sports use in the moving, changing, and living world. Moreover, physical education and sports teachers and professors are able to take their responsibilities from the national and international reality of dances that they should teach to physical education and sports students and followers. Also in this book, I have used the term *movement human*. When we perceive the phenomenon of the dance, we see people moving. In order to express the existence of the moving human being (apart from the technique one may have in one's arms, legs, neck, head, and trunk) in one noun phrase, we say "movement human." This term refers to the entire existence of the human (including the individual as a dancer) and some other as another dancer dynamically working together in both a passive and active relationship.

The term dance human is used to represent collectively all of the various types of dance, such as folk-dance human, creative dance human, ballet human, social-dance human, etc. Each of these terms refers directly to the existence of the working relationship between a human and image in each type of dance. The image means all visualized things that dance human (dancer) creates and remembers inside his head. It becomes the contents of expression of the dance human (dancer). The image is sometimes brought out by music, photos, paintings, etc., in front of an audience. It is made visually an emotional and an intellectual story of the drama that dance human (dancer) thinks in fact. Therefore the image means dance human who belongs to movement image. The image means living, moving images in the phenomenon of dance. It is this relationship, too, that gives life to and maintains the socially significant term *dance*.

Next I would like to explain in detail what is directly indicated by the term *dance*. The object to which the term *dance human* refers is the entirety of the working relationship between a movement image and a movement human in the phenomenon of the dance or in the phenomenon in which an image (coming from a dancer himself) is dealt with. In the world of dance, the movement human and the movement image together make up the dance human. (He is also called a dancer by physical education and sports sociologists.) In this situation, the movement human is a movement human related to a movement image, and the movement image is a movement image related to movement human. Therefore, the two share a common point that connects them together. Specifically, this common point is the existential form in which the dance humans work together in mutual independence and in certain aspects moving in a uniform independence and in certain aspects moving in a uniform motion. However, if we look objectively at them, we are able to divide the dance human and a movement image as a dance human. The images are furthermore accompanied by the music, sounds, and silence. For instance, there exists a dance human without music, as in pantomime.

Therefore, in presenting the theory, in order to refer directly to both the dance human as a movement human and the dance human as a movement image, we will use the term *dance human* for simplification. Only when we wish to make an explicit distinction between the two sides do we use the expression *a movement human as a dance human and a movement image as a dance human*. Therefore, the expression of the dance human refers to both the movement human and movement image side of the dance.

There were many reasons for the creation of the special term *dance human*, but the most important of these was the need to distinguish the general human existence (in abstract dimension) from the existence experienced in the special world in which dance is dealt with in physical education and sports studies and to make this special independence clear. In addition, it serves to help construct theories (dance studies) to explain the unique practice of dance.

The next matter with which we must concern ourselves is taking the special essential existence from the complicated dynamic phenomena of dance in reality, because I think that the essential human existence in the phenomenon of dance works into the specific phenomenon of dance and determines the world of dance. Specifically, in what form does this living phenomenon appear to our eyes? In other words, which actions in the living phenomenon of the dance are essential and nonessential in the specific human existence? Understanding this distinction and synthesis will lead to a clear insight into this living phenomenon of dance.

In order to answer these questions, I will examine the living phenomenon of dance itself, relying on intuitive analysis and the integrated judgment method. As was stated in the hypothesis, the essence of the existence of the living phenomenon of dance and the phenomenon in which an image is dealt with and the nonessence of that existence (auxiliary actions to the existential essence) are manifested in the various aspects of the dance human, such as the track-and-field human, ball human, skating human, skiing human, etc. Please see figure 54 for an explanation of this idea. There are the essential structural elements and nonessential structural elements that form the living phenomenon of dance. (See figure 54).

If we analyze the primary factors that form the movement relying on our perceptions of the dance phenomenon and then integrate these back together, we can come to understand the movement itself. For example, if we look at the action of the dance human, we see that he acts on the ground, water, equipment, ice, snow, air, ball, human, etc., in realities to form the living phenomenon of dance through the moving images. The instant dance human acts in relation to the ground, he begins to exist as a track-and-field human. The instant dance human acts in relation to another person we see the appearance of a martial arts human. Furthermore, in the instant the dance human

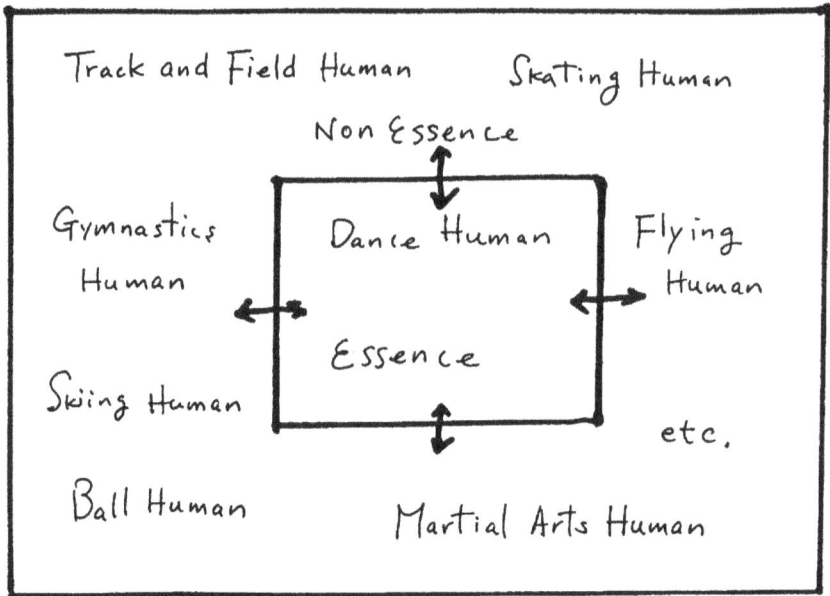

Figure 54. Formation elements of the living phenomenon of dance in each nation in the world

acts on the snow, then he begins to exist as a skiing human. There are the auxiliary actions in the living phenomenon of dance that create motion. They act indirectly on the movement existence of the dance human.

In order to determine if figure 54 is true or false, let us try to return to the living phenomenon (the fact) of each type of dance. For instance, I can explain the living phenomenon of creative dance by using a graph. We can say that the actions of the creative dance human appear as the existential essence in the creative dance. At the same time, the phenomenon appears as a composition of transient aspects of the nonessential, such as the ball human, the martial arts human, the track-and-field human, etc. More specifically, the phenomenon of creative dance human is, most importantly, the actions of the images by which movement is created as a creative dance human and the action of the dance human. However, this creative dance human is also in dynamic contact with the floor of the gymnasium, like the track-and-field human. The living phenomenon of the creative dance in the outdoor falling snow also involves the actions of the relationships between the creative dance human and the snow, the ground, etc., on which he acts, if the creative dance human does it outdoors. However, the determining factors in the valuation of the creative dance, above all, are determined by the actions of the creative dance human (as the movement image for the sake of doing creative dance and the movement human for the sake of doing creative dance).

Therefore, it is possible to say that all of the living phenomena of the various types of dance can be found in every country in the world, being formed by a mixture of the characteristics of the living phenomena of the dance human, the track-and-field human, the skiing human, the ball human, etc. Most important, all of the phenomena are formed from the existential essence of the dance human. Namely, the living actions of the dance human determine the process and result of the dance. As evidence for this, we can say that the points of the dance depend on the actions of the existence of the dance human. The actions of the existence of the dance human provide dynamic variation to the aspects of the phenomenon, and the result of dance is determined by them. They also produce a lot of words in national languages and nonwords like sounds and imitation sounds in the phenomenon of creative dance. Therefore, the actions of creative dance human determine everything in the phenomenon of creative dance.

I would like to put this idea (that the phenomenon of dance is the mutual actions of image, with music, with sentences, with talking, with memories, with voices, etc.) and the human, namely, the dance human, in the form of a hypothesis. However, in order to do this we must know the existential essence of the phenomenon of dance. This would be the factual ground or formation of these words. In order to speak scientifically about the phenomenon of the dance and phenomena in which image is dealt with, we must make this existential essence that will be the object of the analysis very clear. In other words, it is necessary to confirm whether or not the term *dance human* is a term that possesses realistic qualities in the phenomenon of the dance.

Thus I began to think that I could incorporate this method into an ontology of the dance human. In other words, using the term *dance human* I will explain in detail the reality of dance. Thus, should it be possible to prove this hypothesis, dance human would be the existential essence in the phenomenon of the dance and would become specialized terminology whose use would be required any time dance research is being conducted. Furthermore, we would be given the road toward the construction of a theory of dance studies dealing with the entirety of practice and theory. It would be possible to advance the theory by means of a teleology and a methodology and finally to form dance theory (in a world united and different). A distinction would be made between the aspects of dance studies that affect the daily life of humans and special areas of dance studies. When names are given to these boundaries, dance studies will be formed.

I have ascertained that the existence of the dance human can be grasped as three aspects, and in this way I hope to make this existence clear. Specifically, these are the movement-cultural existence of the dance human, the educational existence of the dance human, and the social existence of the dance human. These all point to the fact that in every country in the world the dance human exists in many ways and forms a special world. I will begin from my understanding of the existence of this dance human-the dance human that exists in every country in the world.

3

The Movement-Cultural Ontology
of the Dance Human

The dance human lives in the movement culture, and the dance human exists possessing movement-cultural aspects. This comes from a connotative structure and a denotative structure. Together they maintain independent functions while living and existing as a whole.

The Connotative Structure

The dance human as a movement human is organically composed with a head, a torso, hands, and feet. Internally he is partially muscles, bones, organs, a brain, etc., which all rely on blood for their actions. However, the dance human as movement human is actually made of many materials, such as a certain amount of air, and various other objects, all of which will be acted upon by the existing life energy. These are based on factors of nature, which include gravity, temperature, climate, sunshine, rain, snow, etc., and artificial factors, which include gymnasiums, ground, lighting, etc., and they act on individual or group behavior and skill. However, these factors act together with factors dependent on the dance human as a movement human himself, such as perception, thought, emotion, etc. Therefore, the dance human as a movement human exists as a complex synthesis of the various factors that make up each dance human.

As individual actions, the two sides (the dance human as a movement human and the dance human as a movement image) approach each other, come into contact, and separate from one another. These actions consist of various types, such as receiving, throwing, grasping, kicking, running, jumping, pushing, holding, etc.

As group actions, the two sides (the dance human as a movement human and the dance human as a movement image) approach each other, come into contact, and separate from one another. These group actions consist of various types, such as yelling, using signals, watching, etc.

The actions of the individual and group technical skills are based on the actions of eyes, ears, tongue, skin, etc., of the dance human as a movement human and the actions of bones, bowels, and organs such as the heart, lungs, etc. Finally, the actions of, thought, emotion, etc., also contribute. In other words, while the sensation/thought/emotion system's parts have independent functions, they are organically and dynamically related and participate in the skilled actions of the dance human as a movement human. In making value judgments about skilled actions, such as good/bad, achieved/not achieved, the dance human as a movement human relies greatly on the actions of the sensation/thought/emotion system. The decisions and conflicts are that "My head hurts, but I have to keep playing hard," "I'm tired, so I'll quit soon," "I do dance and my dance will be performed smoothly," "that image is grasped clearly (or I remember it), so I do my best," "my legs hurt, but I have to try harder," "my teacher watches the performances of my dance, so I try to do my best," etc. These phrases point to the dynamic actions of dance human of sensation/thought/ emotion, sensation/emotion/thought/sensation, and so on (figure 55).

The Denotative Structure

The dance human as movement human exists in various movement-cultural aspects. If we were to classify these movement-cultural aspects, we could classify them into the following four types.

The first type includes a kind of dance event in which either the image (dance human) just separates from the human (dance human) or the human (dance human) just separates from the image (dance human). No dance events of this type appear nowadays. However, this kind of dance event might be created by some dance specialists in the future.

The second type includes dance events in which the action of the human (as the dance human) and the image (as the dance human) are mutually disjunctive and conjunctive, such as creative dance, ballet, pantomime, etc.

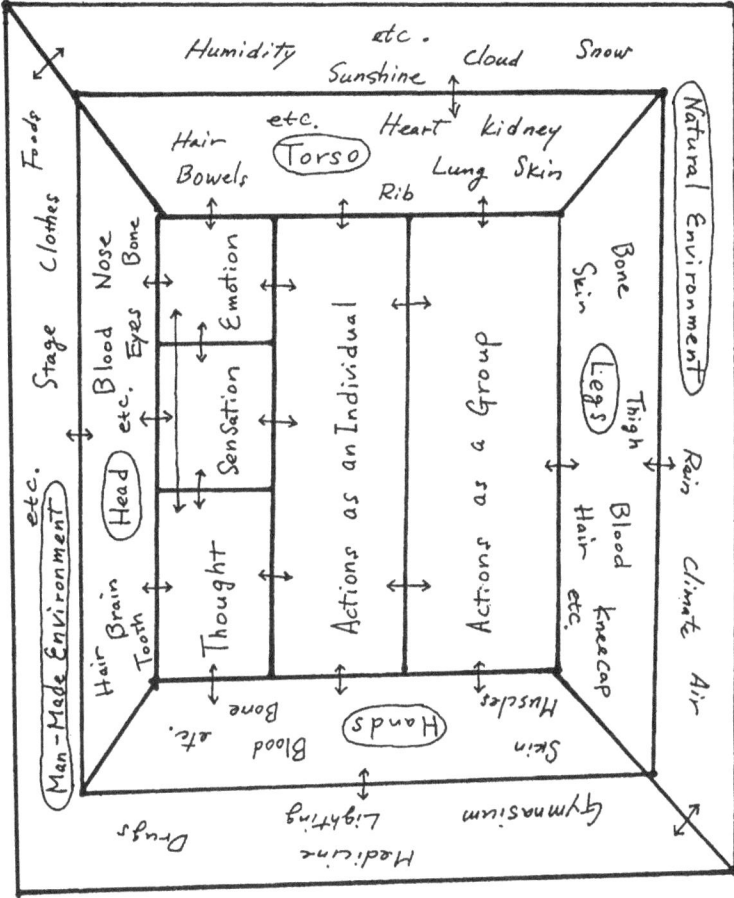

Figure 55. The many kinds of actions of the connotative structure of dance human in each nation in the world

While both type 1and type 2 deal with individualistic movement-cultural properties, both the following type 3 and type 4 deal with movement-cultural properties that are oriented by a group of more than two people from the human (or dance human).

The third type includes dance events in which the actions of the group dance human as a movement human attempt to approach the image or separate from the image. Today dances of this type have not made an appearance in reality.

The fourth type of dance human in the phenomenon of dance is the dance human in which the dance human as a movement human in the group and dance human as movement image in the group repeat actions of mutual approach, separation, and contact. The folk-dance human, ballet human, social-dance human, and creative dance human belong to this fourth type.

In this manner, it is possible to classify the movement-cultural existence of every dance phenomenon based on the substance and type of actions of the dance human. (Refer to figure 56). However, each dance human as a movement human exists in a manner that presents unique aspects. The folk-dance human exists with unique aspects not found in ballet human. (The folk-dance human is absolutely folk dance human.) The creative dance human exists with unique aspects not found in ballet human. (The creative dance human is absolutely creative human, in fact.) Therefore, each type of dance human appears in his own unique movement-cultural aspects.

Ballet-ness (the Ballet Human as Movement Human)

The dance human as a movement human exists in aspects of ballet. For example, there is either a direct or indirect relation to the equipment of ballet, the rules of ballet, the facilities of ballet, the terminology of ballet, etc. The appearance of the ballet human as a movement human forms the unique world of the ballet.

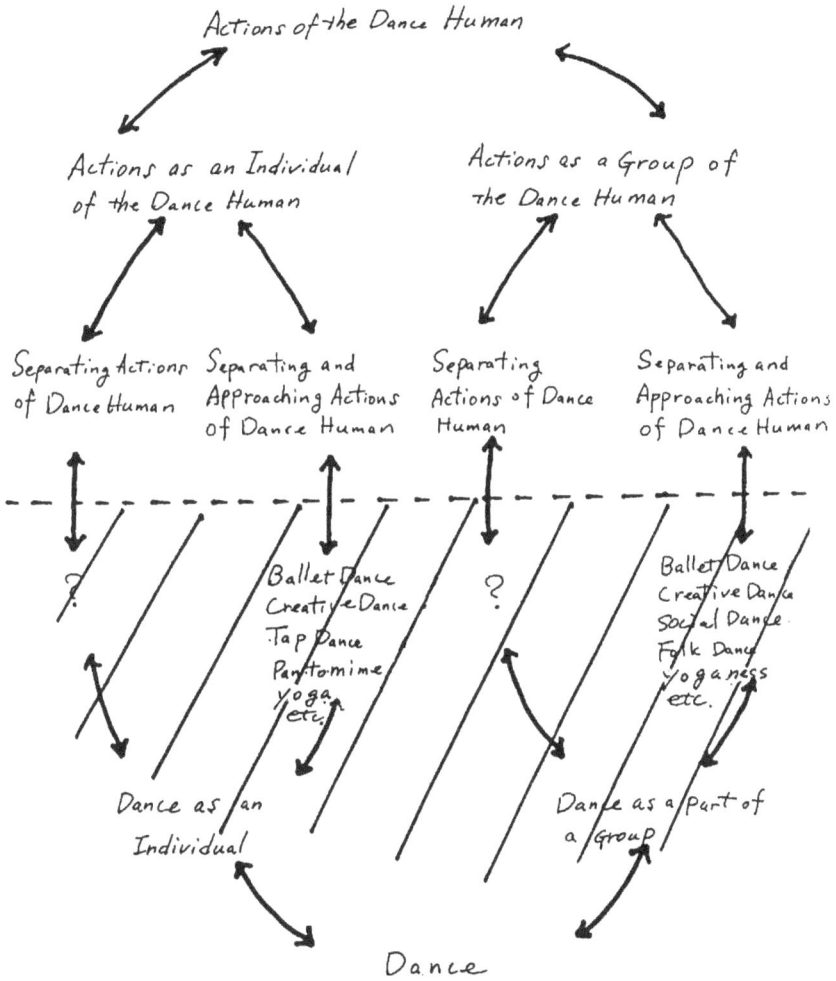

Actions of the Dance Human

Actions as an Individual of the Dance Human

Actions as a Group of the Dance Human

Separating Actions of Dance Human

Separating and Approaching Actions of Dance Human

Separating Actions of Dance Human

Separating and Approaching Actions of Dance Human

?

Ballet Dance
Creative Dance
Tap Dance
Pantomime
yoga
etc.

?

Ballet Dance
Creative Dance
Social Dance
Folk Dance
yoga ness
etc.

Dance as an Individual

Dance as a Part of a Group

Dance

Figure 56. The movement-cultural existence of the dance human in each nation in the world

249

Creative-Dance-ness
(the Creative Dance Human as Movement Human)

The dance human as a movement human exists in aspects of creative dance. For example, there is either a direct or indirect contact with the equipment of creative dance, the rules of creative dance, the facilities of creative dance, the terminology of creative dance, etc. The appearance of the creative dance human forms the unique world of creative dance.

Folk Dance-ness
(the Folk-Dance Human as Movement Human)

The dance human as a movement human exists in aspects of folk dance. For example, there is either a direct or indirect relation to the equipment of folk dance, the rules of folk dance, the terminology of folk dance, the facilities of folk dance, etc. The appearance of the folk dance human form the unique world of folk dancing.

Social Dance-ness
(the Social Dance Human as Movement Human)

The dance human as a movement human exists in aspects of social dance. For example, there is either a direct or indirect, contact with the equipment of social dance, the rules of social dance, the facilities of social dance, the terminology of social dance, etc. The appearance of the social dance human forms the unique world of social dance.

As there are several dances that have been introduced in the above-mentioned, there may increase dance events in future as new dance event we have never seen appear, In this way, the dance human as a movement human exists in all the various movement-cultural aspects in every country in the world, in the United States as Americans, in Russia as Russians, in France as Frenchmen, in England as Englishmen, and in China as Chinese. The dance human exists in these various movement-cultural aspects.

4

The Educational Ontology
of the Dance Human

In the special society of physical education in every country in the world the dance human as a movement human exists, possessing an aspect of the physical education. Every type of dance is evaluated educationally. Certainly, opinions are formed about whether a dance builds a certain strength, develops character, fosters mental growth, fosters creativity, etc. The educational existence of the dance human as a movement human comes from a connotative structure and a denotative structure. Each works based on an independent structure, and as a whole they exist educationally.

The Connotative Structure

In order to make clear the actions of the dance human, we will analyze them and use integrated judgment, by looking both from the social actions of the dance human toward the living energy and from the living energy toward the social actions of the dance human. In this manner, we can grasp fully the entire substance of the actions of the dance human. We have some factors that are expressed, such as body strength, flexibility, etc., while in contrast, some factors are expressive, such as the mind, soul, character, personality, condition of character, morale, flexibility, etc. These factors work in a living, separate manner, and at the same time the actions of dance human are in the integration of all of these living elements. By using these words to inquire about the nature of the actions of the dance human, we can elucidate the concept of the dance human. Therefore, these words refer to the various partial factors that make up the dance human.

They are living words. The source of these words is based upon the supply and demand of living energy produced by the unification (actions of digestion, actions of oxidation) that takes place inside the individual of the mutually conflicting elements of air and food. In other words, the source is the transformation of the various elements, such as body strength, flexibility of body, physique, physical condition, mind, soul, morale, flexibility of mind, personality, condition of character, etc., into a living entity. Therefore, the words *body strength, flexibility of body, physique, physical condition, mind, soul, morale, flexibility of mind, personality*, and *condition of character* are all living words and are words that have come to refer to reality.

On the other hand, we have said that the action of the dance human is formed from a synthesis of the various types of action of the dance human expressed as mind, body, soul, physique, physical condition, body strength, flexibility of body, condition of character, morale, and flexibility of mind. It should be noted that in our analysis of the actions of the dance human we said that there is both an image movement and a movement human side as the dance human, with mutually different objects. Since this is the case, it may not be appropriate to use the same type of language to explain both. However, based on the common point of view that both share as the dance human, we will use the same language to explain them.

The analysis and synthesis of these two sides, the dance human as a movement human and the dance human as a movement image, are shown in figure 57 and figure 58.

Also making up the actions of the dance human are skilled actions, which express technique. However, if we analyze these skilled actions, we can see that they are made up of actions of the conduct of the dance human and the substance of the kind of technique being expressed. In other words, the .actions of the conduct of the dance human, together with the substance of the technique, make up the reality of the skilled action of the dance human and exist united in reality. These exist in a relationship that is mutually life-giving and enlivened, creating the phenomenon of the skilled existence of the dance human.

The Denotative Structure

In regard to the denotative structure of the educational existence of the dance human, I have attempted some analytical speculation that will explain it, as shown in Figure 59.

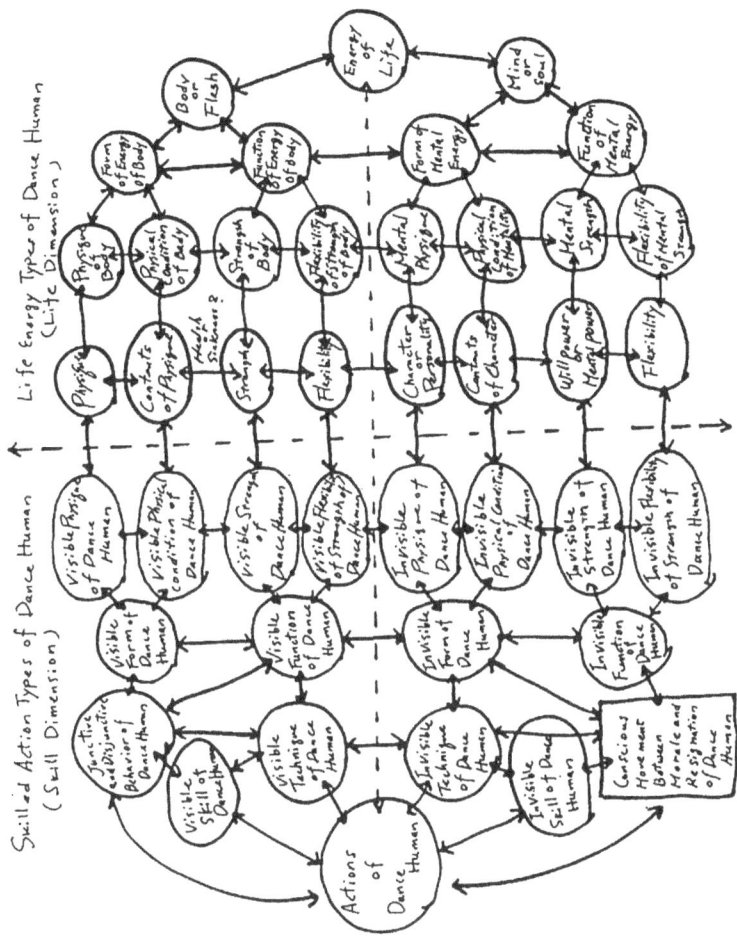

Figure 57. Action types of the dance human in each nation in the world

I The Visible Physique of the Dance Human

   Movement Human : Size. Weight. Color of skin, Stature. etc.
   Movement Image : Image of Size, Image of Weight, Image of Stature. etc

II The Condition of the Visible Physique of the Dance Human

   Movement Human : Condition of Dance Human. For Example, Illness or Health?
   Movement Image : Condition of Image of Dance Human. For Example, Illness or Health?

III The Visible Physical Function of the Dance Human

   Movement Human : Endurance, Speed, Performance. etc.
   Movement Image : Image of Endurance, Image of Speed, Image of Performance

IV The Condition of the Visible Function of the Dance Human
   Movement Human : Adjustable Ability of Endurance, Adjustable Ability of Performance, Adjustable Ability of Speed, etc.
   Movement Image : Image of Adjustable Ability of Performance, Image of Adjustable Ability of Endurance. etc

- -

V The Invisible Physique of the Dance Human
   Movement Human : Invisible Physique of the Dance Human
   Movement Image : Invisible Shape of the Dance Human

VI The Condition of the Invisible Physique of the Dance Human
   Movement Human : Condition of Invisible Physique of the Dance Human. For Example, Illness or Health?
   Movement Image : Image of Condition of Invisible Physique of the Dance Human. For Example, Illness or Health?

VII The Function of the Invisible Physique of the Dance Human
   Movement Human : Mental Endurance. Mental performance etc
   Movement Image : Image of Mental Endurance, Image of Mental performance. etc

VIII The Condition of the Invisible Function of the Dance Human
   Movement Human : Adjustable Ability of Mental Endurance, Adjustable Ability of Mental Performance. etc.
   Movement Image : Image of Adjustable Ability of Mental Endurance, Image of Adjustable Ability of Mental Endurance. etc

581.

Figure 58. The types and contents of the actions of the
dance human in each nation in the world

First Analysis   Second Analysis

Subjective/Objective
Objective/Subjective
in Dynamic Fact

Education al
Phenomenon of the
Dance Human

Entire Expression
of Dance Human
(Social Stand Point)

Partial Expression
of the Dance
Human.

Society
(Objective)

Discoverness
(Subjective)

Cooperativeness
(Objective)

Creativity
(Subjective)

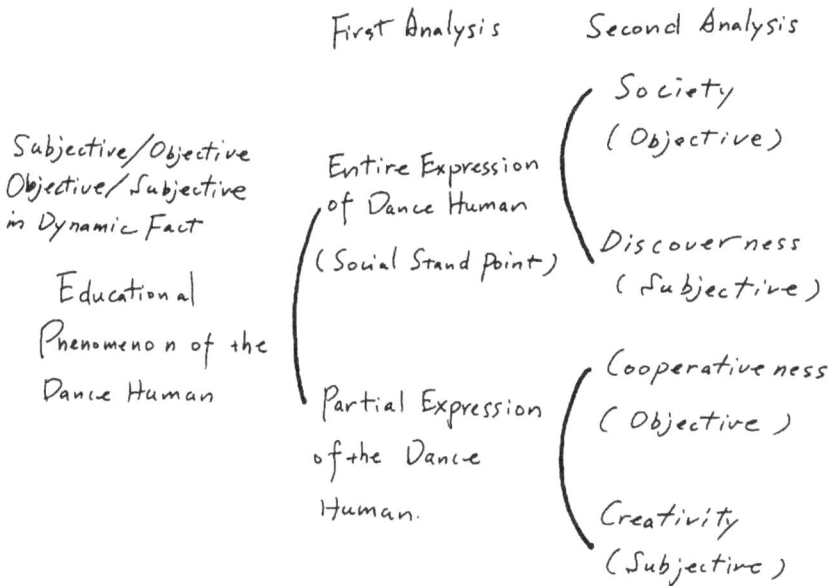

**Figure 59. The educational existence of the
dance human in each nation in the world**

Here I will explain each of the educational elements of the dance human dealt with in the second analysis of the educational phenomenon of the dance human.

Society

The dance human functions in the special society of dance. However, in order to create this special society, he must work by accepting and approving all of the factors. Specifically, the dance human as a movement human that takes on the special social role of player acts both socially and morally The dance human as a movement human (performer) acts in participation with the dance humans that take on the social roles of judges, teachers, leaders, etc., and even with things that are set up for the purpose of becoming a dance human as a movement human, such as unique facilities, equipment, rules, etc. In this manner, the phenomenon of the dance is when, as the dance human as a movement human is enlarged from some person to some thing and from some thing to some person, he acts both socially and morally. However, while the society of the dance human as a movement human provides the nature of a special society, in order that dance occurs in general society, it exists in the twofold relationship with general society and the special society of the dance.

Discovery-ness

The dance human as a movement human acts creatively. At the same time, a dance human as a movement image also acts creatively. In the action of the dance human, there are situations in which new technical content or form, of which no similar example existed in the past, is added. There new techniques are conceptualized and given special names. This itself points to the discovery-ness of the dance human. Names in the events of dance itself point to the discovery-ness of the dance human. For example, we are able to find so many things in the dance of Isadora Duncan of the United States. Her original words for dance that she had created were proof of the discovery-ness of dance human. There is a certain matter in which she brought about the birth of the new dance. In this way, there are situations in which a new dance human is given existence and movement-cultural history is formed. The discovery-ness of the dance human consists of both the creative and historical expansion aspects of these actions.

Cooperativeness

In the phenomenon of dance, there are many cases in which the dance human acts in a group. In these cases, cooperative intentions are demanded of the dance human. This cooperativeness depends on the mutual relationship between acting dance humans that have taken on the social role of the player, and therefore, this is a social action. There is cooperativeness from a unified standpoint and cooperativeness from a different standpoint. For example, the general factors of the school associated with the individual dance human, region, age, sex, etc., may be identical or different. Also, the various factors of the special standpoint of dance, such as skill level of the dance human, the player role, companions, etc., may be identical or different.

In this way, the actions of the cooperativeness of the dance human exist as the nature of the identities and differences of the special things limited only to dance. So if we try to limit it to only the cooperativeness in the special society of dance, the cooperativeness of identity recognition of the dance human is based on the recognition of technical standpoint and the cooperativeness of difference recognition is based on the recognition of existential standpoint.

Creativity

The dance human, in the living, always-changing space of the dance, acts while at every moment being faced with the problem: "In what way should I best handle the image I have?" The dance human as an image movement, which has been acted on by the dance human as a movement image, is a concrete expression of the skill of the dance human as a movement human himself. It is something that indicates the level of skill. Therefore, the dance human as an image movement demands skill from the dance human as a movement human, and conversely, the dance human as a movement human exists while demanding skill from the dance human as an image movement. Through the skill demands of these two sides, the dance human creates. For example, the dance human as a movement image is thrown by the dance human as a movement human, who has taken the social role of a butterfly as a dancer and a skill. Then the dance human as a movement human tries to face this movement image and, through the image of a butterfly as an extension of the individual's body, tries to respond to the skilled action of the movement image as a butterfly. As a result, the butterfly is an image, talking of butterfly. The story of the butterfly, and so forth, will be created.

The creativity of the dance human can be seen in the creativity of the partial cause/effect action of playing and the action of going inside and the action of doing well and the action of failure. Through this partial cause/effect process, the action of winning, the action of losing, and the action of a draw are created. Creativity can be seen in the partial cause/effect actions in the entire process of the dance, from start to finish. Furthermore, the creativity generates the subjective emotions of happiness, vexation, anger, and sorrow at every instant in dance human as a movement human and dance human as movement images, in the special living space of dance, the unknown space of dance, and regulated space of dance, acting creatively in an original way. These actions bring about a reformation of the self-consciousness of the possibilities of ability in the dance human, who has taken the special role of dancer. In this special society, it gives meaning to life.

In this way, the dance human exists educationally. At the same time, he exists as the educational being in scholastic physical education in every country in the world and is an expression of every country in the world by his existence.

5

The Social Ontology
of the Dance Human

The dance human exists within general society. There he exists while possessing an aspect of social existence in which he lives trying to plan original plans. For example, from the factual phenomenon of the dance all kinds of words have been derived, such as *physical education, recreation*, etc. On the other hand, in social actions of dance human, there are various kinds of social language that have been created, such as *fair, unfair, cooperative*, etc. This can be said to be implicit proof that the dance human exists socially concerning the social existence of the dance human. In order to grasp his factual living state as a living state, I will divide this into a connotative structure and a denotative structure and explain each. Therefore, the social existence of the dance human is the entirety of the independent actions of connotative structure and denotative structure.

The Connotative Structure

Let us consider the basic aspects of the actions of the dance human, In the case of the individual, it is the actions of mutual separation/ contact within the dance human. In the case of the group, it is the actions of mutual separation/contact among many dance humans. In other words, the basic principle is the entirety of the motion that occurs when the dance human as an image movement and the dance human as a movement human mutually separate, approach, and have contact.

If we apply this fact to each kind of the entire phenomenon of the dance, it will be understood easily. This is described by figure 60.

In other words, in order to grasp this dynamic separation/contact relationship between the dance humans, one must begin by looking objectively from the actions of the body of the dance human.

Meanwhile, there are also the actions of the mind of the dance human, namely, the separation/contact movement of consciousness. Those actions come from the fact that when dealing with the image, the dance human as a movement human recognizes the image by the action of unconscious-conscious. The strength, or perhaps weakness, of the actions of the consciousness of the dance human as a movement human is located in the polarized structure of the morale and resignation of the consciousness. The strength or weakness depends throughout on the manner in which the consciousness moves between those polarizations (figure 61).

As the dance human as a movement human lives, breathes, and goes to the dance human as an image movement, and as the dance human as an image movement lives, breathes, and goes to the dance human as a movement human, the morale strengthens the consciousness. In other words, the morale strengthens the unified perception of both sides of the dance human, the dance human as a movement human and the dance human as a movement image, as a dance human. It also promotes the manifestation of living as a dance human. For example, in a hotly contested dance competition, the dancer himself and each action that the dancer does comes to be perceived as a unified dimension.

Because the morale is a living thing, it promotes flattering j aspects, but since it is caused through the consciousness's condition of resignation, it moves to the resignation, which is a different kind of element. Primarily, the morale of the dance human is in the dimension of time, which has a passive nature and has some I bad points, but in the dimension of space it has an active nature. The morale possesses these kinds of properties.

However, the resignation of the dance human is the condition of the consciousness of the preparatory steps for displaying the consciousness of morale. Therefore, the resignation of the dance human, in relation b the morale, is an element of denial, but on the other hand, it provides a kind of quality that serves to support morale as well. In the realm of space the resignation of the dance human is weak and passive, but in the realm of time it is strong and active.

The connotative structure of the social existence of the dance human presents the mutual actions of separation-contact within the

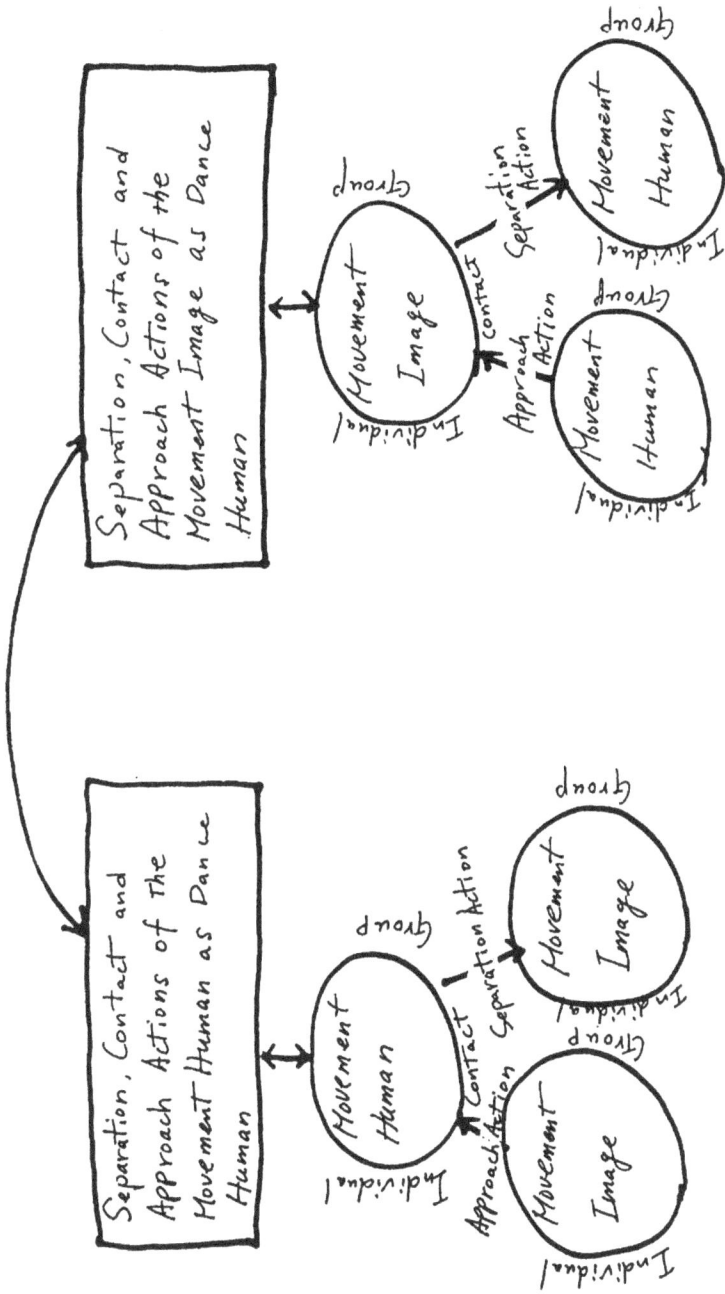

Figure 60. Separation, contact and approach actions of the dance human in each nation in the world

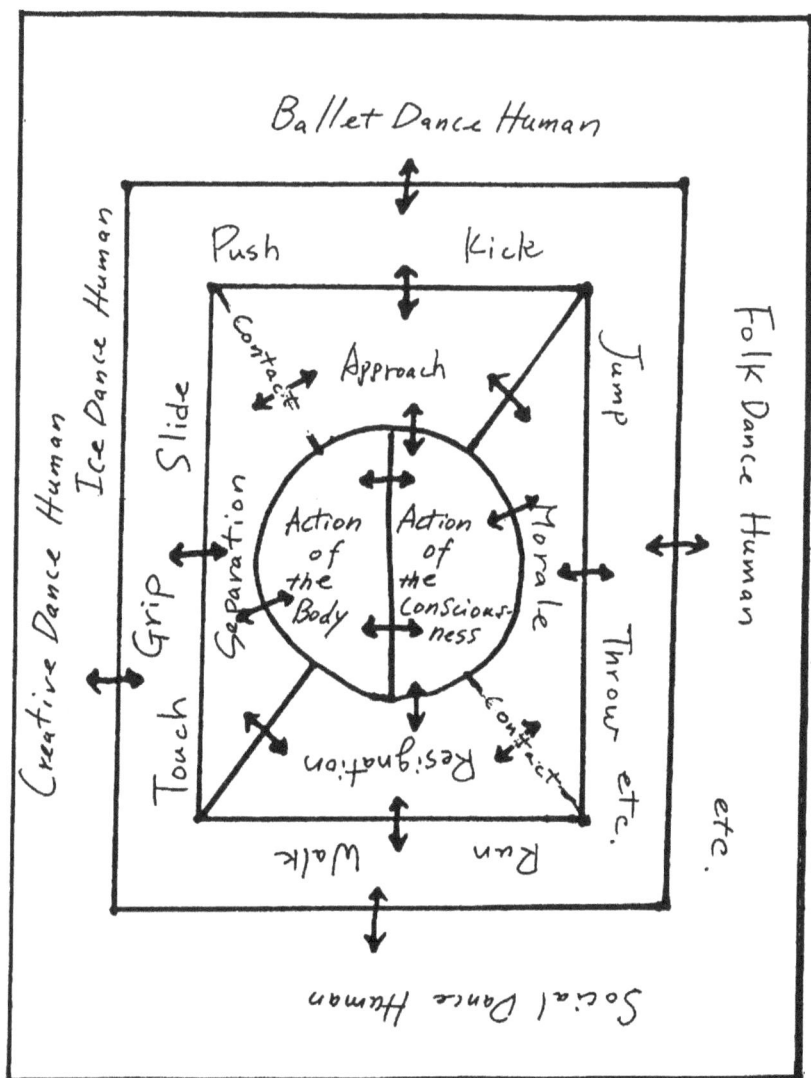

Figure 61. Relation between existence of the dance human and the words or language connecting phenomena of the dance human in each nation in the world

dance human. Objectively, the body acts by the separation- contact actions, and at the same time, subjectively, the mind acts by the separation/contact actions. Together they act as a whole. Within these actions, the changes in consciousness are acting, namely, by presenting the aspects of morale and resignation.

Concerning the actions of the dance human, we use many different expressions to indicate them. These different expressions all rely on the aspects of the actions of dance human. (Refer to figure 62.)

For example, in order to create sentences for classification within the types of dance human, such as the action of the creative dance, one would proceed in the following way.

The dance human as a movement human is performing a rattlesnake at the same time the dance human as an image movement is performed (the action of the creative dance human). The dance human acts by doing at the same time the dance human as a movement image rattlesnake (the actions of the creative dance human).

In the above manner, the actions of the connotative structure of the dance human themselves act in an original way. At the same time, they also act with aspects of denotative structure.

The Denotative Structure

In the following ways, I have analyzed and gained insight into the denotative elements of the social existence of the dance human and attempted to extract the denotative elements themselves. (See figure 63.)

From figure 63, I will explain each of the social factors of the dance human listed in the second analysis.

Recreation-ness/Competitiveness

First there is recreation-ness, in which the dance human amuses himself with entertaining dance, such as when a group of coworkers or a family enjoys dance. There is also competitiveness, which includes tension of the kind of seriousness such as when competitive leagues are commissioned through the sponsorship of all kinds of competitive

Names of Actions of the Dance Human as an Image Movement :	Names of Actions of the Dance Human as a Movement Human:
being performed	Performing
being run	Running
being Walked	Walking
being danced	Dancing
being Crept	Creeping
being jumped	Jumping
etc.	etc.

Figure 62. Natural expressions related to the actions of dance human in each nation in the world

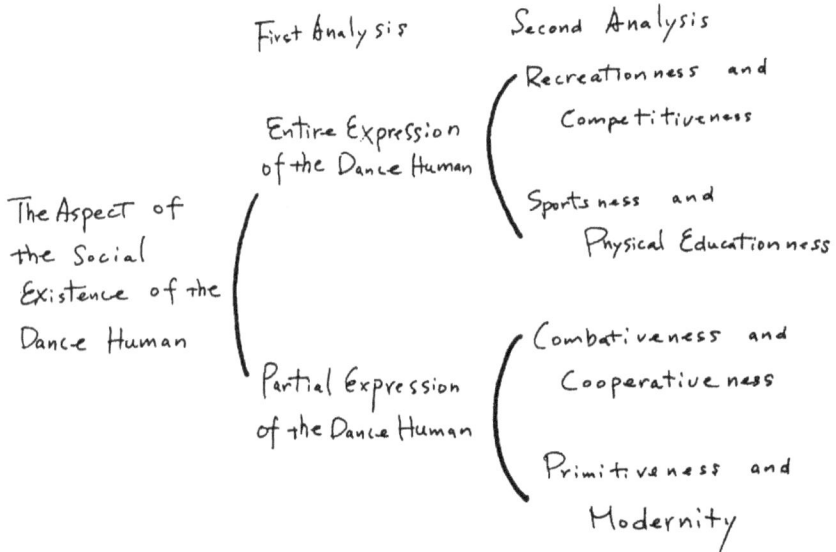

First Analysis

Second Analysis

The Aspect of the Social Existence of the Dance Human

Entire Expression of the Dance Human
- Recreationness and Competitiveness
- Sportsness and Physical Educationness

Partial Expression of the Dance Human
- Combativeness and Cooperativeness
- Primitiveness and Modernity

Figure 63. The social existence of the dance human in each nation of the world

groups. The recreation-ness of the dance human fosters a place for the meeting of the hearts of the dance human as a movement human comrade and the dance human as a movement human and the dance human as an image movement comrade. It is a softening aspect that pursues mutual understanding. Then there is the competitiveness, which is the aspect of the dance human where, within the rules of competition, a dance human as a movement human comrade, or perhaps a dance human as a movement human, and a dance human as a movement image comrade, facing one another, act with bravery and valorous determination. The greater the scale of the competitive league, the more the spirit intensifies, and the competitiveness of the dance human appears more conspicuous. For instance, this is the case in all the types of dancing in international leagues, etc.

Sports-ness/Physical Education-ness

In the phenomenon of dance, based on the fundamental structure of the teacher and pupil, the educational environment and content are given in the school's gym or a corresponding place. This is the physical education-ness of the dance human doing dance. The physical education-ness of the dance human is an educational phenomenon that depends on the sum total of the teacher and pupil. This is an aspect of the special society called school and an aspect of the actions of the dance human that come from a regionally narrow scope. The student who is recognized by the school side, perhaps specially selected, from nursery school through elementary, junior high, and high school, will be acting the role of the physical education-ness of dance human. On the other hand, the phenomenon of the dance in general society is in expression of the sports-ness of the dance human. But we cannot see the sports-ness of dance human now, because a sphere of dance does not belong to sports. It would be possible for dance to belong in the realm of sports. If it were so, the sports-ness of dance human would be the aspect of the dance human in which, in the social phenomenon that relies on the sum total of leaders and followers, a wide range of many Binds of dance would be developed with no relevance to sex, age, or occupation. Furthermore, there are the phenomena of creative dance, folk dancing, social dancing, and ballet. All of these are expressions of the sports-ness of dance human.

Combativeness/Cooperativeness

In the actions of the dance human, there are the elements of the contrasting actions of combativeness and cooperativeness. The action of an individual dance human as a movement human on a team of dance humans is an expression of cooperativeness. This action of the play among companion dance humans creates a oneness of the team/individual and builds many conscious states. It conspicuously expresses the cooperativeness of dance human. This aspect can also be seen in the phenomenon where a group does a dance, whereas actions of the dance human, the skilled actions of the dance human as an individual, are sublimated to the skilled actions of the dance human as a group. Namely, when there is a lack in the skilled actions of one dance human as a movement human, it is compensated for by the skilled actions of some other dance human as a movement human as an individual. In addition, there is also the aspect in which in order for one dance human as a movement human as an individual to do skilled actions, some different dance human as a movement human as an individual tries to give assistance. In these forms, this aspect appears.

In contrast to this, there are also times when, with a severe attitude the other dance humans, the dance human as an individual feels other dance humans to be rivals or opponents. This is an expression of the combativeness of the dance human. It is most conspicuous in the setting of vehement competition between dance humans. Combativeness can be seen in every phenomenon of dance and every phenomenon in which image is dealt with. It is the moment when the skilled actions of the dance human as an individual are steeply opposed to the skilled actions of some other dance human as an individual and they feel each other to be rivals. It also can be the movement of rivals that appears between the skilled actions of dance humans of a group.

Primitiveness/Modernity

In dance, there is the primitiveness of the dance human, in which the dance human engages in indirect image (or body of image) contact. In dances such as creative dance, pantomime, etc., there is direct contact with the image in the actions toward the dance human as a movement human that has taken on the role of player (or performer), such as the situations of flying, walking, creeping, etc. Therefore, the primitiveness of the dance human involves giving a direct impact to the body of image of dance human, but the opportunities to handle the image are relatively frequent.

On the other hand, there is an aspect of modernity of the dance human, in which in the relation between dance humans, the dance human acts by using equipment and music. Folk dancing, social dancing, ballet, etc., are dancing that conspicuously expresses the modernity of the dance human. In the modernity of the dance human, the impact of the image received by the body of the dance human as a movement human is small. The handling of the image is relatively rare, and the freedom is limited.

Moreover, to say that here in the denotative structure we have come up with a comprehensive list of all of the words that refer to the social existence of the dance human would be addled. I have aimed only for a coordinated understanding of the social existence of the dance human and for an understanding of it as a living existence. Furthermore, if we look at all the various elements of the social existence of the dance human, such as the amateurness or professionalness of the dance human, and the fair play-ness of the dance human, and the playfulness of the dance human, we can see that these elements are vital elements that act to stir up the social aspects of the dance human. In this manner, in every country in the world, the dance human expresses the originality of each country and carries on a social existence. In the stream of time of past-present-future, this existence lives in the present as realistic beings and this existence is variable and alive in all national languages in the world.

6

Generalizations from the Ontology of the Dance Human

Up to this point, the three existences of the dance human, namely, the movement-cultural, social and educational existence, have been explained clearly. *Dance human*, when taken as in the hypothesis, is language that refers to the existential essence of the phenomenon of the dance and the phenomena in which an image is dealt with. In other words, we have confirmed the fact that the words *dance human* are alive and exist, forming the special expanding world of dance and dealing with images for dance in every country in the world. We have also confirmed the fact that these words refer directly to a special kind of human. The dance human exists as the expression of each country in the world, in the United States as an American, in Russia as a Russian, in China as a Chinese, in Japan as a Japanese, in Sweden as a Swede, etc. In the present of the ever-flowing stream of past-present-future, with living and variable aspects, it exists and lives.

Now, as a result of the clear evidence of the existential essence of the dance and the clear evidence of the existence of the dance human in the phenomenon of the dance, the following kinds of questions can now be answered:

Question 1: What is the phenomenon of dance?
Answer: The phenomenon of dance is the phenomenon in which a human and image become dance human through doing the dance. It is a special world in which the dance human plays (or acts).

Question 2: What does it mean to do dance?
Answer: This is a matter in which some human becomes a dance human that can be divided into, on the one hand, a movement human and, on the other hand, an image movement for doing a dance.

For example (more concreteness):

Question 1: What is creative dance?
Answer: Creative dance is a practice by which human and image become creative dance human.

Question 2: What does it mean to do creative dance?
Answer: This means becoming a creative dance human that can be divided into a movement human as a creative dance human and a movement image as a creative dance human.

Question 3: What does it mean to do a dance in physical education?
Answer: This is the action by which some humans become dance humans who can be divided into, on the one hand, a movement human and, on the other hand, movement image, and both of these are physical education-ized and tried to become physical education-ized.

Question 4: What does it mean in sports to do a dance?
Answer: This is the conduct in which the human and image become dance human in both sides, and both of these are sports-ized and try to become sports-ized.

For any other questions concerning the phenomenon of the dance itself, they can be answered from the movement-cultural, educational, and social ontologies previously presented.

Furthermore, this dance human encompasses every type of dance human. Namely, it is the existence of the creative dance human, the existence of the folk dancing human, the existence of the social dancing human, the existence of the ballet human, etc. Also depending on the differences in sex, age, race, school, occupation, etc., the above exist as different expressions.

In the above manner, through the movement of speculation, the establishment of the ontology of the dance human, from both an abstract standpoint and a concrete standpoint, from the existence to being and from being to existence, became possible. Here we can generalize this system as the ontology of the dance human.

Finally, while I have referred to the existence of the dance human as a special existence of the human in the dance, I must now go on to present the existence of a purpose in the existence of the dance human. Namely, the existence of the dance human that I have presented up until now is an existence that acts in order to realize the dance human image. It is that purpose for which the existence is acting. Therefore, I must now go on to develop a presentation concerning the dance human image–the teleology of the dance human. I would like to affirm the dance human image that comes from the existence of the dance human, who exists with special aspects in dance.

7

The Teleology of the Dance Human

Until this point, I have contemplated the existential essence in the phenomenon of all types of dance, namely, the existence of all types of the dance human. I have clearly shown and confirmed that in every country in the world every type of dance human exists in the world of each type of dance. However, at the same time, this existence includes the purpose of the dance human, namely, the dance human image. It is not simply the existence of the dance human, but also an existence that tries to realize the ideal image that the dance human must attain. Above all, the practice of all types of dancing that is being conducted in scholastic physical education in every country in the world is being practiced for the sake of the realization of all types of the dance human image by all types of the dance human. Also, there is the necessity for physical education and sports studies research concerning all types of dances in every country in the world (such as physical education and sports studies philosophy, physical education and sports studies psychology, physical education and sports studies physiology, physical education and sports studies sociology, physical education and sports studies history, etc.) in order to plan the realization of the dance human image, in the practice of the dance or the practice where an image is dealt with, in physical education.

At this point I will go on to speculate about what kind of special ideal image is meant by the purpose of the dance human or, more specifically, the dance human image.

The dance human image is, of course, the purpose of the practice of dance, but it is necessary to explain clearly to what in reality it is to which this word directly refers. It refers to the ideal image in which the actions of the dance human as a movement human and the actions of the dance human as an image movement in the practice of dance are existing together, doing superior actions. The dance human image is the ideal image that is living and exists ideally from one era to the next era in every country in the world. This is determined by the research of the physical education and sports theory specialists (such as physical education and sports studies philosophers, physical education and sports studies psychologists, physical education and sports studies physiologists, physical education and sports studies sociologists, physical education and sports studies historians, etc.) that are living in each era in every country in the world. The term *dance human image* refers directly to the ideal existence that adds weight, depth, size, and breadth to that acting existence.

In the nature of the substance of the dance human there are really two different kinds of natures. Also, these two natures dynamically act together and form the firm dance human image. The first is the part of the purpose that has a universal nature that is common, no matter what the time, no matter what the place, no matter what the country. For example, all of the superior actions of the movement human and the image movement–in other words, the attempt to realize the dance human image–even though there are differences between the histories, cultures, ideas, races, etc., of all the countries in the world, share a common universal nature.

The second is the concrete purpose of the dance human, which is variable depending on the time, the society, the nation, age, sex, and other variables from country to country. In every country, there is originality in history, ideas culture, and national language. The dance human image of a certain era in each country of the world has the aspects of that era. Furthermore, from the point of view of age, the various types of the dance human image for children are different from the various types of the dance human image for old people. From the point of view of sex, the dance human images for male and female are different. The images of the dance human are not identical, due to the various differences among people. Therefore, as opposed to the purpose of the universal substance of the dance human, this points to the variable, concrete purpose of the dance human. The constitution of the teleology of the dance human relies on the support/being supported relationship between these two sides, which is a relationship that acts dynamically and mutually to support each side. The dance human image of the former is the purpose of the dance human, while the dance human image of the latter is the goal the dance human. The difference between these words clearly points to the difference between the universal purpose and the variable purpose. Therefore, the dance human image consists if the purpose substance as its core, and that which surrounds the purpose substance is the goal substance. The dynamic relationship between them assumes the character of abstract/concrete-concrete/abstract. Because of this, the dance human image possesses unifying qualities that transcend the realities of time, nationality, age, sex, etc., (time and space) but at the same time, this teleology is also one that sees those realities as realities. This can be summarized in figure 64.

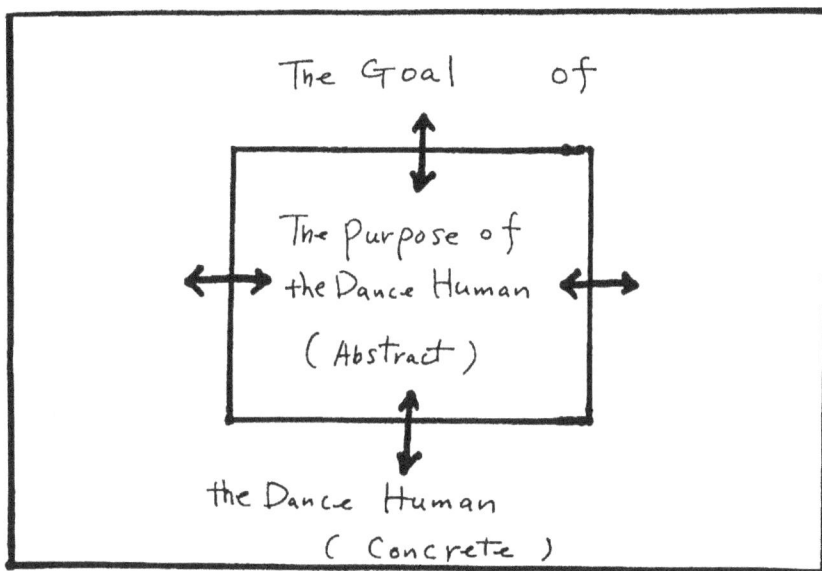

Figure 64. Constitution of the dance human image in each nation in the world

Next I would like to go on to explain the purpose of the dance human. Specifically, of what substance is the dance human image itself constructed? I will now explain this point.

The structure of the dance human image is made up of two types: a connotative structure and a denotative structure. These form the living, unified whole. There are the actions of all of the many element images, and as a whole they act ideally. If we broadly divide these various idealistic elements, they come from the connotative structure and the denotative structure. (Refer to figure 65.)

In physical education and sports, the dance human forms the special society of the dance. He works ideally in a unique way. At the same time, he is regulated in a unique way and exists ideally.

The Image of Connotative Structure

In the actions of the dance human image, there is the image of connotative structure. This acts as the foundation for the generation of the image of denotative structure, and so this is a vitally important area. The image of connotative structure itself is formed from the various element images that become the many different ideals. It is formed from the ideal of the image of life energy that comes from physical education and sports nutrition studies and physical education and sports hygiene, the ideal of the image of the body and the image of the mind (mind-body image) that come from physical education and sports philosophy, the ideal of the image of body strength, the image of flexibility, the image of physique, and the image of physical condition (the image of health) that come from physical education and sports physiology, etc. The physical education and sports studies researchers of every country in the world will go on to prove the realistic existence of dance human. Relying on the leadership of this proof, the previous images of the connotative structure of the dance human will be concretely alive and an acting ideal image. Then, in order that the physical education and sports studies researchers of every country in the world expand on the substance of the words of these various elements, and in order to promote understanding of these words as living things, the research into purpose will proceed. As a result, to the question: "Why are the educational ministries of every country in the world conducting and practicing all kinds of dance in scholastic

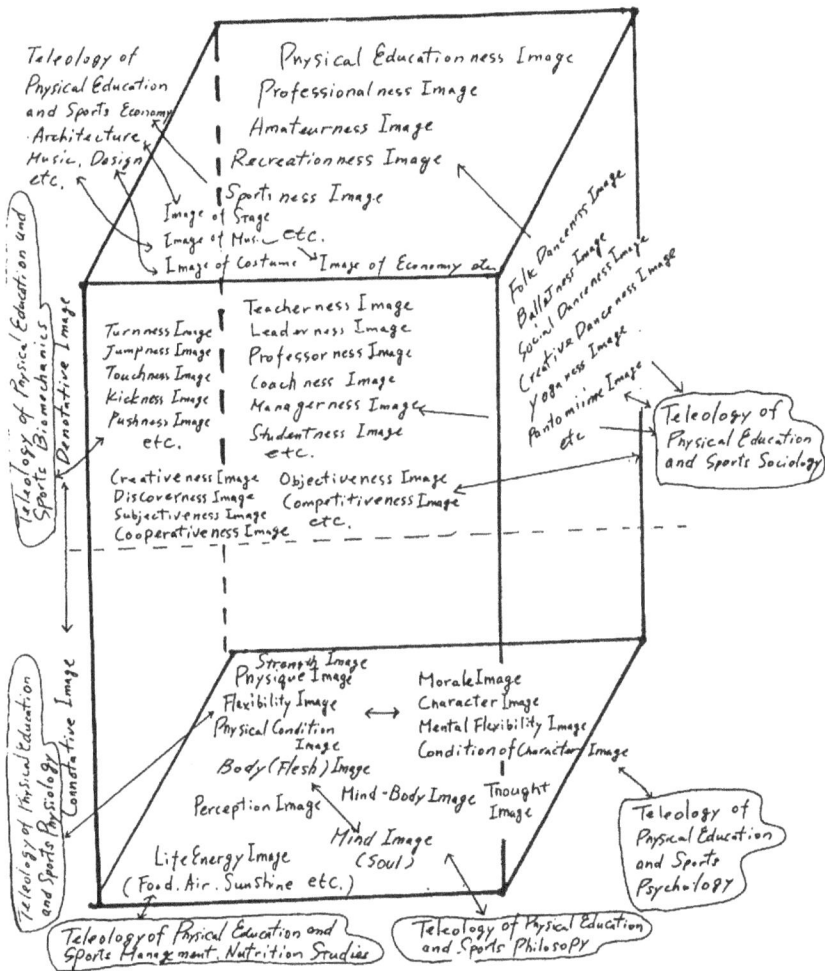

Figure 65. The dance human image in each nation in the world

physical education?" one will be able to provide a direct answer from the various fields of physical education and sports studies, namely, physical education and sports philosophy, physical education and sports psychology, physical education and sports physiology, physical education and sports sociology, physical education and sports history, etc. For example, according to physical education and sports philosophy, all types of dance are practiced in scholastic physical education in order to realize the image of the mind and body of all types of the dance human image. The content of the image of the mind and body can be explained relying on the research of physical education and sports philosophers. Of course, the contents of the partial element images presented here all are ideal contents that are drawn from the proof of all of the specialist researchers in physical education and sports studies, and at the same time, in the space of the various elements in the image of connotative structure, they are doing superior actions.

Also, these are the various elements that do superior actions in the image of the denotative structure as well. For example, the image of body strength formed by superior inner actions of body strength itself, acting in superior actions in relation to the various elements, such as morale, flexibility, cooperativeness, competitiveness, physical condition, creativeness, etc.

As is shown above, the image of the connotative structure in the dance human image is the entirety of the various elements of the connotative structure that have been amassed by the physical education and sports studies researchers in every country in the world and the physical education and sports studies research of every era. However, this image of connotative strum not only acts in the image of connotative structure but works in the image of denotative structure. So, what kind of substance of ideal images makes up the image of the denotative structure of the dance human? I will now go on to deal with this question.

The Image of Denotative Structure

In the actions of the dance human image as a dance human image, there is an image of denotative structure. In the ideal image that is generated from the image of connotative structure, the origin of the formation of the image of the denotative structure is included. Inside the denotative structure itself are the actions of the various elements of the image.

Looking from the specialized point of view of the physical education and sports sociologists and scholastic physical education and considering the existential direction of the dance human, if an inquiry is made to determine the ideal images of that existence, then in the following way, the idealistic elements of the denotative structure become visible: the image of sports-ness, the image of physical education-ness, the image of amateurness, the image of professionalness, the image of recreation-ness, the image of teacher-ness, the image of student-ness, the image of leader-ness, the image of manager-ness, the image of coach-ness, the image of director-ness, the image of follower-ness, the image of creative dance-ness, the image of ballet-ness, the image of sad butterfly-ness, the image of creativeness, the image of cooperativeness, the image of competitiveness, the image of objectiveness, the image of discovery-ness, the image of subjectiveness, etc. From the above kinds of images of elements, the image of the denotative structure in the dance human image is formed. The above various images of elements are the various aspects of the dance human image, and they are things that have been culled from researchers in physical education and sports sociology and scholastic physical education. Then the images of the various elements in the denotative structure act in a way that promotes the idealistic condition of the connotative structure, while at the same time they are the superior denotative elements that act in a way that promotes the idealistic condition of the elements in the image of the denotative structure. Therefore, each of the elements in the denotative structure themselves is an element that is superior and acts ideally.

In the above manner, the dance human image himself is the purpose of the existence of the dance human in every country in the world. Therefore, this is limited by the existence of the dance human, and in reality there is a purpose in straining to derive the dance human image from this existence. For example, in order to explain this dance human image as a dance human in reality, we can divide the dance human image into its various different types, such as the creative dance-ness image, the ballet-ness image, the folk dancing-ness, image the social dancing-ness image, and so on. We can concretely express the goal of the dance human if we look, for instance, at the creative dance from various points of view. From the point of view of school level, there are the elementary school dance human image and the high school dance human image. From the point of view of sex, there are the male creative dance human image and the female creative dance human image. From the point of view of age, there are the ten-year-old social dance human image and the forty-year-old creative dance human image. From the point of view of nationality, there are the creative dance human image as an American, the creative dance human image as a Japanese, the creative dance human image as a Russian, the creative dance human image as a Swede, the creative dance human image as an Australian, the creative dance human image as a Frenchman, the creative dance human image as a German, the creative dance human image as an Italian, and so on. In other words, because the existence of all types of the creative dance human in every country of the world is different, the purpose of the dance human can be materialized as different goals by the nationalities, national languages, backgrounds of national histories, and other national differences. On the other hand, while dance human image can make as its purpose the various unique dance human images of each country in the world, from a global, humanistic, common point of view, it can also present a purpose that is the dance human image as a world citizen, provided that the existence of all types of the dance human practicing all kinds of dances in all places around the world can be confirmed, this purpose can be erected as a common purpose of all types of the world citizen, or perhaps mankind, dance human image.

Above I have presented the purpose of the dance human or, more specifically, the substance of the dance human image (limited to only the important substance necessary in dance theory). As a result, we have reached a point at which the following kinds of questions can be answered:

Question 1: Why are the educational ministries of every country in the world practicing all types of dancing in scholastic physical education?
Answer: All types of dance are being practiced in scholastic physical

education in every country in the world in order to realize all types of the dance human image as the dance humans of every country in the world.

Question 2: Why are the educational ministries of every country in the world offering classes on the theory concerning all types of dance in scholastic physical education?

Answer: This is so that in the scholastic physical education of every country in the world physical education teachers will show the peaceful practice of all types of dances to the students and explain the practice of all types of dances to the students and the students will understand them.

Question 3: Why are the physical education and sports researchers of every country in the world needed for conducting research in fields such as physical education and sports psychology, physical education and sports philosophy, physical education and sports physiology, physical education and sports history, physical education and sports sociology, etc.? Furthermore, is it necessary in human society, the human nation, and the human world?

Answer: It is absolutely necessary for development of physical education and sports studies (including dance study). This is so that the place of dance in every country in the world will be realized. This research is the guarantee of the sound practice of dance in every country. Also, through this research we, all physical education and sports scholars can build the national theory of the dance in every country in the world that supports human nations and the human world.

Question 4: Why must a World Physical Education and Sports Academy be established?

Answer: Relying on the development of this type of research, the dance human image in every country in the world and the dance human image of each era of mankind will be constructed, thus developing the guarantee of peace in every country and world peace. Also, the academy will nurture physical education and sports researchers who will contribute to peace in every country and to world peace or will work as responsible professors at colleges, universities, and graduate schools who support the nation and world as a human society through their true theory or knowledge.

Question 5: Why must a Physical Education and Sports Academy be established in every country in the world?

Answer: Physical education and sports researchers (from all the fields) are necessary to conduct national dance theory in every country and guarantee that the practice of dance in every country in the world is a peaceful practice. And through these efforts, we are able to promise prosperity of nations and prosperity of mankind. (The ministry of education in every nation currently has to answer all of the questions concerning dance in public because of letting students practice some kinds of dance, performing from elementary school to graduate school. Instead of the ministries of education in all nations, we scholars of physical education and sports in all nations must take responsibility to answer the questions concerning dance in public.)

In addition, any questions concerning the purpose of formation related to all types of dances in every country in the world can be answered from the teleology of the dance human. Also, from this purpose it is necessary to go on to develop support for peace in every country and world peace.

Furthermore, from the presentation of the ontology and teleology of dance human in every country in the world, we must now go on to develop the methodology of the dance human in every country in the world by which the existence of the dance human in every country in the world realizes the dance human image of every country in the world. This will deal with the method by which the existence of the dance human in every country in the world realizes the dance human image. The methodology will be organically connected to the ontology and the teleology and will have the unique quality of working together with them. This kind of undertaking will work through the realization of the establishment of universal dance theory, which unites all countries in the world and accepts differences among all countries in the world.

8

The Methodology of the Dance Human

The methodology of the dance human is an original theoretical area that deals with both the movement human and the movement image sides of the phenomena of all types of dance. These two sides, which are referred to directly by the term *dance human*, can be said to work together to emphasize the movement image. Only the ability required for the movement image is required of the movement human as a dance human. On the other hand, if we emphasize the movement human, only the ability required for the movement human is required of the movement image. Therefore, achieving the required ability that is possible when both sides accept each other's demands is imperative. This type of method is the only advanced method by which the dance human image can be realized in each nation in the world. Toward that end, there are notably two methodologies: one in relation to time and one in relation to space. The former considers the experience of becoming a dance human in terms of time, while the latter considers the experience of becoming a dance human in terms of space. Therefore, the method that realizes the dance human image must give the appropriate weight to experience in time and experience in space.

Theoretical Foundation and Ground for the Formation of the Dance Human Methodology

Before presenting the methodology of the dance human, it is necessary to first make clear the reasons why it is possible to present such a methodology. In order to do this, we must look at the theoretical foundation and the ground for the methodology. The theoretical foundation for the formation of the methodology of the dance human relies on the movement-cultural, education and social ontologies of the dance human and the teleology of dance human already presented. The ground for the formation of this methodology is the fact that in scholastic physical education in every country around the world dance is being practiced. The former is based on the development of the theory, while the latter comes from the practice of dance.

The Characteristics of the Methodology of the Dance Human

There are two characteristics associated with the content of the methodology of the dance human. First, it is an unchangeable, universal, abstract methodology, applicable to any country at any time. Second, as country (space) and era (time) change, it is a concrete, realistic methodology that changes accordingly. The methodology of the dance human is constructed with the former at the core, while the latter surrounds it, both working together to preserve the relationship. More specifically, the former is the area of the methodology based on the common qualities of all countries and constructed by the physical education and sports researchers of every country in the world so that the practice of dance in scholastic physical education in every country in the world serve to realize the dance human image. Meanwhile, the latter is the area of the methodology that has the quality of grasping the differences between the realistic aspects of the dance human by country, era, age, sex, school, etc., as differences in realistic aspects.

Elements of the Formation of the Contents of the Methodology of the Dance Human

In regard to the formation of the methodology of the dance human, both the theoretical foundation and the practical ground have already been presented. However, I believe that the latter, the practical ground, gives an extraordinarily important reason for the formation of the methodology of the dance human. Namely, because of the existence of the practice of dance in physical education programs, the existence of the practice of dance in society, and the existence of physical education teachers, mentors, and students who play a function in society, the need for the methodology of the dance human becomes apparent.

In that case, physical education teachers and mentors are those who lead students to become dance human and realize the dance human image, while students and followers who receive all forms of dance education are those who look toward becoming all forms of dance human and realizing all forms of the dance human image. Therefore, the human relationships of the teachers and mentors and students and followers in the phenomenon of the dance will all become the dance human and realize the dance human image. It is a mutual relationship that exists to realize the dance human image.

Those fostering the dance human have experience in the past of fully (deeply and widely) becoming a dance human in order to realize the dance human image. They are those who possess the leadership qualifications to be able to realize the dance human image. On the other hand, those becoming dance human must receive leadership in order to realize the dance human image. They are those of whom study ability is demanded.

With the relationship between physical education teachers who try to realize the dance human image and foster students as dance humans, who study while looking toward becoming dance humans, realizing the dance human image, as the ground, the various structural elements of the methodology of the various kinds of dance human are formed. Specifically, these elements include study, leadership, evaluation, curriculum, educational resources, study ability, study processes, leadership ability, skill, etc. Classifying these elements into large groups, we may divide them into study, leadership, and educational resources. The terms *skill, study ability, study process*, etc., are technical terms connected with the student or follower becoming a dance human and trying to realize the dance human image, and therefore are study terms. The terms *leadership ability, evaluation, curriculum*, etc., are all terms connected with the teachers and mentors trying to realize the dance human image and turn their students into dance humans, and are therefore leadership terms. Finally, that which brings the leadership and study together at the place of the dance is the educational resources. The structural elements of the methodology of the dance human are systematized in the manner described in figure 66.

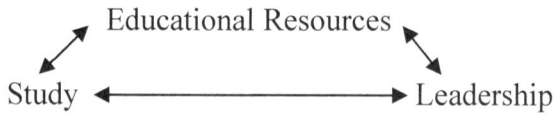

Figure 66. The structural elements of the methodology of the dance human in each nation in the world

Study. This is the state of those becoming dance humans in which they learn all of the various things they must learn from those helping them to become dance humans in order to realize the dance human image.

Also, we will call students those who, under the supervision of those fostering the dance human, strive to learn that which they need to become dance humans. Furthermore, study ability is ability that students possess to learn all the constructive knowledge required in order to become a dance human and realize the dance human image. Skill is a part of study ability and is the condition of the mastery of the necessary techniques required to become a dance human and realize the dance human image. Also, the study process is the process by which, under the leadership of those fostering the dance human, those becoming dance humans learn all of the relevant knowledge.

Leadership. This is defined as the ability to lead those who will become dance humans by those who will foster their becoming dance humans by giving them all the various knowledge they will need toward the goal of realizing the dance human image. Leadership ability is the ability of those fostering dance humans, with the goal of realizing the dance human image, to fully develop those becoming dance humans. The leadership process is the process by which those fostering dance humans, with the goal of realizing the dance human image, lead those becoming dance humans. Furthermore, evaluation is the process by which those fostering dance humans decide what level those becoming dance humans have reached and how far they have advanced in approaching the realization of the dance human image. Curriculum is the study route through which those fostering dance humans lead those becoming dance humans in order to realize the dance human image.

Educational Resources We collectively use this term to refer to all materials those fostering dance humans use to lead those becoming dance humans to realize the dance human image, along with all study materials used by those becoming dance humans aiming to realize the dance human image. Therefore, the educational resources play the role of intermediaries in the formation of the leadership and study of the dance human and are a necessary methodological element in the realization of the dance human image. The educational resources include natural educational resources and man-made educational resources. The former are sunshine, air, weather (clear, rainy, snowy, cloudy), air pressure (wind), water (water in pool), earth (ground), etc. The latter include gymnasiums, lighting, clothes, tools, shoes, stages, etc. Therefore, in the broad sense of the term, *educational resources* refers to the combination of natural educational resources and man-made educational resources but, when taken in the narrow sense of the term, refers mostly to man-made educational resources.

The Construction Method of the Methodology of the Dance Human as National Theory in Every Nation in the World

It is imperative that we use the terminology of the structural elements of the methodology of the dance human, namely, *study* (*skill, study process*, etc.) *leadership* (*evaluation, curriculum, leadership process, leadership ability*, etc.), and *educational resources*, in order to realize the dance human image. However, it is also necessary to answer the question of how the content of these elements can be given substance. I will now present these kinds of problems related to the construction of the methodology of the dance human.

From the standpoint of those dealing with the fundamental theory of physical education studies, it is possible to construct a methodology that answers these kinds of questions. The methodology of the dance human should use the original specialized vocabulary from each specialized area of physical education, and considering study, leadership, educational resources, etc., we can create a separate methodology from each field of physical education that serves to realize every partial image of the dance human in each era and each nation that emerges from that field. In regard to the methodology of the dance human from physical education physiology, for instance, while considering study, leadership, and educational resources we can construct an original methodology, using the specialized terms of physiology, such as *strength, physique, health*, and *flexibility*, that serve to realize the strength image, the physique image, the health image, and the flexibility image of the dance human.

Likewise, in regard to the methodology of the dance human from physical education psychology, while considering study, leadership, and educational resources we can construct an original methodology, using the specialized terms of psychology, such as *character, morale, mental health, flexibility*, etc., that serve to realize the character image, the morale image, the mental health image, and the flexibility image, etc., of the dance human. In regard to the methodology of the dance human from the physical education philosophy, while considering study, leadership, and educational resources we can construct an original methodology, using the specialized terms of philosophy such as *mind, body, mind-body relationship, soul, flesh*, etc., that serve to realize the mind image, the body image, the mind-body relationship image, the soul image, the flesh image, etc., of the dance human. In regard to the methodology of the dance human from physical education educational science, while considering study, leadership, and educational resources we can construct an original methodology, using the specialized terms of educational science, such as *creativity, subjectivity, objectivity, cooperation, competition*, etc., that serve to realize the creativity image, the subjectivity image, the objectivity image, the cooperation image, the competition image, etc., of the dance human. In regard to the methodology of the dance human from physical education sociology, while considering study, leadership, and educational re- sources we can construct an original methodology as a national theory, using the specialized terms of sociology, such as *performer, dancer, amateur; professional, sports, physical education*, etc., that serve to realize the performer image, the dancer image, the amateur image, the professional image, the sports image, the physical education image, etc., of the dance human. In regard the methodology of the dance human from biomechanics, while considering study, leadership, and educational resources we can construct an original methodology as a national theory, using the specialized terms of biomechanics, such as *grasp, run, catch, walk, creep*, etc., that serve to realize the grasping image, the running image, the catching image, the walking image, the creeping image, etc., of dance human. Moreover, the construction of the original methodology of the dance human for each of these specialized fields of physical education must be living, changing entities, taking into account the realistic existence of things such as nationality, race, age, sex, etc., to always be the best methodology for physical education researchers at the current time. Therefore, the research specialists in each field of physical education must, while referring to the knowledge in physical education history for advice, construct separate methodologies as national theories responsible for each specialized field.

In the above manner, it is possible to construct a methodology of the dance human for every country in the world. Thus we are able to form a national methodology of dance study in each country in the world in each national language.

Part VII

About Physical Education and Sports Studies in Each Nation in the World

Concerning responsibility to the nation as a scholar of physical education, we must answer the following: What is education? Is education becoming true education in reality as we hoped? *Education* does not mean "teasing" college students. Therefore, the educators in every nation have to be shown a blueprint of the universal theory that of necessity must come from our real life in order to gain the social trust of all people in every country, but not a blueprint from the books. All faculties in colleges and graduate schools must show the blueprints to all people in public if college and graduate schools are to gain national and international trust. All the books come from the necessity in real human life. All faculties in college and graduate school must have more objective theory that explains a necessity in fact. The college, the university, and the graduate school seem to be similar to the company where fine merchandise must be produced, in fact, if the real education demands true education eventually. In fact, the real college education is in the spoiled situation in which professors misuse the national language in a playful stage without production of national and world acknowledgement of people in all nations because the government does not have a universal blueprint of each study. I think the education is originally for the people, in the people, and with the people, but not for the governments. Now the time is coming to reconsider the education in all nations, especially physical education faculties in all nations, for which we have taken responsibility on behalf of the nation and world as physical education scholars. Despite the real education not being connected with social, national, and world responsibility, the doctoral program by the ministry of education has been made, in fact, without the theory that can guarantee doctoral programs and doctors. We found out about the national problem of permitting doctoral courses in graduate school by the ministry of education. We must cross-examine who permitted the doctoral programs for graduate school in physical education faculties. The problem is a thing that the doctoral program by the ministry of education has been made in no connection with personal achievements of scholars of physical education. In fact, none can make a doctoral program of graduate school in physical education faculties in all nations in the world. Masauki Tamaki said in the newspaper, *Asahi*, on January 12, 1994: "Sports has been used by governmental education and advertisement of company." I can see there a lack of sports theory becoming independent.

The ministries of education in all nations have to take responsibility for what teachers and professors of sports have done in the educational programs from elementary school to graduate school. For example, if the universities use many kinds of sports events, the universities have to offer theory classes for the practice of each sports event, because professors let the students participate in many kinds of sports events in fact. The government has an obligation to answer to all people in all nations why the government needs doctoral programs in physical education. In fact, why are the professors needed and why do they use all national languages for the physical education studies and research? Why does the government need many kinds of sports events in the practice of physical education? Why does the government employ professors on physical education faculties, doctors of philosophy, medical doctors, doctors of education, etc., who are valuable on the faculties of physical education in all nations? We have to question the real responsibility of the ministry of education in each nation for people who the government obliges to pay taxes. In world history, sports have been created by the people in the nation. The government cannot use many kinds of sports events in the practice of physical education in the schools, the colleges, the universities, and the graduate schools because the governments in all nations do not have the true theory or the principle of physical education by which the governments can guarantee the doctorate. Therefore we, physical education scholars have to create the theories for people, with people, and in people instead of the obligatory ministries of education in all nations. We have already been creating a principle of physical education and sports studies beyond the different national languages and different countries. I have to question the corrupted reality of the government, for what are the governments? Don't the governments need to take responsibility for educational programs to society, the nation, and the world? We have to ask immediately of the governments of all nations: "Why do the sports practices in physical education deserve just one credit for the sports classes that the students take at the colleges?" We have to know a correct answer without personal opinion from the government, which we can understand clearly. We must request that the participation in sports events definitely deserve three credits for students. We have to say to all the governments: "All the practices of physical education are the practices of the peace that all students practice at school." Why are many sports events in physical education worth the education through the physical activities? I request strongly that this hypothesis must be made not by someone's opinion but by factual proof. We have to have a responsibility for the human nations and for the human world.

All national languages have been created by citizens of the respective nations. These languages have been based on national traditions, reflected in the expressions of people in all nations. We must not deny the existence of languages in all nations. They mean a neutrality of values. All national languages in education have to be used for peace in order to guarantee mankind's existence. Why do we need all national languages for physical education and sports studies? Because we have social, national, and world responsibilities for the special existence of humans in the phenomena of sports and physical education instead of national ministries of education in all nations. I believe that real democracy is based only on a principle of the majority, but also a principle of the truth that people have always experiences in reality. Therefore, all national languages show the proof of the human existence in public that people are living now and people were living in the past and people will live in the future. So all expressions of national language must live in reality and act to the real nations. The skills of the national languages, for example, speaking, writing, and reading, must be based on human existence in each era and each nation. We have to learn inside the words (the grammar of national language) and outside the words (the whereabouts of national language). And we really need to know both elements of national language. The scholars of physical education are not translators but people who generate true knowledge to all students. Our mission for the nation and the world is this. For example, the words *doctor* and *professor* must be defined in each nation and in the world, because these people, whom many people believe unconditionally in societies and nations, must take responsibility for the nation and the world. Therefore, there are inside (function) and outside (function) words (national language) and the common functions of the words (national language) that show the responsibilities for the nation and the world in each era. It means that they are people who have created their own theory, which they can teach to all students at colleges, universities and graduate schools. The responsibilities of the doctors and the responsibilities of the professors in all nations we must trust internationally and nationally. This does not mean irresponsible people of national languages at colleges, universities, and graduate schools. We see that here education is not education but play of the national language in realities. For example, the excessive examinations make students undergo mental torture. We have to define authorized words such as *doctor* and *professor* in all nations in order to get social trust, national trust, and world trust for physical education and sports scholars. It is a way of the restoration that we, all physical education scholars, have been living without a universal theory, by which I mean principle. That has caused the irresponsibility and the disordered knowledge of the past. Why do we need all national language for the physical educational and sports studies and research? We can answer that there are existences of golf ball human, crawl human, 100-meter human, etc., and they have their own purpose coming from specific human (sports human and physical education human) existences in all nations. They speak their own national languages in reality in order to make the national theories of physical education and sports studies, which realize a peace of the nation and a peace in the world. Therefore, all national languages are the proof of special human existences in all nations coming from the peculiar national languages.

All national languages are the neutral standpoints by which researchers and scholars express their research papers in public. Fundamentally, physical education scholars are not translators, but scholars who can create the true knowledge for students and other people. We do not need professors who cannot have their own theory, because they bring irresponsibility to the nation and world, and our society's trust of us as professionals is lost in such a reality. The social trust is the most important thing in human society, because colleges and universities define authentic words such as *doctor* and *professor* Therefore, we have to define the authentic words in order to recover people's trust. It is our obligation, because the doctor and professor have to take responsibility for the nation and the world. I believe that real democracy means the qualities of national languages that people in all nations speak in reality, because all national languages are just the proof of the existences of humans in all nations. When we study papers from someone's research, we have to investigate them if they are to become true knowledge. The estimations of the research papers are very important, because professors cannot give doctoral degrees to students without the true theory or the principle, although the responsibilities belong to the governments. We have national and world problems at present.

All national languages have limitations as expressions of humans by which people strive to understand each other according to the rules of national languages. For example, American English means matters in relation to human existence in all of the United States. Therefore, American English does not show the matters in relation to human existence in France in reality. This means that American English is an absolute proof of the human existence in the United States but not a proof of the human existence in France. Moreover, all national languages are changeable, because the expression of the national language is the proof of the human existence in all nations in each era. Therefore, the human existence or people, if I may express "human" by another word, are eventually changeable in comparison to 100 years ago and 100 years in the future. The personal skills of foreign languages are different matters from their translation. We have to distinguish clearly between an essence of national language and an essence of the translation. That means that research or study and translation differ. The research is the research. The translation is not research but the translation. The real research has responsibilities to the nation and the world. On the other hand, the behavior of translation does not mean the behavior by which the translator takes responsibility for the nation. It is just a matter of creating an information world.

We always have to act as adults in government, not children. Our tragedy has come from the ignorance of the governments about the physical education and sports practices, because the governments do not have the theory that guarantees the justification of the sports practice. We have been compelled to anguish because of the ignorance of the governments. All governments have to provide all scholars of physical education sports studies with the right to independence, because we scholars of physical education and sports studies have the universal theories that can explain the real physical education and sports practices in all nations. The time has come when we instead of the governments have to lead all scholars in all nations. We have to help the governments. Our field could create a brilliant future for the development of physical education and sports studies with the support of the people of the world, because our studies create real doctors and researchers who protect the human nation and human world and support all human existence in all nations. We know that democracy likes the true but not the fake, as the Olympic Games have been showing until now. We will decide to take this way for human nations and the human world forever.

We have to take responsibility for authorizing words such as *doctor, professor,* etc., so that people can trust their professionals in public. *Doctor, professor,* etc. are words that are concerned with responsibilities of the human nation and mankind. They are not the words that mean the personal decorations in the public society. They are the words that are accompanied by the responsibilities of the human nation and mankind in each era. We make the true definition of the authorized words coming from our true theories, because we need to gain the social trust of the people of all nations. Then we will hold democratically a world conference of scholars in all nations. Our physical education and sports scholars are people who take responsibility for sports and physical education experiences. At the same time they are people who eventually want to protect the human nation and mankind with the social, natural environment in the earth from the specific standpoint of a physical education and sports scholar,

I think that they are very important people for all nations and the world. Therefore, the physical education and sports scholars in all nations have to be supported financially and socially by all the governments. They are also people who support all civilians in 'the nation, who love democratically the nation and the world, and who are loved by many people coming from all nations. They are people who bring up students or other people to become gentlemen and ladies through physical education and sports practices. The physical education and sports studies would become only a real study that remains in world history forever as long as the sports practices will be carried out at schools by the government.

A final goal of our studies and research and practices at schools, colleges, universities, and graduate schools in all nations is peace in the world. Our teaching of physical education and sports comes from social, national, and international necessity. Our lectures and teaching both practice and theory have social, national, and international meaning. Therefore, our studies must be independent from other studies, for instance, education, philosophy, medicine, and so forth. Our studies also must be independent from the governments wherever there are the faculties of physical education and sports at colleges, universities, and graduate schools in all nations. Our studies, both practice and theory, are the studies that we protect for all citizens in the nation and the world from the specific dimension. Therefore, the studies are relevant to human rights and thoughts of democracy tied to human existence, because human education must be human education forever. All national languages that teachers and professors use are directly relevant to human existence in all nations. The physical education and studies are the studies having the role of human education.

The ministries of education in all nations have to exercise responsibility for the practice of many kinds of sports events. In fact, the ministries of education have permitted many kinds of sports events in the practice of physical education from elementary school to graduate school, with teachers and professors instructing students concerning the sports events, but the ministries don't have the theories so that they can answer all questions, such as: "Why do you need many kinds of sports events at the school?" Someone said, "Physical education is education through physical activities." Someone else said, "Physical education is education through big muscular activities." All definitions are personal opinions without proof, in fact. They are all hypotheses. They are not true knowledge. The key words in the hypotheses are *physical activities* and *big muscular activities*. The person who creates the definitions has to offer proof through using the key words in the hypotheses. I realize that I cannot provide the proofs in both hypotheses, because the hypotheses are not proper for factual explanation of the practices of physical education. They seem to be irresponsible abuse of national language. Therefore, the ministry of education in the nation has to have justified theory in order to use many sports events from the elementary school to the graduate school. Therefore, we, all the physical education and sports scholars in all nations, have to make the national theories in our own national language under this principle of physical education and sports studies in all nations. I want to emphasize the necessity of these theories for all governments, because they are only true theories to develop the nation and the world.

Limitation of Expression of Human in National Languages

All national languages have limitations in expression is evidenced in research papers. For example, American English is an expression of the human in the United States, Japanese is an expression of the human in Japan, Spanish is an expression of the human in Spain, French is an expression of the human in France, German is an expression of the human in Germany, Italian is an expression of the human in Italy, and other national languages are expressions of the human in other nations. Why is this so? Because all national languages in research papers have a limitation as an expression of the human in all nations and because we have to avoid an abuse of expressions of research papers in all national languages in all nations. At the same time, we have to find the world language that all scholars in all nations can understand in our research fields and can create, of course, all national languages as the official languages so that you can understand the research papers within your country. But the national language has a limitation of expression of the human so that people can understand each other. So we need a world language supporting each national language.

These theories I am formulating are for the sake of fostering good professors of physical education and sports studies in all nations, because we need such people to contribute to peace in each nation and peace in the world.

All scholars of physical education and sports studies must be emancipated from the fear of colonies, as powerful countries dominate and press small countries and promise harmonious prosperity to all nations of the world. This principle accepts all questions concerning physical education and sports studies and practices, including educational programs, national existence of the faculty, etc. As long as we have the principle, we must take the attitude of adults for all people of all different nations. That means responsibility for the human world. Our job must entail this.

Our Standpoint Regarding Physical Education in All Nations

We have many questions we must address in public. For example: Have all the governments in all nations created the true theories of physical education before they built up faculties of physical education in colleges, universities, and graduate schools? Why must we ask this? Because if the ministry of education agrees to build the faculty of physical education, we doubt the functions of the educational program, in fact. The ministry of education in each nation is responsible for the question on behalf of all people in each nation in the world because we humans must ensure the existence of our human nation and human world for future generations. We humans don't admit the study without true theory or without necessity of the nation in public because the study has to take responsibility for all people in each nation. We have to check and negotiate with the faculties of physical education in all colleges, in all universities, and in all graduate schools. These faculties should be important in the educational systems in all nations because the physical education studies eventually will establish the principles of physical education and sports studies. Therefore, we will be able to expect the strong support from the government for faculties of physical education and sports in all nations.

We have another question: Why do we need the physical education theory and practice in colleges, in universities, and in graduate schools? Why do we need the professors on the faculty of physical education in colleges in all nations? We must answer them with the true theories for all people in the world. If we do not have theory to answer all the questions, suspicion of the education in each nation would come out internationally and nationally in reality on behalf of a lack of responsibility. In addition, the evaluation of research papers has to be based on how much responsibility the research papers take for the human nation and to the human world, not how much the research displays skills. Therefore, the evaluation for the research papers absolutely has to be accompanied by the true theory of the faculties of physical education in college and in graduate school. We abhor research with a lack of goals coming from the fact.

Moreover, the problem, I think, is that physical education study has to be independent from politicians in each era, because some politicians personalize their disregard for the government responding to the voices of the people. In addition, the physical education and sports scholars must not lead the faculties of physical education and sports into the bureaucratic system but into the democratic system in all nations. The real teaching of students must involve responsibility for the human nation and the human world through expression of each national language and through the use of the social examination, the experiment, the computer, etc. It does not mean just to teach a technique for writing, speaking, and reading in each national language, technique of experiment and technique of social examination. Accordingly, to education in college and in universities absolutely must be brought responsibility for the human nation and the human world. All the professors have to have responsibilities for their practices and lectures in college and in graduate school. We don't need lectures without social necessity. We need professors in college and in universities who support people in each nation and the ministry of education in each nation. A professor is a person who can teach students. Therefore, the professor has to have his own theory. The teaching of theory is worth a credit for students in colleges and in universities. The credit means support of the human nation and human world so that all professors in each nation trust the credit that students take in college.

Furthermore, the problem I want to mention is that English exists in two forms. One is a national English whose expression is limited nationally, such as American English, British English, etc., and another is world English. The characteristics of English as a national language and English as a world language are quite different. English as a world language means to support or help all the national languages have more or less a limitation expression of human in the world. English as a national English cannot support English as a world language. Therefore, English as a world language is involved with other national languages. We consider English as above-mentioned before we use English for study and research of physical education and sports. Therefore, all the English speeches that the world doctor speaks in public become the world language that can teach or lead to the future professors in all nations and all the national languages' speeches (including American English or British English) that national doctor speaks in public become the national language that can teach or lead to future professors in the nation.

Our social, national, and world responsibility is to bring the true knowledge so all students can learn and know the real practice of physical education and sports. Our specialty does not mean translating from one national language to another national language. We really need professors that take responsibility but do not need professors that play with the national language in front of students in college and graduate school. Because education means the education of students but does not mean a play of national language by which the professor intends to avoid his responsibilities for real society, the nation, and the world. This is a book that will be presented to a real scholar of physical education and sports studies who wants to become a professor in college or graduate school in any nation. And the judgment on doctoral degrees must be made in a National Academy of Physical

Education and Sports Studies and World Academy of Physical Education and Sports Studies but must not be made in graduate school. (Our policy prohibits doctoral degree in graduate school that must not be used in public, because we do not need a doctor of fabrication in all nations that makes trouble internationally and nationally.) Our friend is a person who takes responsibility for the practice of physical education and sports within and without school beyond different nations and different languages. And we will really expect him to realize a peace of nations and a peace in the world. This book is for all scholars of physical education and sports studies in all nations. National doctors and world doctors are people who support and protect all people and all governments in each nation in the world.

From now on, we must devise a way by which all problems of physical education may be solved in all nations. The character of our research and studies in college and graduate school must move from personal interests as research motivation to social necessity, national necessity, and the necessity for mankind. The necessity promises definitely the establishment of justification of our specific research and specific studies separated from general studies and general research in colleges and graduate schools in all nations. We move definitely toward a way of solving current problems and we want actual peace and development of our studies in all nations and peace of mankind in history forever. I expect that all scholars in our field would get a sense of "independence" from everything. We share the responsibilities and happiness for us.

A Conception of Physical Education and Sports Studies in All Nations Utilizing Different National Languages or Different Expressions among National Languages

I think that all studies in general must be universal blueprints created for all nations by professors. There is a lot of knowledge professors have produced up to now, but much knowledge has come from professors' opinions. (I would say in public that this is fake knowledge as I believe that education means absolute education, going to real education, in fact.) So all students have to face the heavy work like a mental torture through the heavy examinations. These phenomena of education show incomplete studies that professors are not able to teach to students in college and graduate school. Therefore, we cannot trust the doctoral degree in graduate school, although many people might believe we can.

I would like to show you about physical education and sports studies in all nations with the chart of them as a living tree. The ground and the sky connected with this tree on the earth are geographically different from each nation. For example, the American tree (meaning the study in American English) grows up magnificently on the American ground and in the American sky. The French tree (the study in French) grows up magnificently on French ground and in the French sky. Other trees grow up on their ground and in their skies. This tree that I want to plant in all nations in the world will grow up on different grounds and in different skies, with scholars of physical education and sports, in history. This tree (like the physical education and sports studies) is a sacred tree of peace that we want to plant in each nation in the world through negotiation among nations by us.

This is also a tree that true physical education and sports scholars, professors, and doctors in all nations can develop, in fact. This tree creates independence from all restrictions that the scholars currently obey in society. The principle of physical education and sports studies grows up from under the ground like the roots of trees in all nations. The direction of the growing roots is the direct opposite of the direction of physical education and sport studies in all nations. The principle goes deep into the ground in order to support trunk and branches. It also creates the necessity for ensurance of the existence of each specific study in public. For example, physical education and sports psychology, physical education and sports biomechanics, etc. The trees (physical education and sports studies) in all nations take different shapes and grow at different speeds (like American scholars use American English in order to make the American theory in American English in each era because the originators of the study and research are Americans who are living in the United States, like French scholars use French in order to make the French theory in French in each era because the originators of the research and studies

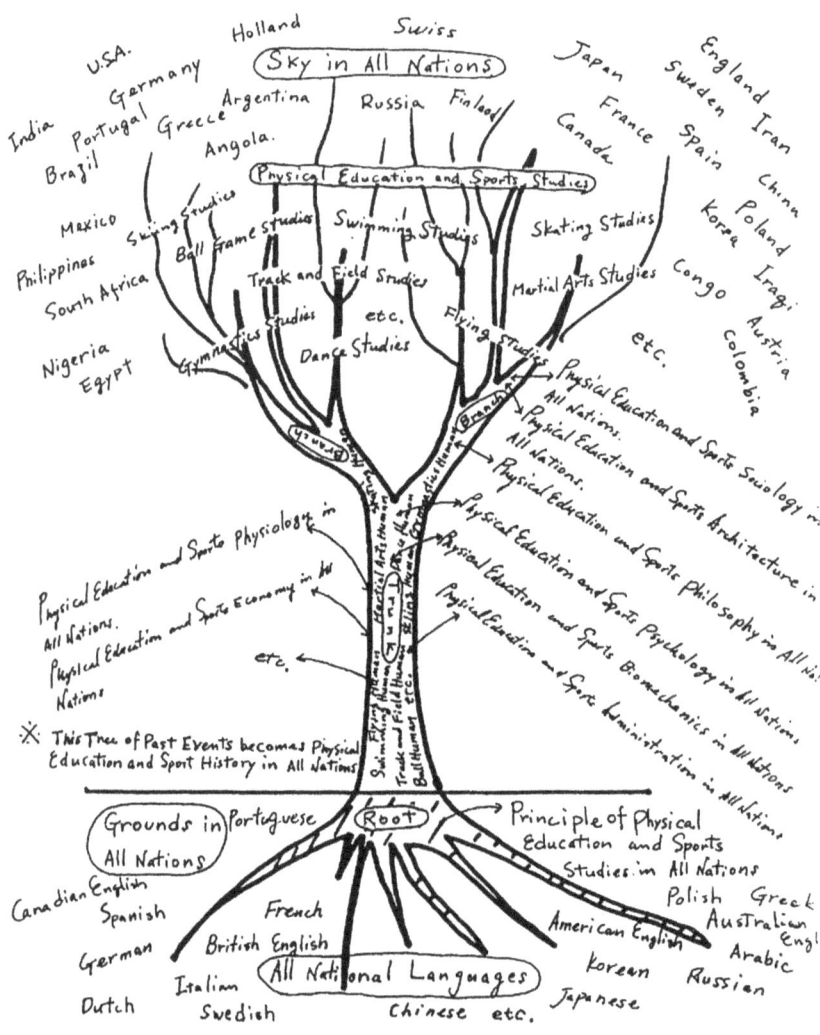

Figure 67. A conception of physical education and sports studies in all nations as the tree of peace theories

are French people who are living in France, and like another country's scholars use their own national language in order to make national theories in their own national language in each era because the originator of the studies and research are that other country's people, who are living in that other country). I am responsible for the establishment of this tree in all nations in order to create the national theory in each nation in the world, I believe that letting this tree grow up in each nation will bring to realization peace within nations and peace in the world. Therefore, physical education and sports studies in college and graduate school must begin the practices of physical education and sports and explain them and define them. And we suppose that there will be Olympic competition held among the national doctors who are chosen in each national academy, with the thought of democracy seeking out truth and under the true judgment without professors' preferences. We expect that this democratic tree will grow up in each nation in the world.

This national theory has to be constructed by national academies of physical education and sports studies. All governments, professors, and national academies must be responsible for the national theory in each era. Because of what they let all students practice, many kinds of sports events or applied movements of sports, they must answer publicly all questions coming from all people with true theory. This principle can only offer an answer to all questions of sports and physical activities that people present in public. The specific terms that are attributed to the physical education and sports studies must be returned to the living practices of physical education and sports and explain the actual practices of physical education and sports. There are many specific terms or words about specific human existence in all national languages. For example, in American English there is *physical fitness*, which our physiologists have created in physical education and sports studies; there is *character*, which our psychologists have created in physical education and sports studies; there is *soul*, which our philosophers have created in physical education and sports studies; there is *amateurism*, which our sociologists have created in physical education and sports studies; there is *jumping*, which our biomechanicians have created in physical education and sports studies; etc. All of the words that we have created, those professional words and specific terms, must return to actual, living existences of specific humans in our practices in all nations on the earth as our professional obligations on behalf of all people.

About My Experience with Japanese Education as an Adult Educator

I received much of my education from elementary school to graduate school in Japan. However, when I think of education in my homeland, Japan, I am aware of some problems with the educational system. I openly say that the educational system was based on a system of bureaucracy and colonialism (*gakubatsu* in Japanese) by the Japanese government. There is abuse of expression in Japanese by Japanese professors despite all Japanese directly connected to human existence (Japanese people) in Japan. For example, when professors use *ningen* (human) in Japanese, almost no professors know the place of the *ningen* (human). I want to ask the professors whether the expression *ningen* is the *ningen* in Japan or the *ningen* in the United States. They think that the *ningen* is living in all nations. In fact, *ningen* means only the human living within Japan, because *ningen* is an expression for human in Japan. Sports practices in school are used by the government, in fact. I cannot find the national necessity for sports practices according to the true theory to answer all the questions of sports. There are doctoral programs in some graduate schools, for example, Tsukuba University, Tokyo University, etc. Those doctoral programs have been irresponsibly created in the darkness. We must investigate who created doctoral programs in graduate schools in Japan, because all authorized words, for example, *doctor, professor*, etc. must belong to those who hold true theories. We must foster the national professor and the national doctor for people, in people, and with people. In fact, freedom of education in Japan has only gone to the surface and not reached inside Japanese education. So I feel that there is a thick wall to prevent democracy Therefore, to realize true education is not easy. I think that the responsibility of the professor is to produce true knowledge on behalf of students, but not to acquire techniques of how to talk jokingly to students in lectures, because most students are people who do not possess professional knowledge. In fact, a result of the examination has become a standardized evaluation of student's ability when teacher and professor evaluate students in school. That means that examination has had absoluteness, despite the research of the examination for students indicating not enough has been done. At this point, we have to see it in the whole process of education. Education is very important for the nation, but we should not forget that fake education brings a fake nation in fact. I believe that Japanese education will not run to fake education.

There are so many skills that professors teach in college and graduate school. However, the important fact we have to realize concerning skills and knowledge in Japan is that they are based on the existence of humans within Japan on the earth, because the human existence in Japan speaks Japanese. That means that the human existence in Japan creates all skills and all knowledge within Japan. If we emphasize an aspect of skill and technique of language and science, professors' recognition of the human existence would lose much despite all skills strongly tied to human existence, in fact.

We need professors and doctors in Japan who really support the people of Japan (who pay a lot of taxes) but do not need to lean on the people of Japan or lean on the traditional colleges and universities, as in playing with the national language in front of students in college in all nations. Our professors also are not translators who steal the knowledge from another country. Professors have to have their own knowledge in order to teach in front of students in all nations. This is our definition of *doctor* or *professor*. Therefore, professors have to have a real entity in all nations so that they can teach students in all nations. This book is very important in order to foster the authorized person for physical education and sports studies in all nations, Japan and all other nations. In the future, all courses of physical education of colleges and graduate schools in Japan must be independent from the ministry of education and must assure democracy among scholars, among famous colleges and new colleges, among national colleges and private colleges, among graduate schools, among professors and students, etc., according to the true principle written down by me. We will evenly create the opportunity to grant national doctorates of physical education to all Japanese scholars of physical education in the Japanese Society of Physical Education and Sports Studies. It must be assured forever by the principle of physical education and sports studies.

Part VIII

What Is the True Principle of Physical Education and Sports Studies?

1

About the Function and Shape
of the Principle in Reality

Principle means a universal theory beyond different languages and different eras with evidence to teach about sports practices and physical education practices in every nation in the world and in every era. The principle is a theory that is not created by personal opinion. It gives fundamental knowledge to all scholars equally in order to begin correct research and study. It is also a theory that will begin correct research and study. It is also a theory that will be able to break out through different languages and different eras as long as sports practices and physical education practices are carried out in schools and society in all nations. It acts directly to support physical education and sports practices within and without school. We can see all physical education and sports practices are practiced according to the principle of physical education and sports studies, because relations between practice and theory are like a paper with back and front. The character of the principle gives a life to each national language. It also is a theory that exists alone in the world. The principle acts to guarantee the awarding of doctoral degrees in physical education and sports studies in public after evaluation of research papers. It is a theory that provides social justification of school education, including physical education faculties in college and graduate school. Now I see a death of physical education study because no professors have found the origin of physical education study for the future. And I submit the principle of physical education and sports studies to all scholars in all nations. The principle is a theory that is able to lead people who want to do studies of physical education and sports in all nations. It also is based on thoughts of philanthropism to help all people in each nation in the world. The principle is a theory that gives the range of the social responsibility and the direction and method of research and studies of physical education and sports to all people in all nations who want to become professors in college and graduate school. The principle is needed in order to guarantee study/achievement to world people in every era and every nation in the world when someone is given authority in the profession of physical education and sports studies, because the authority must be guaranteed forever by the principle. The principle has a true power to enact correctly and support the practices of sports and physical education within and without school. It is also able to build the National Academy of Physical Education and Sports and World Academy of Physical Education and Sports in history in order to foster future professors in all nations.

The principle consists of theory that is able to answer all valid questions in all nations in connection with physical education and sports practice and theory within and without school (from kindergarten to college and graduate school). For example, about the necessity for the existence of professors of physical education in college and graduate school in all nations, about the necessity of existence of the physical education faculty in college and graduate school in all nations, about the necessity of employment of professors of physical education in all nations, about the necessity of college and graduate school programs (curricula) of physical education courses, about the guarantee of a doctoral degree of physical education and sports studies (national doctor and world doctor), about the necessity for a national academy and world academy of physical education and sports, about the necessity for world and national sports practice organizations like the IOC, and so forth.

The principle is a theory that guarantees the necessity for use of all national languages, social examinations, computers, experiments, books, etc., in school. It creates the beginning of all parts of studies included in physical education and sports studies. The departure of real research begins definitely from the principle of physical education and sports. Now all professors of physical education faculties in college, university, and graduate school judge the research papers that all students write, in their national language. Then they see just skills of writing without seeing the content of the research papers. It is not true judgment because all professors see the research papers through glasses in the color of their national language. The principle of physical education denies this method of judgment of research papers. Our judgment means how someone takes responsibility for the physical education and sports practices, in fact, through research of physical education and sports, and our judgment keeps seeing development of the human nation and human world. Then a peace comes to fruition. The principle denies all formality because we must have responsibility for the matters mentioned above.

2

Establishment of World Academy of Physical Education and Sports Studies

This world organization (ICHPERSD in USA) will be an organization that scholars of physical education and sports will support and protect for all people and for all nations in the world as a human nation and human world and also function to guarantee physical education and sports practices within and without college and graduate school in all nations. Based on the principle of physical education and sports studies devised by me, this organization must be guaranteed in all nations in the world forever as long as physical education and sports practices will be enforced for people (or students) within and without schools and societies in all nations in the world. This world organization must ensure democracy for all scholars in all nations in our field, physical education and sports studies and research.

This world organization (ICHPERSD in USA), completely independent from all governments, is the organization that will contribute to peace in .the world and development of mankind. This world organization will ensure equally the values of all national languages, their own cultures, and their own histories forever. This world organization has only the right to grant the authority in physical education and sports studies to people who contribute much toward our responsibility for mankind forever. This organization ensures freedom of research and study for all scholars of physical education and sports in all nations in the world under the responsibility for development and peace of mankind.

This world organization (ICHPERSD in USA) must never be abused by anyone. This organization has responsibility for all names of studies that belong to the physical education and sports studies, for example, philosophy, sociology, history, physiology, psychology, etc., in all nations in the world. We do not recognize those cases like a subject of physical education in education faculty, a subject of physical education in medical faculty, etc., because education faculties, medical faculties, etc., must not dominate the physical education program and degrees in college and graduate school in all nations. We will make strong world policy on behalf of fulfilling the social responsibility for all people in all nations. At present, the study of education, medicine, etc., have not been ensured as study of peace in the world, because nobody has created a "universal world principle for world people."

This world organization will have a right to ensure the independent existence of faculties in colleges and graduate schools under the principle of physical education and sports studies devised by me in all nations in the world forever. All the physical education faculties in colleges and graduate schools in all nations in the world are needed, in fact, and must be helped by all governments in order to realize a peace of nations and a peace in the world forever. This World Academy of Physical Education and Sports has a right to ensure professors' salaries and research expenses in colleges and graduate schools and also have a right to teach correct research education of physical education and sports to people who will become professors in colleges and graduate schools in all nations in the world.

This world organization will have a national academy in each nation in the world created through negotiation with each nation. We will take the negotiation to the president of each national academy of physical education in every nation in the world. The world organization ensures equal respect for all national languages in the research papers as proof of human existences that people are experiencing in all nations and abandons any prejudices about evaluation of research papers coming from all national doctors in all nations in the world. The national academy in connection with the world academy has a responsibility for making national theory in order to support all people in the nation and to ensure for all people in the nation peace in each era.

This world organization will adopt the principles of practical competition of the Olympics held by the IOC and hold the competition of national doctors from all nations every four years and grant to the most skilled people the world doctor degree as world leaders.

We are substantially able to make physical education and sports faculties established by the principle of physical education and sports studies created by me in all nations in the world forever. Of course, the existence of all physical education and sports curricula for all students in colleges and graduate schools in all nations in the world is clearly ensured by the principle. So all physical education and sports faculties are independent from pressures of all national administrations because we, all scholars of physical education and sports, have a right to protect physical education and sports practices and establish a human nation and mankind through the practice and the theory offered in lectures by professors in colleges and graduate schools. All physical education faculties in all nations must adopt the democratic systems inside and outside of the faculty in college. Therefore, we prohibit any prejudices among the nations based on different national languages in the world and also prohibit abuse of all national languages by professors in all nations in the world. Our purpose of the study and research makes each national theory support all people in their different nations with different national languages. Furthermore, we will be ready for Olympics or national doctors in order to recognize world peace in the world academy every four years.

The relationship of personal affairs in physical education and sports faculties in college and graduate school must be based on democracy in Japan, the United States, and other nations by the principle in connection with human rights in all human nations. The relationship between professors and students in college and in graduate school must be, too. All faculties of physical education and sports in colleges and in graduate schools in all nations in the world are ensured democratic relationships by the principle of physical education and sports studies created by me. All students in college and in graduate school in all nations in the world must not be subjected to brutal mental tortures by professors in phys cal education faculties again. I have had this brutal experience done to me by professors. I feel like I have been in slavery to professors in my college and graduate school in Japan. The will of professors to teach students in practice and theory class must produce true knowledge of physical education and sports practices. This principle ensures the democratization of physical education faculties in colleges and in graduate schools in all nations of the world.

For All Professors of Physical Education
in All Nations in the World

Up till now all professors have been leaning on educational systems that the governments have created, but we knew that these physical education programs were not able to foster professors as specialists in physical education. They were people that emphasized their national languages but not true knowledge. We must make accusations about the current situation, in which we are not able to foster authorized people like doctors and professors. Therefore, we, as scholars of physical education, must complain to all current professors in all nations in the world that are irresponsible about all things in physical education programs in college and graduate school in all nations in the world because there is no universal principle of physical education study. All current professors in all nations in the world are irresponsibly inclined to physical education programs that the government made despite the government not taking responsibility for the principle. They forget to serve the nation and world despite working as professors in public.

There is no true standard for evaluation of research papers that professors must do in public. Now they are giving doctoral degrees to the graduate students according to professors' preferences within an educational system. We must complain nationally and internationally about those worse situations of scholars of physical education in order to protect the human nation and human world. They are people that are sucking the blood of civilians and cannot teach in public. A professor is a person who serves the people and government. We must say in public that professors should not abuse their social status in college and graduate school. We request professors who have real identity as scholars of physical education and sports in all nations in the world.

All the professors in colleges and graduate schools in all nations in the world must produce true theory that they can teach students without adding their opinions. We will no longer be teachers of the national language. We will be scholars of physical education and sports. All professors must act to answer all questions about physical education and sports practices within and without schools in all nations. We should not teach all students in college and graduate school fake knowledge. All professors must have responsibility for production of true knowledge in order to lecture in college and graduate school. National languages do not have any values, in fact. So all professors must recognize that all national languages are a means by which to create national theory appropriate to allowing many kinds of sports events to be practiced from elementary school to college and graduate school in all nations in the world, To master all national language is not the final purpose of all nations in the world, All civilians in all nations have a right to know how professors of physical education and sports studies work, in fact, because all civilians pay taxes to the government in all nations. Therefore, professors of physical education and sports do not have time to play with the national language for students in class. All the professors must not cheat civilians living in all nations in the world as they abuse their social status. Professors in college and graduate school are people who have their own theory to teach for students. We must say now that the existence of physical education faculty in college and graduate school in public does not have social necessities because there is no theory to protect the physical education faculty in college and graduate school in all nations in the world. It means that faculties of physical education are not equally important in educational systems in all nations in the world. All the governments do not learn a value of sports events and ignore it. All of sports in school must not be offered by the government's opinions in each era. All of sports in school must not be used by teachers' opinions and professor's opinions. All professors cannot have a right to reject our accusations of the current situation of physical education. I think that this problem is on a governmental level so we must eventually discuss it with the president of the United States because we work truly to support the government and all the people as a human nation. All our work becomes the government's task, in fact.

There is no necessity to have doctoral programs for the Ph.D., etc., because those doctoral programs are not based on true theory to ensure uniformity in graduate schools in all nations in the world. Therefore, we in physical education faculty cannot use the name of doctor in public because the doctoral programs have been secretly made by personal opinion on the governmental side.

All the professors and researchers must learn about the role of all national languages, pointing out the principle of physical education and sports studies before they speak and write about topics of physical education and sports studies in their national language for students in college and graduate school. All expressions as words in national languages must finally return to all the people in the actual nations in which people were living, are living, and will be living during each era on the earth. All national language displays things that people are independently, traditionally, and culturally experiencing in all nations in the world, as all national languages lead national education in the world.

Part IX

Our Social, National, and World Responsibilities

None of the activities of physical education and sports should be abused by the government in each era and in each nation of the world. And to all governments we should offer the true theories of physical education and sports studies before the nations promote the practice of physical education activities and sports activities by pupils in schools, colleges, and other places. Moreover, we have discussed the relation between professors' salaries and people's payments in the forms of taxes and student's tuition, so we must be responsible for physical education and sports studies in all nations of the world and professors must have their own theories in order to teach the true knowledge to students in college and graduate school. This means the thought of democracy should come into the research of physical education in all nations. I think that we have to check research achievements of professors in colleges and in graduate schools in all nations, because we are responsible for teaching a specific study for all students in all nations. I also think that we should not recognize the doctoral programs and the doctoral degrees deriving from any other studies because those doctoral programs do not work properly for fostering physical education and sports doctors.

Fundamentally, our thought does not take just a Western way as fragmentary knowledge of the human is produced, but a mixed Western and Eastern way of going to unified knowledge of the mankind, like building national theory up. These principles come from the thought of coexistence in all nations and the thought of competitions in all nations. The true lead in education means that teachers and professors give true knowledge to students without personal and national egoism (like making prejudice). What is the true knowledge? It means the knowledge coming from practice of our lives on the earth, beyond different national languages. We will put true evaluation of physical education in order to foster future professors and doctors beyond different languages when we see all research papers from the point of view of true education within and without college and graduate school. The expression of each national language (in all the publications) has a limited scope, acting within the nation in fact. For example, American English is the expression of the human within the United States, French is the expression of the human within France, Korean is the expression of the human within Korea, and so forth.

Because I have the true theories, I have to say to the people of the world that physical education as sports practiced in each nation has been misled with irresponsible purpose by each government in the world. No government in the world has any theories that ensure all kinds of sports events despite each government (or teacher and professor) letting all students do many kinds of sports events from elementary school to college, in fact. So the government must transfer the responsibility for the physical education faculty in college to scholars of physical education in each nation in the world, because the government does not have the true theories of physical education as sports practices, in fact. The government cannot practice many kinds of sports events because they go to misuse in each era. I demand of each government that all sports courses in the physical education programs in colleges and in universities in all nations must offer three credits, because all sports practices in the colleges and universities are the practices for peace according to our theories, On the contrary, the government should expect that the efforts of scholars of physical education in all nations will definitely lead toward development of physical education and sports studies. Each government also should entrust the responsibilities for practices of physical education to scholars of physical education in their nation. The prosperity of our nation will depend on efforts of our country's scholars in college and graduate school. Our slavery to medical doctors, doctors of literature, doctors of education and other doctors in college and graduate school will end completely in all nations because we will have the true theories of physical education and sports studies. We really need physical education doctors (as national doctors and world doctors) in all nations that provide national theories that can support citizens as humans and also support governments as humans. I confirm that they will bring true knowledge to all students in college and graduate school in all nations. We must not recognize all things in our field without true theory, which guarantees doctoral programs and doctoral degrees because we have responsibility for education, for human society, for the human nation, and for the human world on the earth in each era. All scholars in all nations have to have responsibilities for peace of nations and for peace of the world on behalf of protection for people in all nations. Therefore, professors in physical education faculties in all nations must take their theoretical lectures to colleges and in graduate schools in all nations as long as physical education faculties have the practices of many kinds of sports events and exercises of applied sports events. We declare to the governments in all nations that physical education and sports studies and the faculties in colleges and in graduate schools are important for the nation because they are the studies of peace for people, with people, and in people in all nations.

I think that we physical education scholars have to go toward establishment of the World Academy of Physical Education and Sports Studies with cooperation between the United States and Japan in order to lead correctly the practice and study of physical education and sports at schools in all countries. The world academy (ICHPERSD in USA) must function to lead national scholars of physical education and sports in all nations beyond different languages of the world, to all nations of the world, under our true theories for the human nation and human world and for peace in the world. We must disclose abuse of some national languages that national education by the government has had, in fact. The world academy can recognize all national languages equally when it sees and evaluates the research papers from all scholars of all nations, because we really need to contribute to peace in the world. A way of solution moves with these questions: Why do we need a national language for physical education and sports studies? Why is American English important for our studies and research? Why is Spanish important for our studies and research? Why are other languages important for our studies, too? First of all, we must answer to all people of all nations on the earth from the principle, because all professors in colleges and in graduate school in all nations use the national language in front of students in their lectures. Our answer is that because of building up national theory for peace and development of the human nation and human world, we need physical education faculties in educational systems in all nations.

Message to the U.S. President

I have been seriously and honestly considering the principle of physical education and sports studies and intend to build a national theory of physical education and sports studies up due to my social, national, and world responsibility as a scholar of physical education. Thus, I have completed the principle of physical education and sports studies linked in my first book. I now must request, Mr. President, that physical education and sports scholars in all nations be released and independent from general studies (for example, medicine, pedagogy, etc.) that have influenced and dominated physical education and sports studies before.

We will take a democratic way and substantial way for evaluation of our specialty. We deny the way that graduate school professors secretly give doctoral degrees, because nobody can guarantee physical education doctoral degrees to anyone in graduate school in any nation in the world. The character of our doctoral degree is to signify a national doctor to support the nation and all people of the nation and world doctor to support mankind and all people in all nations. Our selection of national doctors and world doctors will be open, in the Olympic competitions. Under the true judgment (the principle of physical education and sports studies in all nations of the world) we will view research papers and foster our professors and our doctors in the future beyond different national languages in the Olympics.

We promise you that physical education and sports scholars will bring true democracy, responsibility for mankind, and peace through efforts of their research and studies. Mr. President, please understand "the principle" I have patiently devised in places in the United States and Japan in order to give equal happiness and responsibilities of mankind to all people in all human nations.

I expect that the United States will lead all nations from the standpoint of the principle of physical education and sports. We need researchers and professors in our specialty who love and support the

United States as a humane nation. We also expect contributions to peace in the world (world doctors) that will come from the United States. Please cooperate with us for future nations and future generations. God bless America.

My Identification as a Physical Education and Sports Scholar Working for All Nations of the World

I was ostracized by Japanese professors in the past because I announced one of my theories for peace in the Japanese Society of Physical Education. Now I have a sense of shame that I was born in Japan when I look back at my past. I have mentioned to many scholars in Japan that they must support the government functioning as a human nation through building national theory as a human nation from the principle, even though I have never gotten aid for research from the government. In this situation, I have really been disappointed. On the contrary, I thought that all professors in the Japanese Society of Physical Education must be investigated for their research achievements. My struggle began from this point in my past because all professors' salaries come from payments of taxes to the government and students or students' parents or other relatives pay tuition for studies in college and graduate school. I came to the United States from Japan in order to foster physical education and sports professors for the future. I believe that true democracy does not depend on the principle of the decision of the majority (opinions), but true theory under the justification of humanity because many people in the world history have committed evil when the principle of decisions of majority take advantage of principles of democracy. I think that the true democracy in fact must hold true theory that people can make common sense of.

After World War II, Japanese education was directed by the American government under thoughts of democracy Although Japan needs democratic education, we do not need educational irrespon-sibility for the real society, real nation, and real world coming from just individualism of professors without theories. We must say that we need doctors on physical education faculties (for peace and people) in colleges and in universities, but we cannot approve of the current doctoral programs in the educational system because the true theory (principle) that secures for the human nation and mankind as physical education studies and can answer all real questions of all people in the United States has not been created. I feel it dangerous that we recognize doctors and professors as authorized professionals in the current educational system without the assurance. The current situation evokes misuse of authorized positions by doctors and professors, especially in Japanese society.

We Need Healthy Nationalism for True Education in All Nations

We need sound nationalism in order to create objective knowledge for students, but not morbid nationalism like that that engendered thoughts of war in the past. On the contrary, sound nationalism would accelerate the production of more progressive knowledge in schools in all nations.

I must display the structure of American English in public; what is American English, fundamentally? American English is one of the national languages in the world that American people can understand within the United States. American English has an internal structure and exterior structure. The internal structure consists of American grammar for writing and speaking. The external structure is the proof of the human existence in the United States (as a philosophical expression) the proof of American people (as a sociological expression) that the human uses words as evidence of the human. People should not be used by words (all national languages) but use them in order to build national theory up in all nations. This is an international rule in all national languages in the world.

I would like to mention many necessities of physical education and sports studies that, in fact, we have to emphasize in public under the principle. I list the following items:

- Physical education and sports science and other studies are needed for development of physical education and sports studies.

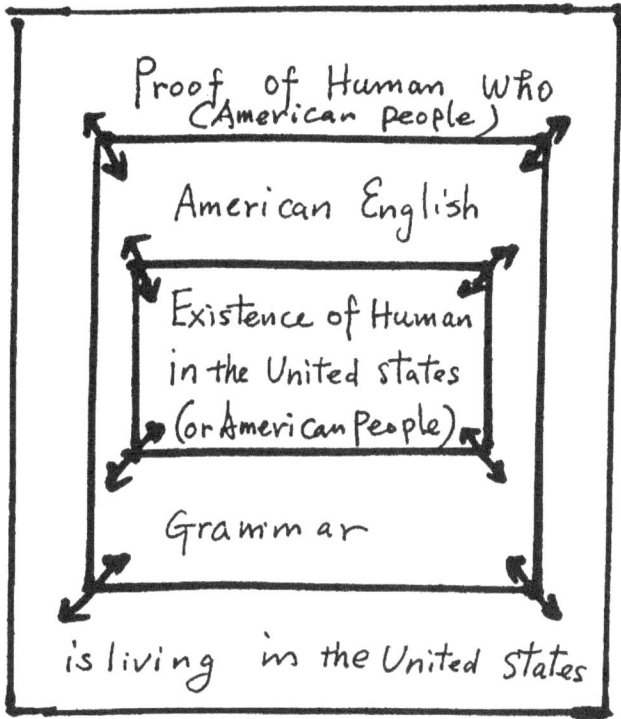

Figure 68. National language as an expression of the human in the nation; for example, American English

- Physical education and sports practices are important for ideal mankind and each practice of physical education in college and graduate school should offer three credits to the student.
- In graduate school, master and doctoral programs must be provided by national doctors.
- Lectures on theory in college and graduate school are unconditionally needed for all students.
- The physical education faculties in college and in graduate school in all nations must be ensured for people.
- All sports organizations like the IOC must practice sports under the theories of sports and physical education studies.

- Professors of physical education and sports in social status as a specific profession must be guaranteed forever by all nations in the world.

The Democratization of Our Faculties in
All Nations in the World and the Olympics

We support the Olympics as a sports practice. Baron Pierre de Coubertin of France founded the Olympics. World theories must be provided by world doctors of physical education and sports studies in the future because all sports practices in the world must belong to physical education and sports scholars in all nations. Then our physical education faculties within and without school get real democracy. Sports does not require formalism but meritocracy. Democracy likes real meritocracy for prosperity of mankind. Our democracy of physical education cannot be protected by the government but by our principles of physical education and sports. In the future, a world doctor of physical education and sports will hold the post of president of the IOC because he will be a person who has contributed to peace in the world. We need a person as a president of the IOC who can support Baron de Cubertin by theory of the physical education and sports studies that can contribute to peace in the world. We do not recognize presidents of the IOC who cannot have the true theories of sports practices. Why is it so? Because the practices of the Olympics have lost the true meaning of necessity for mankind. The IOC might lead to the death of mankind through the practice of sports without being ensured by theories of sports in the future.

The president of the IOC must know theories of sports, as this is the obligation of the president on behalf of people in the world. We, as true scholars of physical education and sports, are afraid of personal possession of the Olympics by the president of the IOC. The IOC must administer the Olympics on behalf of people in all nations of the world. It is the duty of the IOC to the world's people.

Message to Japanese Government

I have made much effort toward the establishment of the principle of physical education and sports in Japan. This principle of physical education and sports is a theory that the ministry of Japanese education must hold forever, whenever the government offers sports practices to the Japanese people. I have insisted in the Japanese Society of Physical Education that physical education professors must take responsibility for all Japanese people and the ministry of education. Unfortunately, in those days I was ostracized by Japanese professors and members of the Japanese Society of Physical Education. My struggles for peace in the world have begun since I opposed Japanese establishment. I must say to the government that they are anticitizens. I know that the ministry of education must have a theory of physical education practices and sports practices in order to get the trust of the citizens of Japan. I have suffered much spiritual damage in my private life because the announcement of my theory to the Japanese Society of Physical Education was greeted reluctantly by some professors and some members of the Japanese Society of Physical Education. I actually despaired of living in Japan as a scholar of physical education. My freedom of research was encroached upon by some professors. And they have apparently abused their social positions as professors to gather benefits for their family and themselves, and finally, they have stolen my idea. Since then I have lost my right to speak in public as a scholar of physical education in Japan. I know that Japanese society strongly supports formalism, in fact. At the same time Japanese society faces internationally a danger to them because their defense of formalism. I must insist on our rights and responsibilities for all Japanese people and the ministry of education in Japan. In fact, all professors' salaries in colleges and graduate schools come from payments that people make in the form of taxes and students or students' parents make as tuition. Therefore, I cannot permit the professors' behavior I witnessed in my past. Until now I have protected my theory as a scholar without the government's help. Now I must say to the government that this task is one the Japanese government must undertake as long as all schools in Japan offer many kinds of sports to all students. I know that real scholars take a productive view toward physical education. In fact, my theory was rejected due to the preference of professors in Tsukuba University and Tokyo University. I have to say to all Japanese people: Why does Japan need Tokyo University and Tsukuba University? What is education? Encouraging colonialism (*gakubatsu* in Japanese) is education at present in Japan, isn't it? I say to my prime minister that real education means service to the Japanese people, with the people, and in the people. (Dr. Earle F. Zeigler of the United States mentioned it as "General Education for Peace" in the *Journal of Comparative Physical Education and Sports* in 1992, published by Verlag Karl Hofmann.) I believe that the necessity of education comes from requirements for development and peace in the human nation and human world. Therefore, all professors in all nations must put efforts toward this.

I hope that I will establish a new Japanese Society of Physical Education and Sports Studies for peace in the world in the future in order to foster real professors and doctors of physical education and sports in Japan. We as scholars of physical education and sports wish to understand our responsibility to the Japanese people and to the Japanese government. Our work always must go to public tasks, not personal gains. But we wish economic aid to be provided to us in order to establish national and world organizations of physical education and sports.

Now that Japanese colleges and graduate schools are running to corruption we cannot foster the professors of physical education and sports studies in graduate programs in Japan. Their lectures are irresponsible for students and play with the Japanese language, in college and graduate school. They do not have a universal blueprint (principle) behind their lectures in all colleges and in all graduate schools. Therefore, professors' lectures are substantially fruitless for students. We real scholars of physical education and sports studies have a responsibility for rectifying this situation, which I appealed in the Japanese Society of Physical Education. All research papers (or knowledge of research papers) that professors grade are torn to pieces without national integration in physical education study. They have not created physical education study as their own study but gathered knowledge borrowed from general studies and the United States. This has also not functioned well in actual sports practices. First we need basic theory (principle) before the government creates physical education faculties, before the government plans doctoral programs in graduate schools, before the government employs someone as a professor in college and graduate school. I feel that this is a national and international issue that the government must take care of us scholars of physical education and sports in reality. The time has come to appeal that the rights of physical education and sports scholars must be insisted upon in public. I hope that my prime minister understands our efforts as scholars of physical education and we will share responsibility and happiness with the Japanese people and world's people. We promise that we will also contribute to national peace and world peace through building the national theory of physical education and sports studies in each nation.

The Evaluation of the Research of National Doctors of Physical Education and Sports Studies

Evaluation of research is very important, and we must be very careful in evaluating research papers. Our job is not that of translator from one national language to another national language. Our responsibility is to create a national theory of peace that must have the strongest power in reality to support all people in practices of physical education and sports and the governments that approve the practice of sports from elementary school to graduate school in all nations in the world. We must guarantee that a national doctor possesses true theory that ensures a value for the human world forever. We know that Ph.D.'s, Ed.D.'s, and other professors are not able to guarantee the doctoral program and the value of doctor in fact. Therefore, we know that the principle is the most important theory, which can give all rights of physical education and sports study and practices within and without schools in all nations in the world. And we know that we should evaluate how much responsibility a professor has taken in order to develop the physical education and sports practices, not how much he has played skillfully with the national language and with experiments in the research papers. And we also must add historical evaluation of physical education and sports when we evaluate the research papers of each part of physical education and sports studies.

Our way as true scholars of physical education is toward a system of Olympics (the most democratic way), not the government system of nations. We must be independent from governments in all nations in the world. The government cannot create doctoral programs and also cannot dominate the physical education faculties in all nations. Governments cannot practice sports events and teach theory of sports for students from elementary school to college and graduate school, because the governments in all nations do not have true theory the governments can teach to the students.

We do not recognize any doctoral degrees and doctoral programs (Ph.D., Ed.D., etc.) that governments have created for graduate school students, because they are personal doctoral degrees granted by professors of graduate school without the theory that should guarantee the doctoral degree. Our physical education scholars can create national academies and world academies (ICHPERSD in USA) that can foster national doctors and world doctors as authorized leaders of physical education and sports. So we as scholars of physical education and sports studies must be independent from domination of the governments in all nations.

We must work toward an Olympics in which national doctors chosen by each National Academy of Physical Education and Sports Studies compete. They will be people working to lead students in public and produce public knowledge that all students have a right to learn. Therefore, the society, nation, and world must recognize the existence of scholars of physical education in the society, nation, and world.

What is the National Language in Each Nation in the World?

The national language is words that humans use in real life in order to communicate with each other. Therefore, all national languages (American English, Chinese, French, German, Russian, Japanese,

Korean, Italian, etc.) are the proof that humans are living in all nations in each era. Humans in all nations use national languages' grammar in order to write and speak correctly in each nation. However, mastering the national language is a means of doing something in society but not the purpose of the human in society. The national language has a limitation of expressions for humans. For example, American English is an expression of humans (people) within the United States. Japanese is an expression of humans (people *ningen*) within Japan. Therefore, all national languages finally offer proof of human existence in their nations through creating the national cultures. Therefore, all national languages are important for doing the research and for the studies of physical education and sports. All scholars of physical education and sports in all nations must know what all national languages are in fact before they begin to do the study and research for physical education and sports.

While all the physical education and sports scholars use national languages for students in their lectures, they must know that mastering the national language is a method in order to appeal for realization of peace of nations and peace in the world. The scholars must have responsibility for the practice of physical education and sports separate from exhibition of the national language. The necessity for the lecture comes from responsibility for physical education and sports in schools. Then the democratization of physical education in all nations would occur in all nations in reality, if we demand this in public.

All things that researchers of physical education and sports in college and graduate school in all nations in the world are doing in terms of books recommending, assigning laboratory work and experimentation, administering oral examinations, etc., are absolutely methods in order to testify or to evidence his hypothesis. Why do we need a book list, laboratory work, oral examinations, etc., for study and research of physical education? They are also methods used in each era and each nation on behalf of realization of peace in the nation and peace in the world, but not the purpose of physical education studies and research. The purpose of research and studies of physical education and sports is to make national theory and world theory on behalf of realization of peace within the nation and peace in the world.

So all researchers in all nations in the world have to learn for what the purpose of research is and what the method of research is. Therefore, all researchers have to learn the principle of physical and sports education before they try to research physical education and sports in college and graduate school.

What Are Physical Education and Sports Studies?

I must answer this question as a scholar of physical education and sports studies for the world's people in order to get social, national, and world trust.

When humans do sports and physical education they create special human existence as movement humans–for example, tennis ball humans, baseball humans, judo humans, social dancing humans, and so forth. And each specific human from elementary school to graduate school practices, working toward ideals of specific human existences in all nations. So physical education in schools in all nations of the world is not education through "physical activities" and not for the "health of the human," because these phrases come from personal opinion without evidence. Therefore, people who proclaim thus in public must offer proof of these hypotheses (personal opinions), and I request them to show the proof to the world's people. I vote against them because we, as scholars of physical education, must ensure the human nation and human world through practice of physical education and sports and theories of physical education and sports in college and graduate school. The practice of physical education and sports in schools will make the origin of peace to spread peace in the world. So physical education and sports studies in all nations are studies to create peace. Physical education and sports studies have had a character of social justification I as human education in each nation forever.

Afterword

I have witnessed human existence in both nations, the United States and Japan, but not American English and Japanese, although learning the national language is, finally, a method in order to fulfill human life. I have also learned through studying philosophy the importance of human existence, which can produce national languages, cultures, history, etc., connecting human society. When I started to think about the principle of physical education and sports studies and research in Japan, I was so fascinated by the phenomenon of sports that I completely forgot my private life. This means, in fact, that these theories have been giving much influence to my life until now and these theories have given sadness, happiness, bravery, desperation, etc., to me. I wanted to become a person who, as a lover of truth, lived in order to change reality for the better, like many great people of the past (for example, Albert Schweitzer) indicated was a way of human life in world history. Schweitzer's philosophy of reverence for life (Harold E. Robeles, *Albert Schweitzer, an Adventurer for Humanity*, Millbrook, Press 1994) apparently created my strong interest in human existence.

I have published this book in order to realize the development of physical education and sports studies and research in each nation and peace. All principles that I have created are basic theories in order to build up objective knowledge for students as the national theory of each nation in the world. All the objective knowledge for students is produced by all scholars of physical education and sports in each nation of the world. Therefore, this book must not be abused by governments, organizations, and any people. This is also a book that contributes to the democratization of physical education and sports research and studies among scholars in each nation in the world. And I hope your nations will adjust to change better than before. Our duty as a profession is to serve humanity and to develop humanity forever.

I have proposed that we should hoist national flags and play national anthems at national academies and the World Academy of Sports and Physical Education. We can approve the social, national, and world existence in public, but not by governments in each era, because we must teach all governments how to work toward all nations in the world forever. We must ideally show each government how to help people live and coexist with people of other nations. If the government does not learn from us, the nation will move toward corruption of the people of the nation. The more the government refuses to learn wisdom, the more the nation will go to corruption, without heeding the voices of the people. And finally the nation will go to war. Therefore, I really feel that we must establish a World Academy of Physical Education and Sports and the organization must continue in order to serve and to adjust democratically, humanistically, for all nations in the world. I feel that we really need the organization in the world. From now on I will move toward the establishment of the world academy.

Frankly, I would like to say regarding the government, especially that of the United States, I have several times faced scenes that American people have much pride in, as they speak American English, especially concerning people who teach students from college to graduate school. I have learned from my life in the United States that their range of view is very narrow concerning American English, as if American English is the best language in the world. These people's recognition of American English has a possibility of being abused internationally. In our era, any colonialism–that is, an idea of a powerful nation, group, or person dominating a powerless nation, group, or person–must end up among each nations of the world under the principle.

I also have to speak of Japanese education in the world. Japanese teachers and professors have not learned the truth of Japanese (one of the national languages in the world). They have just learned how to write and speak Japanese grammatically. I see current Japanese education has been influenced so much by the United States since the Second World War. All nationalism in Japan was killed among the people. The sound nationalism coming from humanity was killed, too. Instead of it, thoughts of disorder coming from individualism or egoism have been developed. In fact, the extreme individualism or egoism coming from incorrect education has been destroying the human nation and human world.

These situations have come about through abuse of national education. Many Americans evaluate people in reality by how well the people know American English. But they ignore how people take responsibility for the United States as a human nation and for Americans as humans. Japanese education has been distorted by the government because the government did not have a universal blueprint for national education. And American education, too, without a universal blueprint (principle) made mistakes in national education in each era of the human nation.

Both governments have been using many kinds of sports events in schools until now without any permission from sports founders and any scholars of physical education and sports. It is clearly shown in history that governments have abused many kinds of sports events in schools without any principles. It shows a historical sin by the government.

We recognize that both national languages are important for the American and Japanese people. At the same time, the Japanese people and American people have to know that each expression of research papers, magazines, and books in American English and Japanese belongs to the American people and Japanese people as the proof of human existence in both nations. We will end evaluating researchers by just their facility in the languages, because this measurement means that the government will not have standardized evaluation in order to foster professionalism in the future. The standard of evaluation depends on how much a person has taken responsibilities for the human nation and human world, not on how much the person skillfully played with the national language, avoiding the responsibility in public. We really need true development of physical education and sports studies in all nations in the world.

We will move substantially to establish the World Academy of Physical Education and Sports Studies (ICHPERSD in USA). Our efforts are fundamentally for the people, with the people, and in the people, because we have to take responsibility for the human nation and human world (as the truth). Therefore, we physical education and sports scholars declare in public that we have a right to be independent from any governments. And we promise that we will put forth an effort toward development of physical education and sports studies in all nations in the world and contribute toward peace of nations and peace in the world. I am proud that we can also change for the better national educational system for all nations in the world without formality. We will see flags of human nations and hear national anthems every four years because it shows the heart and body of people (human) and precious life of people (human). I pray that peace will actually come true for us someday.

In general, the necessities in reality for all national languages of the world, education in all nations in the world, and computers and experiments in laboratories by researchers in all nations of the world exist, coming from the human existence (existence of all people in all nations of the world) that people are experiencing in reality. And the social, national, and world necessity for studies and research into physical education and sports comes from "specific human existences" (see each principle) in all nations of the world. We must respect the specific human existences in all nations and must respect equally all national languages of the world. All national languages are living and moving in each era, just as people are living in all nations in the world.

The true purpose of teaching is to give actual, true knowledge to students, not to give credit and degrees to students. We ask that the quality of the teaching in all nations of the world change for the better.

Bibliography

Edmund, Fusserl. *Ideen* 1. N.P.: Verlag Von Max Niemeyer, 1922.

Hegel, Georg Wilhelm Friedrich. *Samtliche Werke 4; Wissenshaft der Logik Zweiter Teil (The Research for Logic in the Second Volume)* N.p.: George Lasson, 1923.

Hideo, Kondo. *Taiku no Tetsugaku (The Philosophy of Physical Education).* Tokyo: Reimei Press, 1951.

Kitaro, Nishida. *Zen no Kenkyu (Research on Virtue).* Tokyo: Iwanami Press, 1966.

Lindsay, A. D. *The Philosophy of Bergson.* N.p.: J. M. Dentsons Ltd., 1911.

Nishida, Kitaro. *Tetugaku Rombun shu (Collection of Philosophical Essays)* Vol. I, 7. Tokyo: Iwanami Press, 1945.

Kuki, Shuzo. *Iki no Kozo (The Structure of the Beauty of Consciousness).* Tokyo: Iwanami Press, 1974.

Earle F., Zeiglar. *Sport and Physical Education Philosophy.* Camel Benchmark Press, 1989.

www.ingramcontent.com/pod-product-compliance
Lightning Source LLC
Chambersburg PA
CBHW031458270326
41930CB00006B/153